Understanding the Ethics of Generative AI

The book discusses the ethical complexities that software developers face as they build AI systems capable of autonomous creation. It explores the ethical decisions developers must make when building generative AI systems, from mitigating bias in training data to protecting user privacy and navigating regulatory compliance. Through real-world case studies and actionable frameworks, it equips technical professionals with both the understanding and tools to build AI systems that are fair, transparent, and worthy of public trust.

This book covers the following topics:

- Identifies and corrects algorithmic bias in training datasets, ensuring AI systems produce equitable outputs that don't systematize discrimination.
- Designs privacy-first AI architectures and implements transparency practices that comply with data protection regulations while building user trust.
- Navigates evolving legal and regulatory landscapes (GDPR, AI Act, sector-specific rules), helping teams stay ahead of compliance requirements.
- Applies ethical frameworks to real-world decisions: what to do when fairness and accuracy conflict, how to audit AI systems for hidden harms, when to say no to a project.
- Provides a governance model for embedding ethics into development workflows, not as an afterthought but as a core design practice.

Understanding the Ethics of Generative AI

A Developer's Guide

Loveleen Gaur

CRC Press
Taylor & Francis Group
Boca Raton London New York

CRC Press is an imprint of the
Taylor & Francis Group, an **informa** business
A CHAPMAN & HALL BOOK

Designed cover image: Shutterstock

First edition published 2027
by CRC Press
2385 NW Executive Center Drive, Suite 320, Boca Raton FL 33431

and by CRC Press
4 Park Square, Milton Park, Abingdon, Oxon, OX14 4RN

CRC Press is an imprint of Taylor & Francis Group, LLC

ISBN: 9781041153184 (hbk)
ISBN: 9781041155409 (pbk)
ISBN: 9781003679974 (ebk)

DOI: 10.1201/9781003679974

Typeset in Times
by Deanta Global Publishing Services, Chennai, India

Contents

Preface....................xiv
About the Author....................xvi

Chapter 1 Demystifying Generative AI 1

1.1 Emergence of Generative AI....................1
1.1.1 Definition of Generative AI....................1
1.1.2 A Concise Historical Overview: Transitioning from Theory to Practice....................2
1.2 The Power of Creation: Applications in Various Industries....................3
1.2.1 GenAI in Art and Entertainment....................3
1.2.2 Revolutionizing Healthcare Through AI-Driven Innovation....................5
1.2.3 AI in Commerce: Automation, Innovation, and Further Developments....................6
1.3 Ethical Frontiers: Addressing the Challenges of Generative AI....................7
1.3.1 The Ambivalent Nature of AI Creativity....................7
1.3.2 Prejudice and Equity: Guaranteeing Justice in Artificial Intelligence....................8
1.3.3 Privacy Issues: Safeguarding Data in an AI-Driven Environment....................8
1.4 The Ethical Framework for Generative AI....................9
1.4.1 Tenets for Ethical AI Development....................9
1.4.2 Governance and Regulation: Influencing the Future....................10
1.4.3 The Function of AI Ethics Committees and Review Boards....................11
1.5 Case Analyses: Ethical Quandaries in Generative AI....................12
1.5.1 Deepfakes: The Subtle Distinction Between Creativity and Deception....................12
1.5.2 AI-Created Art: Who Holds Ownership of the Creation?....................13
1.5.3 GenAI in Medicine: Reconciling Innovation with Patient Rights....................14

1.6 The Way Ahead: Constructing a Responsible AI Future........15
1.6.1 Collaborative Initiatives: Reconciling Technology and Ethics........15
1.6.2 Education and Awareness: Empowering Future Generations........15
1.6.3 Advancing a Human-Centric AI Future........16

Chapter 2 Comprehending Training Data 19

2.1 Basis of Artificial Intelligence........19
2.1.1 Definition of Training Data........19
2.1.2 Categories of Training Data: Structured and Unstructured........19
2.2 The Significance of Quality in Training Data........21
2.2.1 Data Quality: The Foundation of AI Precision........21
2.2.2 The Influence of Data Volume and Heterogeneity........21
2.3 The Negative Aspect: Prejudice in Training Data........22
2.3.1 Comprehending Bias: Its Infiltration into AI........22
2.3.2 Prevalent Forms of Bias in AI Training Data........23
2.4 Practical Implications: Case Studies of Biased Artificial Intelligence........24
2.4.1 Discriminatory Algorithms in Recruitment........24
2.4.2 Racial Prejudice in Facial Recognition Technology........24
2.4.3 Gender Bias in AI-Driven Virtual Assistants........25
2.5 Addressing and Alleviating Bias in Training Data........25
2.5.1 Methods for Identifying Bias in Data........25
2.5.2 Approaches for Acquiring More Representative Data........26
2.5.3 The Significance of Human Oversight in AI Development........27
2.6 The Future of Training Data: Ethical and Inclusive Artificial Intelligence........28
2.6.1 Advancing Ethical Data Collection Practices........28
2.6.2 The Importance of Transparency and Accountability........29
2.6.3 Imagining an Inclusive AI Future........30

Chapter 3 Strategies for Mitigating Bias in AI Development 33

3.1 Methods for Generating Equitable and Representative Training Data........33
3.1.1 Data Augmentation: Improving Diversity in Training Datasets........33
3.1.2 Compiling Inclusive Datasets: Optimal Practices........34

3.1.3 The Function of Synthetic Data in Bias Mitigation....37
3.2 Bias Mitigation Implementation: Exemplary Cases from Generative AI Initiatives....38
3.2.1 Mitigating Gender Bias in AI-Generated Content....38
3.2.2 Addressing Racial Bias in AI-Driven Decision-Making....39
3.2.3 Guaranteeing Equity in AI-Driven Healthcare Solutions....40
3.3 Optimal Strategies and Suggestions for Bias Reduction....41
3.3.1 Incorporating Bias Mitigation into the AI Development Lifecycle....41
3.3.2 Cooperative and Interdisciplinary Methodologies....41
3.3.3 Ongoing Surveillance and Feedback Mechanisms....42
3.4 The Prospects of Bias Mitigation in Artificial Intelligence....43
3.4.1 Novel Techniques and Innovations....43
3.4.2 The Function of Policy and Regulation....44
3.4.3 Establishing a Bias-Free AI Future....45

Chapter 4 Techniques for Ethical Calibration of AI Models 48

4.1 Introduction....48
4.1.1 Definition of Calibration in AI....48
4.1.2 Calibration and Ethics: An Essential Relationship....48
4.2 The Function of Calibration in Advancing Ethical AI....49
4.2.1 Equity via Calibration: Its Significance....49
4.2.2 Mitigating Bias via Efficient Calibration....50
4.3 Techniques for Calibrating AI Models....52
4.3.1 Post-Processing Calibration Methods....52
4.3.2 Calibration Throughout Model Training....52
4.3.3 Calibration Measurement: Metrics and Instruments....55
4.4 Challenges in Attaining Neutrality and Equity in Calibration....56
4.4.1 The Compromise Between Precision and Fairness....56
4.4.2 Calibration in Imbalanced Datasets....57
4.4.3 The Complexity of Multidimensional Fairness....58
4.5 Case Studies: Calibration in Action....58
4.5.1 Calibrating AI for Fair Lending Decisions....58
4.5.2 Calibration in Healthcare: Ensuring Equitable Outcomes....59
4.5.3 Addressing Bias in AI-Powered Hiring Tools Through Calibration....59
4.6 Future Directions: Advancing Calibration for Ethical AI....60

4.6.1 Emerging Techniques and Innovations in Calibration 60
4.6.2 The Role of AI Governance in Calibration 60
4.6.3 Toward a Future of Fair and Neutral AI Models 61

Chapter 5 Addressing Privacy Challenges in Generative AI 65

5.1 Introduction: The Convergence of Privacy and Generative AI 65
5.1.1 Defining Privacy within the Framework of AI 65
5.1.2 The Importance of Privacy in GenAI 65
5.2 Identifying Privacy Risks in Data Collection and Utilization 66
5.2.1 Data Collection: The Initial Point of Risk 66
5.2.2 Data Utilization in AI: Harmonizing Innovation and Privacy 68
5.2.3 The Function of Third-Party Data in Privacy Vulnerabilities 69
5.3 Industry Best Practices for Protecting User Privacy 70
5.3.1 Privacy by Design: Incorporating Privacy into AI Development 70
5.3.2 Federated Learning: A Privacy-Conscious Method for Model Training 70
5.3.3 Differential Privacy: Protecting Personal Data 71
5.3.4 Secure Multiparty Computation: Augmenting Data Security 72
5.4 Real-World Case Studies: Privacy-Centric Approaches in GenAI 73
5.4.1 Case Study: Privacy-First AI in Healthcare 73
5.4.2 Case Study: Privacy in AI-Enhanced Social Media Platforms 74
5.4.3 Case Study: Privacy Protections in AI-Enhanced Financial Services 75
5.5 The Future of Privacy in GenAI 75
5.5.1 Emerging Privacy-Preserving Techniques 75
5.5.2 The Role of Regulation and Policy in Protecting Privacy 76
5.5.3 Establishing Trust in GenAI: The Way Ahead 77

Chapter 6 Ensuring Transparency and Accountability in AI Systems 82

6.1 Overview 82
6.2 Comprehending Transparency in AI 83
6.3 The Necessity for Accountability 85

6.4 Principal Obstacles to Attaining Transparency and Accountability ... 87
6.4.1 Algorithmic Opacity and Complexity of AI Technology ... 87
6.4.2 Data Provenance and Inherent Bias ... 87
6.4.3 Commercial and Competitive Dimensions ... 87
6.4.4 Lack of Consensus and Benchmarks ... 88
6.5 Strategies to Enhance Transparency ... 89
6.5.1 Frameworks for Transparency-by-Design ... 89
6.5.2 Standardized AI Documentation Instruments ... 89
6.5.3 Techniques for Explainability and Interpretability ... 89
6.5.4 Open-Source and Collaborative AI Initiatives ... 90
6.5.5 Transparency Requirements Driven by Regulatory and Policy Frameworks ... 90
6.5.6 Autonomous Audits and External Evaluations ... 90
6.6 Mechanisms for Ensuring Accountability ... 91
6.6.1 Ethics Review Boards and AI Governance Committees ... 91
6.6.2 Algorithmic Auditing and Impact Evaluations ... 91
6.6.3 Protocols for Documentation and Record-Keeping ... 92
6.6.4 Frameworks for Legal and Regulatory Compliance ... 92
6.6.5 Explicit Assignment of Responsibility and Liability ... 92
6.6.6 Transparency and Public Disclosure Systems ... 92
6.6.7 Feedback Mechanisms and Stakeholder Involvement ... 93
6.6.8 Whistleblower Safeguards and Reporting Mechanisms ... 93
6.7 Case Studies on Transparent and Accountable AI ... 93
6.8 The Significance of Multi-stakeholder Collaboration ... 95
6.8.1 Multidisciplinary and Cross-Sector Collaboration ... 95
6.8.2 Collective Design and Participatory AI Development ... 95
6.8.3 International AI Governance Discussions ... 96
6.8.4 Partnerships Developing Ethical AI Through Cooperative Business Models ... 96
6.8.5 Civil Society and Advocacy Organizations ... 96
6.8.6 Academic Institutions and AI Literacy Programs ... 96
6.8.7 Independent Research and Think Tanks ... 97
6.9 Future Perspectives: Cultivating a Culture of Ethical Accountability ... 97
6.9.1 Integrating Ethics from the Beginning ... 97

6.9.2 Commitment of Leadership and Governance of Organizations ... 98
6.9.3 Encouragement of Ethical Behavior ... 98
6.9.4 Public Involvement and the Discussion of Ethical Issues ... 98
6.9.5 Continuous Evaluation and Ongoing Improvement ... 99
6.9.6 Creation of Systems of Regulatory Guidelines and Legal Frameworks ... 99

Chapter 7 Ethical Considerations of Autonomous AI Decision-Making 103

7.1 Overview of Autonomous AI and Ethical Considerations ... 103
7.2 Fundamental Ethical Dilemmas in Autonomous Decision-Making ... 104
7.2.1 Obligation and Liability ... 104
7.2.2 Clarity and Comprehensibility ... 105
7.2.3 Prejudice, Equity, and Inequity ... 105
7.2.4 Human Agency, Consent, and Control ... 105
7.2.5 Privacy and Data Management ... 106
7.3 Practical Implementation of Transparency and Accountability ... 106
7.3.1 Documentation of Models and Systems ... 107
7.3.2 Data Transparency and Traceability ... 107
7.3.3 Transparency in Decision-Making and the Right to Explanation ... 107
7.3.4 Responsibility Throughout the AI Lifecycle ... 108
7.3.5 Regulatory and Organizational Conformity ... 108
7.4 Governance and Risk Management for Autonomous Artificial Intelligence ... 108
7.4.1 Governance Based on Lifecycle ... 109
7.4.2 Mechanisms for Human Oversight and Intervention ... 109
7.4.3 Auditing and Independent Evaluation ... 110
7.4.4 Incident Reporting and Response ... 110
7.4.5 Harmonizing Governance with Regulation and Organizational Culture ... 110
7.5 Case Studies on Autonomous Decision-Making Failures and Acquired Insights ... 111
7.5.1 Autonomous Decision-Making in Healthcare ... 111
7.5.2 Autonomous Systems in Criminal Justice and Law Enforcement ... 112
7.5.3 Autonomous Vehicles and Safety-Critical Determinations ... 112
7.5.4 Integrative Ethical Insights from Case Studies ... 112

7.6 Practical Guidelines for the Ethical Implementation of Autonomous AI 113
7.6.1 Clearly Define Purpose and Boundaries 113
7.6.2 Designate Accountability Prior to Implementation 113
7.6.3 Incorporate Transparency into System Design 113
7.6.4 Assessment for Bias, Safety, and Contextual Relevance 114
7.6.5 Guarantee Significant Human Supervision 114
7.6.6 Implement Monitoring and Incident Response Protocols 114
7.6.7 Synchronize Practices with Legal and Regulatory Standards 115
7.6.8 Consider Ethics as a Continuous Organizational Obligation 115
7.7 Conclusion and Principal Insights 115

Chapter 8 Navigating Regulation and Governance in Generative AI 118

8.1 Overview 118
8.2 The Present State of AI Regulation 119
8.2.1 The European Union: Leading in Risk-Based Regulation 119
8.2.2 The United States: Sector-Specific and Decentralized Regulation 119
8.2.3 China: Governance Centered on the State and Focused on Security 120
8.2.4 Innovative Frameworks: Canada, Singapore, and the United Kingdom 120
8.2.5 Principal Obstacles in the Regulatory Framework 121
8.3 The Significance of Ethical Governance 122
8.3.1 Transparency: A Fundamental Element of Democratic Oversight 122
8.3.2 Accountability: Correlating Authority with Obligation 122
8.3.3 Equity and Non-Discrimination 123
8.3.4 Human Supervision and Autonomy 124
8.3.5 Inclusivity and Stakeholder Engagement 124
8.4 Global Collaboration and the Necessity for International AI Regulation 124
8.4.1 The Issue of Fragmentation and Regulatory Arbitrage 125
8.4.2 Multilateral Institutions and Their Functions 125

8.4.3 The Necessity for Binding, Interoperable Frameworks 126
8.4.4 Comprehensive and Fair Global Governance........ 126
8.5 Regulatory Case Studies........ 126
8.5.1 Case Study 1: The European Union's AI Act—A Pro-active Rights-Based Framework 127
8.5.2 Case Study 2: Canada's Artificial Intelligence and Data Act (AIDA)—A Risk-Based Compliance Framework 127
8.5.3 Case Study 3: Singapore's Model AI Governance Framework—Co-Regulation and Soft Law 128
8.5.4 Instructional Lessons and Comparative Insights........ 128
8.6 Challenges and Critiques of Existing Governance Models........ 129
8.6.1 Legal Inertia and the Velocity of Innovation........ 129
8.6.2 Technical Opacity and the Constraints of Explainability........ 129
8.6.3 Risk of Regulatory Capture and Corporate Self-Regulation 130
8.6.4 Ethical Relativism and Absence of Normative Coherence........ 130
8.6.5 Global Disparities and the Threat of AI Colonialism........ 130
8.6.6 Advancing Reflexive, Inclusive Governance 131
8.7 Prospective Trajectories: Advancing Adaptive and Inclusive AI Governance........ 131
8.7.1 Adaptive Regulation and Anticipatory Governance........ 131
8.7.2 Collaborative and Multi-Party Governance........ 132
8.7.3 Establishing Global AI Governance Frameworks........ 132
8.7.4 Ethics by Design and Technological Alignment........ 133
8.7.5 Empowerment and Worldwide Inclusion........ 133
8.8 Conclusion........ 133

Chapter 9 Developers' Responsibilities in Promoting Ethical AI 137

9.1 Developers as Ethical Decision-Makers in Artificial Intelligence Systems........ 137
9.1.1 Mitigating Harm Beyond Technical Malfunction........ 137
9.1.2 Transparency as a Prerequisite for Accountability........ 138
9.1.3 Ethical Agency and Professional Disagreement........ 138
9.2 Integrating Ethics Throughout the AI Development Lifecycle........ 139
9.2.1 Ethical Anticipation in Problem Identification and System Architecture........ 139
9.2.2 Data Curation as an Ethical Obligation........ 139

9.2.3 Equity and Responsibility in Model Development . 140
9.2.4 Human-Centric Assessment and Implementation ... 140
9.2.5 Ongoing Surveillance and Post-Implementation Accountability ... 140
9.3 Organizational Conditions Facilitating Ethical AI Development ... 141
9.3.1 Ethical Instruction as Professional Proficiency ... 141
9.3.2 Team Diversity as a Risk Identification Mechanism ... 141
9.3.3 Governance Frameworks That Facilitate Ethical Decision-Making ... 142
9.3.4 Leadership, Dissent, and Ethical Responsibility ... 142
9.3.5 Ethics as an Organizational Practice Rather Than a Slogan ... 143

Chapter 10 Future Directions: Toward Sustainable and Ethical AI Development 145

10.1 Overview ... 145
10.2 Enhancing Regulatory and Policy Frameworks ... 146
10.2.1 Proactive Regulation and Adaptive Governance ... 146
10.2.2 International Alignment and Transnational Regulation ... 147
10.3 Expanding Ethical Considerations in AI Engineering and Implementation ... 148
10.3.1 Automation of Ethical Audits and Risk Prediction ... 149
10.3.2 Integrating Ethics into Development Pipelines ... 150
10.4 Mitigating the Risks Associated with Synthetic Content and Misinformation ... 151
10.4.1 Deepfakes, Misinformation, and Public Confidence ... 152
10.4.2 Authenticity Framework and Digital Provenance ... 153
10.5 Guaranteeing Equity, Access, and Inclusion in GenAI Futures ... 154
10.5.1 Mitigating Data Colonialism ... 154
10.5.2 Designing Culturally Attuned AI Systems ... 155
10.6 Promoting Multidisciplinary and Human-Centric AI Research ... 157
10.6.1 Interdisciplinary Collaboration ... 157
10.6.2 Incorporating End-User Perspectives ... 158
10.7 Advancing a Sustainable and Equitable AI Ecosystem ... 158

Index ... 161

Preface

This book started off with an increasing sense of uneasiness. I have watched AI develop over the years, from specialized algorithms that could sort emails or forecast stock prices to generative systems that can create legal documents, write poetry, or mimic human voices. Innovation has advanced at an astounding rate. Our collective endeavor to comprehend the significance of all of this, however, has been slowertoo slow, in fact.

Technically, no. Morally, yes.

Performance measures, benchmarks, and innovations continue to dominate most discussions on AI. That makes sense. However, we somehow missed the more difficult and subdued queries.

Questions such as
Whose data was used to train this model?
What presumptions do these systems have built in?
When something goes wrong, who is responsible?

I have tried to reintroduce those questions in this work. To promote a more careful discussion about the systems we are creating, not to lecture or scare. It is intended for developers who are tired of hearing that ethics is someone else's responsibility; for students who aspire to build not only impressively but responsibly; and for researchers and policy experts trying to stay focused on what matters while navigating a rapidly changing environment.

A crucial component of the ethical puzzle bias, privacy, calibration, transparency, regulation, and accountability—is covered in each chapter. These problems are not new. However, they acquire significant complexity and urgency in the setting of generative AI. Reacting systems are no longer an issue for us. We are working with creative systems. Furthermore, creating systems devoid of conscience is harmful.

The book does not claim to know everything. In addition to case studies, real-world examples, and useful tactics, it does seek to provide a clear, organized framework for thinking about the difficulties. I have made every effort to avoid abstractions and to anchor concepts, because morality only matters when it can be put into practice.

Now for my acknowledgments, which are equally important but more difficult to write.

Without my mother's love, encouragement, and silent strength, this book would not be possible. Her faith in me and the value of education have always been the driving force behind my actions. I am grateful to my family for their patience and grace in putting up with my long writing sessions, half-finished dinner table ideas, and an inbox that frequently went unchecked. This journey would not have meant much without my husband and kids, who have supported me with unflinching kindness, compassion, and encouragement.

To the numerous students, coworkers, and friends who have pushed my ideas, made me re-evaluate my presumptions, and helped me ask better questions: you have influenced this work more than you realize.

Finally, I want to express my sincere gratitude to my publisher for recognizing that ethical AI merits a special place on the bookshelf, for believing in this project, and for supporting it through each round of editing.

This book is also dedicated to all those who have contributed, directly or indirectly, to the pages that follow.

Let us do more than simply create smarter AI.
Let us put more positive intentions behind it.

Loveleen Gaur, PhD
Author

About the Author

Dr Loveleen Gaur is a senior academic, researcher, and international examiner with over two decades of experience in higher education, doctoral supervision, and research evaluation. She holds a PhD in Computer Applications and specializes in Artificial Intelligence, Generative AI, Data Science, and Business Analytics, with strong interdisciplinary applications across management, healthcare, and digital systems.

She currently serves as Faculty Lead of the Doctoral Program in Deep Technologies at Universidad Nacional Mayor de San Marcos, Lima, Peru, and as Dissertation Committee Chair of the DBA Program at Golden Gate University Worldwide, San Francisco, USA. She is also Research Professor at Alliance University, Bengaluru, India, and Adjunct Professor at the University of the South Pacific, Fiji. In addition, she serves as an Assessor for Innovate UK (UK Research and Innovation) and as a Judge for the QS Reimagine Education Awards. Earlier, as Professor at Amity University, India, she founded its postgraduate programs in AI and Business Analytics.

Dr Gaur has served as an External PhD Examiner and doctoral committee member for several international universities, including Taylor's University, Malaysia; Auckland University of Technology, New Zealand; Alliance University, India; and the Symbiosis Centre for Research and Innovation.

She has an extensive publication record, with more than 150 research outputs and over 5,000 citations in high-impact journals indexed in Scopus and Web of Science, and has authored and edited multiple scholarly books with leading publishers such as Elsevier, Springer, Taylor & Francis, Wiley, and IGI Global. She serves as Co-Editor-in-Chief of *Communications in Statistics: Case Studies, Data Analysis and Applications* (Taylor & Francis) and as Series Editor of *Concise Introductions to AI and Data Science* (Wiley-Scrivener), along with several editorial and reviewer roles across reputed international journals.

Recognized globally for her research impact, Dr Gaur is listed among the Elsevier and Stanford University World's Top 2% Scientists (2024 and 2025) and is a Senior Member of IEEE.

1 Demystifying Generative AI

1.1 EMERGENCE OF GENERATIVE AI

In this chapter, we discuss the apparent rise of Generative AI (GenAI) and how this relates to our earlier questions of whether a machine might create (i.e., produce) a copy of a work of art or write a book (i.e., create literature). If yes, what will it be worth? What's the difference if we "dignify" these machine-born works by calling them art? GenAI raises a lot of unanswered questions, and we need to engage in this multidisciplinary research area examining culture, economy, legality and the relationship between technology and creativity. Academics are currently working on these investigations into how GenAI is shaping our culture and aesthetics, what ownership and attribution of a work born of machine might be, how it might change our conceptions of the future of creative work, and how GenAI affects modern day media (Epstein et al., 2023).

1.1.1 Definition of Generative AI

Generative AI (GenAI) has become one of the fastest-growing branches of artificial intelligence, and it is now widely used by the public, software developers, and within universities. GenAI systems produce new text, images, audio, and video by learning the statistical patterns found in large training datasets (Figure 1.1). They rely mainly on machine learning, and in particular on neural networks and deep learning, which allow the models to capture complex patterns and create new content rather than only classify what already exists. Three model families do most of this work today: Generative Adversarial Networks (GANs), Variational Autoencoders (VAEs), and diffusion models. These have been used to generate photorealistic images and to write coherent text across many tasks Bengesi et al. (2024); Gozalo-Brizuela and Garrido-Merchán (2023); Dasgupta et al. (2023); Epstein et al. (2023).

In particular, the AI industry has come up with several different methods of producing new forms of content (GenAI models), which have the characteristics of actual content of specific use adjusted for (customized content generation, artwork generation, scientific data synthesis, etc.). In contrast to much of the remaining use of AI, such as traditional AI systems used to classify, observe and predict, as well as recommend, GenAI is more about the assessment (or the interpretation) of previously existing types of content (Bengesi et al., 2024; Dasgupta et al., 2023; Epstein et al., 2023; Gozalo-Brizuela, 2023; Gozalo-Brizuela & Garrido-Merchán, 2023).

DOI: 10.1201/9781003679974-1

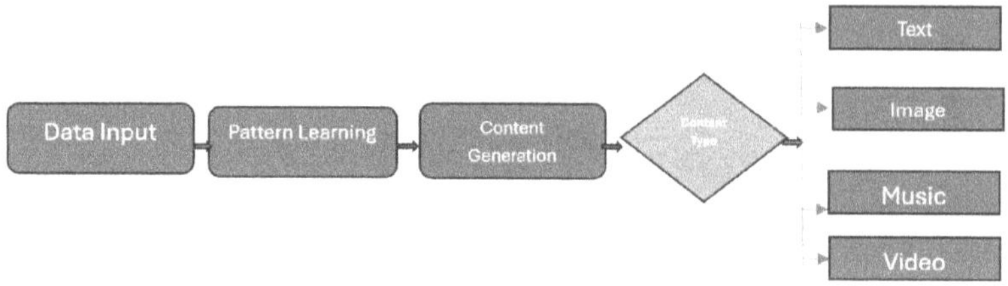

FIGURE 1.1 GenAI process. Source: Authors.

In brief, the major, very commonly deployed technical methods of creating data, GenAI, are based on machine learning (ML) and neural network (NN) technology. ML techniques (in particular, the use of deep learning models) leverage the huge amounts of data amassed to look for the underlying rules and structures of the data being attempted to create. These found models and structures enable a model to create a new but realistic version of the original training data. Two factors define the rapid evolution of GenAI. One is the huge quantity of insights available for computer system browsing; the additional technological increment is the building of advanced networks intended to permit the computer searching through that information. This has resulted in the creation of an extremely reliable generative model. GenAI will have significant opportunities, gaining access to science, art, and entertainment, across the globe. The continuing evolution of GenAI will define how improvement in the areas of human–computer communication occurs, as well as how we will communicate with and utilize visual media and technology.

1.1.2 A Concise Historical Overview: Transitioning from Theory to Practice

The history of GenAI (see Figure 1.2) started long ago with research into general-purpose computer technology by researchers hoping to create robots capable of producing original, amusing works. Alan Turing postulated that robots might be able to write (and paint!) original works, an early contribution to GenAI development. In the ensuing years since Turing first pondered machine-generated content, GenAI grew stronger. Better generative models are made, making photogenic pictures and clear, fun prose (and more) possible through neural networks, a kind of ML algorithm. With the ability to supply more information and accelerate our computing speed, the generative ability of these models has been improved by training more complex neural models on larger datasets. An enormous leap for GenAI came with the creation of GAN (Bengesi et al., 2024). GANs are complex neural nets consisting of a generator and a discriminator that change the game for machine-generated content and enable the creation of images, video, music composition, and more applications (Bengesi et al., 2024). Along with GANs, GenAI came up with VAEs and diffusion models. Interest and engagement with GenAI in the last decade have exploded, and countless models and cutting-edge tools have popped up to enable machines to run wild and do things like compose music, conduct scientific research, and create videos, text, and

FIGURE 1.2 Evolution of generative AI: Significant milestones. Source: Authors.

more (Bengesi et al., 2024; Gozalo-Brizuela & Garrido-Merchán, 2023; Dasgupta et al., 2023; Epstein et al., 2023).

1.2 THE POWER OF CREATION: APPLICATIONS IN VARIOUS INDUSTRIES

The various applications of GenAI are shown in Figure 1.3.

1.2.1 GenAI in Art and Entertainment

GenAI provides a novel approach to content development and production, with the potential to revolutionize thinking and making art across a myriad of industries. With GenAI, artists can create new kinds of creative work, whether that is high-quality furry artwork or gaming content. Thanks to diffusion models, artists are

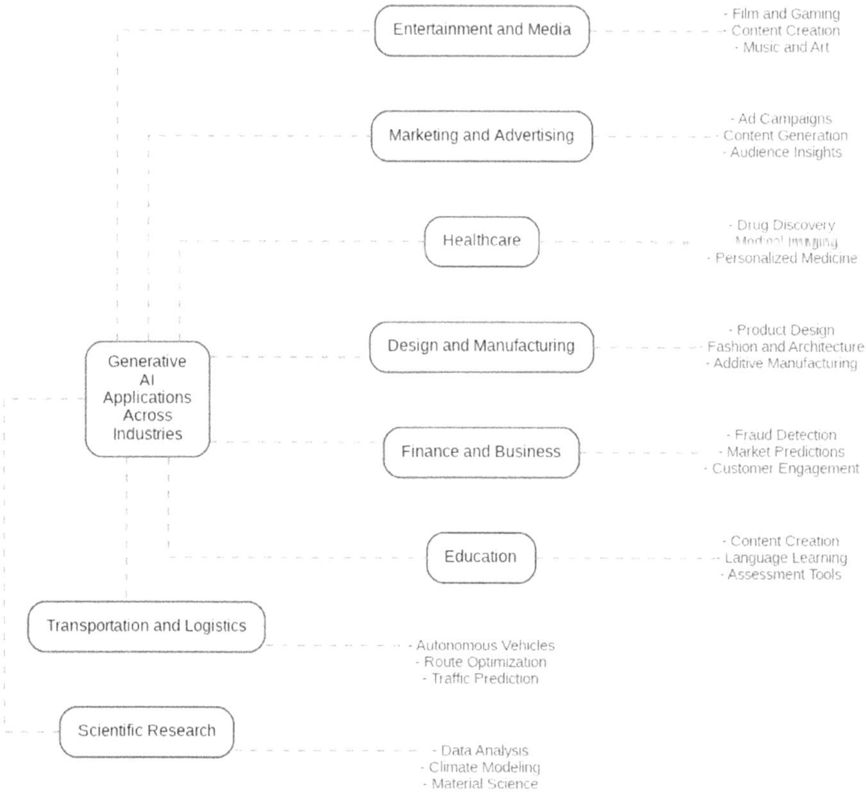

FIGURE 1.3 Applications of GenAI.

exploring the ever-reaching plains of high quality, high-def images and bringing back new types of art that they may not have created before. Writers of poetry and prose find in the development of LLMs the ability to combine words and sentences in new ways to bring exciting new works for ears and eyes to listen to and behold. Out in the world, both arts are getting introductions to new avenues of artistic expression.

In a recent evaluation, Crimaldi and Leonelli (2023) describe how "the creation of human-computer interaction tools applicable to the artistic creation process and the development of AI technologies that generate new kinds of creative output are altering the way the public thinks about these things." GenAI's creative power has outstripped any expectations in the entertainment industry as when "used in games, GenAI can create a plethora of dynamic compelling game worlds, individual storylines, and characters to negligibly alter the user experience of the video game world" (2023). As GenAI continues to develop, there is no telling what its true impact on creative things in the future will be. We will need multidisciplinary research to get anywhere close to grasping the implications of GenAI on commerce, culture, and creativity (Crimaldi & Leonelli, 2023; Epstein et al., 2023; Ghosh & Fossas, 2022).

1.2.2 Revolutionizing Healthcare Through AI-Driven Innovation

GenAI, the term commonly used for AI that generates unstructured data such as text, has reshaped the healthcare industry and changed how drug development and personalized treatments are approached. The impact of GenAI will revolutionize how we conduct pharmacological R&D, enhance speed, productivity, and data quality by removing human error in data collection, research, and decision-making. The discovery of new drugs is vastly impacted by GenAI and how AI technologies are being used to identify and develop new drug compounds via AI analytics and ML algorithms in drug development. The rapid development of large-scale datasets in biological sciences will allow even more companies specifically aimed at applying AI to conduct drug discovery research. AI companies are entering partnerships with pharmaceutical companies to maximize the benefits of GenAI by using it in the development of new strategies and modalities for treatments, and for the discovery of novel drug candidates and drug repurposing.

Partnerships between larger pharmaceutical companies and smaller AI companies (like the one between Pfizer and IBM as they work together to develop a new AI system called Watson) are helping change the way drugs get discovered and developed. Collaborations between the academic and pharmaceutical industries are vital to developing newer and more innovative AI applications in drug discovery and development (Hasselgren & Oprea, 2024). The effects of GenAI on personalized medicine are no less significant. AI applications can analyze massive datasets on a host of different dimensions of an individual patient's health, including genomics, medical history, and social determinants of health, and produce a treatment regimen tailored to a patient's unique needs so they experience greater levels of treatment effectiveness and satisfaction. GenAI has also had an impressive impact on medical research; AI will help radiologists and other providers of diagnostic medicine in searching images, locating anomalies, and providing greater accuracy in diagnostics (Quer et al., 2017; Shamszare & Choudhury, 2023). The healthcare industry faces challenges currently. GenAI's entry has caused rising costs, limited resources, and the need for more effective and personalized care.

An entire treatment plan for every patient in diabetes is being created by GenAI. Relying on genomic data, medical records, and clinical evidence, GenAI algorithms can identify individual biomarkers useful for predicting disease development and determining the ideal treatment plan for each diabetic patient. In this way, the effectiveness of treatment on diabetes will be maximized, and the risk of serious adverse drug reactions to the medications will be reduced, improving the outcomes of patients with diabetes. While making individual patient treatment plans, GenAI also impacts making new medical images and interpreting old medical pictures. Medical image analysis is performed by GenAI editing MRI, CT, or X-ray and allowing medical image analyzers to produce medical images more accurately than ever. With this greater accuracy come more informed treatment decisions and the early discovery of medical conditions (Quer et al., 2017).

GenAI is also being used to develop personalized drug therapies and prescriptions for diabetic patients. Based on "data and genes from patients and other recorded medical information," GenAI models can "dispense advice about the development of personalised drug therapies," resulting in better outcomes and less risk of adverse drug reactions. Beyond individualized therapy and drug development, GenAI is being used for many other applications in healthcare and health IT. For instance, GenAI is being used to improve clinical imaging capabilities, which are critical for diagnosis and clinical planning. GenAI can be employed to automate the image analysis of MRI, CT, and X-ray images, and it is 99% accurate. GenAI can be used for early disease detection and to make better-informed treatment decisions (Quer et al., 2017). While there are limitations as to the use of GenAI in healthcare, its potential utilization for patients and clinicians exists right now, and as technology progresses, the future holds exciting possibilities for GenAI applications in all areas of healthcare.

1.2.3 AI in Commerce: Automation, Innovation, and Further Developments

The blistering pace of GenAI has now more organizations prototyping leading-edge methods in customer service, marketing, product development, and a hundred more areas of the business where advanced applications of AI are being applied. From the increased use of advanced AI technologies on site in organizations, firms have learned to embed better consumer experience, stimulate creativity, and excise waste in process. Organizations are gaining access to a new level of efficiency beyond what paper-pushing voids can yield from GenAI deployment and its impact on content production in marketing. Organizations with a deployment of GenAI can churn out tons of marketing content about their product, its product descriptions, emails, etc., their Social Media; and so businesses can save time (Won't say it thrice, got its first trick out of the air), make funny relatable tweets that actually resonate with their target, improve conversion rates, and win client loyalty. GenAI has changed the game for customer service experience—that's the least of the good an organization can now reap. Organizations can now hit the GenAI-powered bots and virtual assistants to handle queries from order tracking to making product recommendations, creating 24/7 customer support for delivering an experience at volume that is both pristine in its consistency and above the line of the expected quality. Threading its way through the features above, and the examples of organizations going live with GenAI to deliver customer service, we covered so much of the footprint of GenAI that it appears transforming, has the power to elevate creativity in organizations to light a fire in organizations. In pharmaceuticals, GenAI enabling itself into the mix, and GenAI speeded the blends of research and clinical trials massively, increasing productivity, and massively reducing turnaround times and massively improving their decision-making ability. GenAI might transform the current paradigm for delivery of the messages of learning to our children through their environments for learning, filling their learning environment with custom learning materials throughout, rich interactive and cooperative learning spaces, and new and improved means to assess how well students are learning. There's a clearly vibrant and interesting commercial landscape as companies can now discover new commercial prospects opened by the gorgeous possibilities GenAI seems to appear to have and then revolutionize customer service and surface fresh opportunities for automation and repeat. GenAI opens boundless possibilities looking toward the real direction and progress of level of achievements in predictive analytics and the true power of decision-making capabilities.

1.3 ETHICAL FRONTIERS: ADDRESSING THE CHALLENGES OF GENERATIVE AI

1.3.1 The Ambivalent Nature of AI Creativity

The rapid development of GenAI technologies presents an entirely new realm of creativity and creation, requiring us to reconsider both authorship and authenticity along with the conceptualization of creative expression. While GenAI's algorithms allow people to be creative in ways that were previously impossible, they also introduce tremendous ethical dilemmas that must be examined and addressed carefully. On the positive side, the technologies associated with GenAI have the potential to create entirely new and innovative ways for people to express themselves and generate high-quality creative content in minutes or hours using different types of media (e.g., text, images, etc.). Furthermore, the democratization of creativity provides people with the opportunity to participate in the creative process, helps to build and support a vibrant and strong creative economy, lowers the barriers to entry to creativity, and ultimately opens limitless possibilities for innovation. However, many of the very qualities that allow for creative expression present such challenges to the fundamental tenets of artistic and creative practice that create difficulties associated with balancing the output of human-created works with those of machine-generated works, especially relative to copyright and intellectual property concerns. As the emergence of GenAI presents considerable concerns relative to the future of the livelihoods of authors, artists, and others whose livelihoods depend on copyright and intellectual property (Ghosh & Fossas, 2022; Healy, 2023), it is imperative to understand that issues related to copyright and intellectual property are "timely" topics specifically related to generative AI. Creative works generated by GenAI algorithms will produce more creative works than ever, and as such, it will be increasingly more difficult for creators to determine whether original or derivative work was produced. Consequently, authors may be at a higher risk for being taken advantage of, with their works being less distinguishable from virtually identical works of other creators that were generated by GenAI algorithms. Thus, intellectual property is also a significant topic in the context of GenAI technology since the technology produces collections of creative works through AI algorithms using already existing creative works as input. Many are concerned as to what degree human-made creative works will retain their societal value and/or if there will be a difference in the value assigned to a machine-made creative work and a human-made creative work. At the same time, the use of machines in the creative process raises questions about the definition of "artist," or whether a machine can be classified as an artist. Therefore, the increasing proliferation of GenAI will require a careful assessment of how to balance being an individual creative thinker with the ability to generate innovative and/or new ideas and fully realize the transformative potential of GenAI as higher education can fundamentally change the way creative people operate in the creative industries. The emergence of GenAI relative to creative professions will create significant ethical challenges that will require a systematic and comprehensive response (Shams et al., 2023).

1.3.2 Prejudice and Equity: Guaranteeing Justice in Artificial Intelligence

How is AI transforming people's lives, including the criminal justice system and health care, at a rapid pace due to too much dependency on AI algorithms? There are growing concerns regarding bias in OpenAI systems (AI) that can undermine fairness among members of society and cause inequities to marginalized or disadvantaged communities by being trained with biased data. As such, there is an urgent need to develop fair and inclusive GenAI systems that produce output of images/content/other forms without the bias produced from society's assumptions. Numerous researchers have provided evidence of biased AI algorithms, and they have concluded that having multiple perspectives during the design and development phases is essential in preventing AI bias. Biases in AI algorithms can appear in several ways, including lack of representation of certain demographic groups within the training datasets; reinforcement of stereotypes; and exclusion from critical contextual information. To mitigate AI bias, it is imperative that we both prioritize representation and diversity regarding how the training datasets used to create the AI systems were constructed. Thus, to ensure that there is representative training data for marginalized groups, the training data must be selected carefully to ensure that it includes diverse perspectives and experiences from which to draw. In addition, to fully identify and address the potential for bias to occur due to data collection, model training, and model deployment, the culture of openness/accountability must exist in the AI development community. Many researchers have urged that true progress in combating bias and fairness issues in AI can only be achieved through collaborative, interdisciplinary efforts. There are many opportunities for the computing community to learn about how to address societal issues that accompany AI when working in concert with various groups of stakeholders representing a diverse set of stakeholders such as ethicists, lawmakers, and content experts (Radanliev & Santos, 2023; Turner & Critchlow, 2021).

1.3.3 Privacy Issues: Safeguarding Data in an AI-Driven Environment

The assessment of the security, ethics, and consent required when collecting and using personal data must be revisited considering the advanced capabilities of the next-generation GenAI systems as they continue to be deployed in every area of our lives including but not limited to scientific and educational use. The ethics associated with the deployable technologies built on GenAI continue to be examined with respect to the security of the personal data used in building these systems, as well as how that data is shared or disclosed with third parties. To enhance privacy protections and maximize the benefits of the successful and ethical use of AI technologies, researchers have indicated the need for new advanced algorithmic solutions—including, but not limited to, differential privacy, homomorphic encryption, and federated learning (Radanliev & Santos, 2023). One of the main challenges in achieving these goals is placing the power of individual control of their personal data and providing individuals with the ability to make well-informed decisions about how their data is used in their hands. In addition to the fact that GenAI provides differentiated solutions to individual users and opportunities for assessing the cognitive operations of the individual user, it will complicate educating consumers about the possible implications of their data usage. One commonality between existing AI systems is that they frequently lack transparency; therefore, there is a clear risk of bias in any use of those systems, justifying a need for more interaction from researchers and educators with GenAI systems to fully comprehend their advantages and disadvantages (Radanliev & Santos, 2023).

Assessing the potential societal impacts arising from the widespread incorporation of GenAI into society is an essential responsibility for numerous reasons. As we continue to have access to more technological solutions, we will not only be required to redefine our understanding of trust in terms of communicating with others but also readjust our educational curriculum as well as adapt to changing cultural standards. We must provide supportive, educationally focused frameworks and strategies to educators as we continue to implement GenAI into learning environments to help them comply with ethical standards and create robust privacy protection mechanisms to allow effective use of this technology to positively influence teaching and learning (Turner & Critchlow, 2021). A comprehensive, multilayered strategy must be developed to adequately address these issues. Such strategies should include developing secure technology-based solutions, establishing regulatory frameworks, and reinforcing the ethical use of artificial intelligence in our society. Our proactive approach toward the privacy issue associated with GenAI will allow society to utilize these transformative technologies while still protecting individuals' rights and freedoms within the growing digital environment.

1.4 THE ETHICAL FRAMEWORK FOR GENERATIVE AI

1.4.1 Tenets for Ethical AI Development

There are valid concerns about accountability and transparency arising from the rapid expansion of AI (artificial intelligence) for producing content. Deciding who deserves credit for successful results, and who is responsible for the errors or negative outcomes caused by AI, is a complex and multifaceted question that will likely take time to resolve. The accountability for the decision produced by the AI agent should be based on the algorithm and data set used to create the outcome. Thus, it is critical that an ethical framework, principles, and community norms surrounding these types of systems are established. A chain of accountability must be established for who and what created the AI decision and how the different parties involved in the process influence the outcome, e.g., users, owners, designers, and developers should connect to the chain of accountability. Responsible AI development is strongly dependent on transparency. The algorithm design should allow people and other stakeholders to view how AI arrived at the outcome. Trust creation and demonstrating responsible behavior are contingent on transparency. Shoaib et al. and Saberi et al. has established that there is an equal degree of importance in developing methodologies to derive responsible development methodologies for AI as well as in establishing the principles behind the same. AI vendors can provide the governing authority, the public, and other stakeholders with confidence by providing sufficient documentation to support their AI-developed actions. However, the ambiguity and lack of transparency associated with AI-developed content will be challenging to establish accountability and transparency for AI-generated decisions. For example, due to the complexities of the logic behind AI content generation, the rationale for these decisions is frequently impeded, thereby hampering efforts to establish accountability for the AI agent's decision-making.

In addition, the complexity of artificial intelligence (AI) systems and the many AI stakeholders make it difficult to assess the role of each stakeholder in the development of an AI system. Resolving this issue requires a broad and somewhat holistic, comprehensive approach.

1.4.2 Governance and Regulation: Influencing the Future

As AI technology continues to permeate our lives at an increasing rate, it has become increasingly obvious to all relevant stakeholders that strong and inclusive governance and regulatory regimes are necessary for this technology to be developed. The primary authors of both standards and regulations governing the ethical development and implementation of AI technology will be governments, trade associations, and international organizations. Due to the magnitude and sometimes disruptive nature of the effects that AI will have on society, regulatory agencies and policymakers must take into consideration how to balance the need for innovation and development versus the potential negative consequences of technology. To accomplish this, a comprehensive approach to developing and implementing ethical AI technology will necessitate incorporating ethical considerations into every phase of the life cycle of AI technology (deployment, monitoring, design, and execution). Legal rules and regulations, complex ethical frameworks, and continual engagement with stakeholders will all be necessary components of an inclusive and holistic approach. As most AI systems are driven by data and are generally difficult to comprehend, conventional models of regulation by governments will be challenged in their application. In addition to working with industry to achieve collective goals related to AI and its effects on society, governments must collaborate with the industry to develop effective, adaptable regulations. Legislative initiatives should also include creating a collective vision of the impact of AI on society, including the significance of establishing an open and accountable decision-making process, and the establishment of AI technologies based on human-centered design. The governance of AI technologies by humans, in a manner that is compatible with human and societal values, will necessitate a diverse group of stakeholders working in unison to develop a legal framework that supports the continued ethical development of AI. To include the range of perspectives and concerns regarding the governance of technology within the overall framework of legislation, all segments of society should be engaged in the development of policies regarding AI.

1.4.3 The Function of AI Ethics Committees and Review Boards

GenAI technologies (including large-scale language models and computer-vision-based image generators) are advancing rapidly and will have a profound effect on many aspects of our day-to-day lives, as well as how businesses operate. They are also spreading rapidly through commercial avenues, and as these technologies continue to grow in strength, they will present multiple ethical issues. Strong governance frameworks must be developed to ensure that GenAI is used ethically and responsibly by all organizations using them. The establishment of AI ethics committees and/or review boards within organizations is the initial step in creating a framework to govern and oversee the ethical use of GenAI development. AI ethics committees will establish, implement, and enforce ethical standards and procedures as they relate to GenAI development and application.

The primary purpose of AI ethics committees is to protect against the potential risks and unanticipated challenges associated with the use of GenAI by establishing ethical standards. AI ethics committees are designed to uphold both societal norms and the values of the organization using AI systems. In addition, they provide directions for how AI systems can affect other people and make recommendations on how AI systems can comply with both societal norms and organizational values. By addressing ethical issues related to GenAI development at the earliest point in time possible, AI ethics committees can mitigate the potential for bias, privacy breaches, and other detrimental effects of GenAI.

There is a growing body of evidence supporting the need for the regulation and standardization of AI ethics as well. Organizations are struggling to implement ethical practices in the use of AI even though many have created such practices. AI ethics committees will play an important role in bridging the gap by providing clear and comprehensive ways to evaluate the ethical implications of GenAI projects. Furthermore, these committees will create transparency and accountability about the ethical trajectory of GenAI; therefore, AI ethics committees should oversee the development of GenAI projects at all phases of development. As the advancement of GenAI continues, so does the necessity for reviewing and advising upon ethical considerations with AI ethics review boards/committees. These boards/committees will assist organizations in the challenges of navigating the ethical challenges that arise from the use of GenAI and ensure that GenAI is used in a responsible manner to create long-term positive impacts for both organizations and society. The typical composition of AI ethics committees consists of multidisciplinary professionals, including ethicists, legal scholars, subject matter experts, and stakeholders that will be affected by GenAI's development. The duties of AI ethics committees include the establishment of ethical guidelines for the development and implementation of GenAI systems and the enforcement of such ethical guidelines. The ethical guidelines established by AI ethics committees address many ethical issues associated with the use and implementation of GenAI, including, but not limited to, privacy, bias, accountability, transparency, and unintended consequences resulting from the implementation of GenAI. By involving AI ethics committees during the entire development of a GenAI application, organizations can ensure that GenAI is created in accordance with socially and ethically responsible standards. In addition, AI ethics committees provide advice and recommendations regarding risk mitigation and bias reduction and help organizations use GenAI to advance human rights while providing benefits to society. AI review boards established prior to the implementation of a GenAI initiative will serve as critical evaluative bodies to assess the ethical and societal impacts resulting from the use of GenAI. AI review boards will evaluate the advantages and disadvantages of the proposed use of GenAI and evaluate whether the use of GenAI complies with established ethical standards and poses an unacceptable level of risk to individuals or society. Granting increased authority within organizations to AI ethics committees and AI review boards will demonstrate an organization's commitment to developing GenAI in a socially and ethically responsible manner and assist in developing trust in the use of GenAI from the public. Therefore, the establishment and use of AI ethics committees and AI review boards is a very effective mechanism for organizations to navigate the ethical challenges associated with using generative AI. These organizations will provide the necessary oversight to ensure that GenAI is developed in accordance with the established ethical guidelines and that GenAI continues to comply with established ethical standards. AI ethics committees consist of multidisciplinary professionals, including subject matter experts, legal scholars, ethical scholars, and representatives of the individuals and families affected by using GenAI.

1.5 CASE ANALYSES: ETHICAL QUANDARIES IN GENERATIVE AI

1.5.1 Deepfakes: The Subtle Distinction Between Creativity and Deception

Generative artificial intelligence (AI), most notably in the context of deepfake technology, has made remarkable strides in its capabilities and has created a very serious and complicated dilemma concerning our relationship with both creativity and deception as well as their impacts on humankind, society, and the overall information ecosystem (Shoaib et al., 2023; Saberi et al., 2023). The phrase "deepfake" describes AI-generated content that depicts a person as having done or said something they have not. Deepfakes are incredibly creative because they make compelling visual effects or create a novel form of storytelling, as well as create a likeness of an individual who has passed. However, while the creative potential of these technologies increases, there are concerns about their misuse, including using them to propagate misinformation, commit fraud, injure people, or threaten national security. The production of hyper-realistic media using deepfake technology threatens national security, commits election fraud, and undermines trust in digital media. Although there are numerous detection methods available to identify AI-generated content, the ability to discover factual from fictitious media is becoming increasingly challenging as the sophistication of deepfake technology continues to grow while the cost of entry decreases. To address the ethical dilemmas surrounding the creation and distribution of AI-generated content and mitigate the associated risks of the harm caused by this media type, an all-inclusive solution that incorporates innovative detection technologies, multi-platform collaboration, and policy-oriented approaches is required (Shoaib et al., 2023; Saberi et al., 2023).

1.5.2 AI-Created Art: Who Holds Ownership of the Creation?

The advent of new technology, particularly artificial intelligence, has changed society as a whole and has greatly affected various art forms. GenAI models that create visual, literary, and audio pieces of content introduce many new concerns regarding the definition of creativity or authorship; therefore, the primary focus to date of this discussion is on issues surrounding authorship of GenAI-developed artworks—the GenAI models create a new piece of art based on analysis of prior works by the developer, which may result in a finding of authorship of newly created works. Conversely, the definition of authorship for traditional artistic works is clearly defined and established by the artist. The algorithms that create art through GenAI perform this by examining large databases of human-created work to determine the content of GenAI-developed works, which leads to uncertainty regarding the originality and ownership of art developed by GenAI. Copyright laws will not provide sufficient protection against the challenges posed by the development of art using AI, and legal scholars and legislators will continue their discussions regarding the impacts of the evolution of AI-created works. Independent artists have initiated multiple lawsuits against AI companies (Midjourney and Stability AI) for the practice of using copyrighted physical artwork as training materials without the creator's knowledge or permission from the artist, resulting in increased litigation and protests. As the development of art through GenAI occurs, it will be necessary to amend and clarify the definition of fair use, sampling, and derivative works in the context of copyright to ensure adequate protection for traditional artists as well as those who will create art with the assistance of AI technologies.

The ethical and legal ramifications associated with AI-generated art will be many, far-reaching, and difficult and complicated to navigate. Many artists feel that AI will replace human creativity, which could ultimately result in many of them becoming obsolete, since AI can likely recreate works they created, in whole or in part, thereby replacing them. This deeply concerns many independent artists, as it threatens to reduce their income and creates obstacles for others to pursue their creative passions. Compounding the matter, many copyrighted works are used to train AI without the knowledge, authorization, or consent of the artist, thus raising serious concerns about privacy, due process, and fairness. Due to the continued complexity that will continue to surface as this industry continues to evolve, all parties involved in AI-generated artwork should formulate a plan of action with respect to the ethical, legal, and cultural implications of AI-generated art. Policymakers, creators, and technology developers should work together to establish guidelines that protect the rights and interests of those who use AI-generated art while also responsibly and fairly using the technologies of generative AI.

1.5.3 GenAI in Medicine: Reconciling Innovation with Patient Rights

Innovations in artificial intelligence (AI) through the development of generalized artificial intelligence (GenAI) technologies have enabled novel ways to improve patient care and medical research. The extensive volume and high quality of data utilized by AI systems coupled with their capabilities to detect patterns will provide opportunities for enhanced prevention, diagnosis, and selection of therapeutic strategies for a myriad of diseases. Conversely, with advancements in AI/GenAI technologies applied to medicine, there are significant ethical issues regarding patient rights and the ethical use of AI technology that must be addressed in future investigation projects.

The primary ethical issues are those relating to informed consent and the security of confidential data. GenAI applications are developed through training using very large datasets. Often, those datasets include extensive amounts of varied data from numerous sources, which may include highly sensitive medical information. Obtaining informed consent from all patients whose medical information is part of a dataset used to build or develop GenAI technology is critical to the ethical use of the technology by physicians. Cybersecurity is essential for the security of patients' private data using GenAI systems. Additionally, the potential for unintended bias and discrimination in AI-generated decisions is an ethical issue.

AI-generated algorithms have the potential to continue or even exacerbate the already existing disparity in healthcare outcomes based on non-representative training data from developing the GenAI algorithms that comprise them. As such, the creation of diverse and representative datasets, fair algorithmic practices, and regulatory oversight to limit the disparity in healthcare outcomes are crucial. In addition, healthcare practitioners will benefit from ongoing work to establish AI transparency and awareness around AI-based clinical decision-making. Patients should accompany recommendations or findings from AI systems with a rationale that qualifies their validity or appropriateness for the patient, as the implications of these decisions are significant given the potential impact on patient outcomes. Consequently, a thorough review and approval process of GenAI diagnosis or treatment recommendations made, without detailed oversight, could produce a negative impact on the safety of patients. The utilization of GenAI to develop an individualized treatment plan and to produce synthetic medical data has considerable potential benefit to patients; however, the use of these technologies will present additional risk to patients if not closely monitored and validated. Therefore, the establishment of solid proof-of-concept and routine post-deployment monitoring processes, as well as systems to provide assurance, and to create an environment of accountability for the effective and secure delivery of AI-based healthcare services will aid in reducing the risks. To support the viable implementation of these AI-based technologies into healthcare, a thorough and inclusive governance framework must be established. An inclusive governance framework can only be achieved through a collaborative process involving policymakers, healthcare providers, ethicists, and AI technology experts, and the work of all parties needs to produce an appropriate level of regulation that appropriately balances the potential for GenAI technology benefit with the need to protect the rights and welfare of patients.

1.6 THE WAY AHEAD: CONSTRUCTING A RESPONSIBLE AI FUTURE

1.6.1 Collaborative Initiatives: Reconciling Technology and Ethics

GenAI constructions ramping up the accuracy/anomaly detection. There's still not much cooperation between all parties involved with these projects. There'll be success at creating supplemental value to society through the collaborative efforts of engineers/ethicists/politicians/public alike. Identifying whether there is perceived adequate utility (i.e., value derived) will help develop solutions for both current/future GenAI constructions with respect to their respective impacts, compliance, tracking/reporting, payment processing, etc. By examining the elements associated with the blending of ethics/jurisdiction/technologies in the development of independent generative artificial intelligence systems, it is possible to establish a more rigorous process when evaluating technology ethics. The fundamental components of this framework include assessing the identified variables; fostering human development; cultivating trust/transparency; and instilling values to generative artificial intelligence. The research demonstrates that there needs to be collaboration among the major participants involved with AI development; establishing the trustworthiness of technologies/AI frameworks is essential to facilitating the successful development and implementation of generative AI solutions. In addition to promoting the development/implementation of technologies that do not negatively impact society, AI leaders carry responsibility to ensure the accurate definition of technology and the ethical frameworks on which technologies are developed. The stakeholders set forth by policymakers, i.e., regulatory agencies and their representatives, will create the supporting infrastructure necessary for the successful development/implementation and utilization of generative AI by clearly defining and implementing policies and standards of operation and determining how such systems will be monitored for compliance or urgent modification. Collaboration is the common thread between all parties and must therefore be a strategic priority when partnering to successfully build trust with the public, as well as to build an understanding of the ultimate benefit of AI technologies. Ultimately, the continued success of generative AI depends on the continued commitment and collaborative efforts of all stakeholders toward maximizing the synergistic potential of technology to significantly improve both individuals' lives/communities/etc.

1.6.2 Education and Awareness: Empowering Future Generations

Because of the rapid growth of artificial intelligence (AI) technology, we need to provide education about and raise awareness of the ethical implications of these technologies. AI development will have an impact on every part of our lives: business, government, scientific research, health care; thus, we must develop a comprehensive ethical framework around AI development and use with the overall goal of enhancing people's health and wellness. Given the scope and significance of AI technology's impact on society, we must create a culture of responsible innovation by collectively working toward developing a holistic approach that brings together (1) ethical training, (2) legislation, (3) professional development, and (4) innovation to achieve this overarching goal. To ensure that the next generation of AI developers and users understands the complexities and challenges presented by the rapid growth of AI technology, we must create and incorporate comprehensive ethical frameworks into their professional training.

The engagement of multiple stakeholders (e.g., researchers, representatives from civil society & legislators) is vital for developing and implementing effective AI systems. Therefore, this research proposes a model for a holistic approach to integrating ethics into the regulatory process, innovation and education regarding AI by (1) recognizing the need to create comprehensive ethical frameworks, (2) ensuring that ethics are incorporated into AI professional training, (3) conducting ethical impact assessments, and (4) engaging with relevant stakeholders during the design and development of AI systems. The holistic approach proposed in this study will facilitate human progression, foster alignment between technological progress and our morals/interests and promote trust and transparency in AI development.

This study emphasizes that accountability and substantiated claims are fundamental elements associated with the development of AI technologies. As described, the number of AI applications has increased significantly because of recent technological advancements in AI. The increase in AI applications parallels the tremendous growth in the public's understanding of the implications of AI systems today; thus, current ethical standards and regulations (in the business and academic contexts) are no longer sufficient to support responsible and ethical AI development. The establishment of a culture of transparency and ethical innovation will give the next generation the knowledge, skills, and capabilities to address the ethical issues associated with the use of AI.

1.6.3 Advancing a Human-Centric AI Future

The ability of GenAI to support and enhance creative and innovative processes requires careful consideration. Society's fascination with generative AI continues to grow as the pace of generative AI development and the implementation of generative AI technology continues to accelerate; thus, there are questions regarding what this means within the realm of the creative industries. As generative AI provides support for augmenting/enhancing human capabilities—previously unseen there will be new opportunities for collaboration between human beings and AI. Several studies show that generative AI systems have developed new methodologies for developing creatively; therefore, generative AI technologies can now be considered equal to or surpass human creativity in several categories associated with creativity. However, the introduction of generative AI also raises ethical and philosophical questions regarding the overall implications for the creative industries and their future. Philosophers are beginning to examine the relationship between creativity and consciousness through the lens of philosophical inquiry as this area of interest becomes increasingly important. Questions regarding how far AI has advanced in attempting to replicate human creativity, if at all, are also becoming an important ethical question; however, the advent of generative replicas and their implications for making machine-generated creative works indistinguishable from human-generated works continue to blur the lines between human made and machine-generated works. Furthermore, questions regarding whether the incorporation of generative AI into the creative process diminishes the perceived superiority of human-created creative works, or strengthens the relationship between individuals and technology will also need to be addressed by individuals/organizations that continue to build the application of generative AI technologies. If the development of generative AI continues to grow and become even more advanced, then it is reasonable to expect that the amount of original concepts and creative works produced using generative AI is going to increase dramatically; therefore, it is likely that those who create and utilize the most advanced tools will have the biggest impact on achieving their desired innovative accomplishments. Accordingly, if philosophical principles and applied psychology are integrated into applications of generative AI, then researchers will have a deeper understanding of the relationship between creativity and reflection, through the application of psychological principles, and therefore researchers will be better equipped to augment human intelligence and create synergistic interfaces between human and AI hybrid intelligent systems. Additionally, researchers will be able to create collaborative co-creative platforms for generating, selecting and producing ideas for a wide variety of creative projects and enhancing human experiences, rather than detracting from them. To realize the full benefit of generative AI technologies, we need to ensure that the development of generative AI follows a strong commitment to using ethical and socially conscious values as the guiding principles. Only by doing so can we embrace the future of generative AI with a sense of confidence; by adopting a genetically assisted strategy of supporting and enhancing positive human creativity and developing extraordinary innovations and advancements for mankind because of continuing to develop generative AI technologies.

REFERENCES

Bengesi, S., El-Sayed, H., Sarker, M. K., Houkpati, Y., Irungu, J., & Oladunni, T. (2024). Advancements in generative AI: A comprehensive review of GANs, GPT, autoencoders, diffusion models, and transformers. *IEEE Access*, *12*, 69812–69837. https://doi.org/10.1109/ACCESS.2024.3397775

Crimaldi, F., & Leonelli, M. (2023). *AI and the creative realm: Current and future applications.* arXiv. https://doi.org/10.48550/arXiv.2306.01795

Dasgupta, D., Venugopal, D., & Gupta, K. D. (2023). *A review of GenAI from a historical perspective.* TechRx iv. https://doi.org/10.36227/techrxiv.22097942

Epstein, Z., Hertzmann, A., Herman, L., & Shkolnik, A. (2023). *Art and the science of generative AI.* arXiv. https://doi.org/10.48550/arXiv.2306.04141

Ghosh, A., & Fossas, G. (2022). *Can there be art without an artist?* arXiv. https://doi.org/10.48550/arXiv.2209.07667

Gozalo-Brizuela, R., & Garrido-Merchán, E. C. (2023). *A survey of GenAI applications.* arXiv. https://doi.org/10.48550/arXiv.2306.02781

Hasselgren, C., & Oprea, T. I. (2024). AI for drug discovery: Are we there yet? *Annual Review of Pharmacology and Toxicology*, *64*, 527–550. https://doi.org/10.1146/annurev-pharmtox-040323-040828
Healy, M. (2023). *Approaches to generative AI: A social justice perspective*. https://doi.org/10.2139/ssrn.4544617
Quer, G., Muse, E. D., Nikzad, N., Topol, E. J., & Steinhubl, S. R. (2017). Augmenting diagnostic vision using AI. *The Lancet*, *390*(10091), 221. https://doi.org/10.1016/S0140-6736(17)31764-6
Radanliev, P., & Santos, O. (2023). *Ethics and responsible AI deployment*. APSA Preprints, https://doi.org/10.33774/apsa-2023-f1fkq
Saberi, M., Sadasivan, V. S., Rezaei, K., et al. (2023). *Robustness of AI-image detectors*. arXiv. https://doi.org/10.48550/arXiv.2310.00076
Shams, R. A., Zowghi, D., & Bano, M. (2023). *Challenges and solutions in AI for all*. arXiv. https://doi.org/10.48550/arXiv.2307.10600
Shamszare, H., & Choudhury, A. (2023). Clinicians' perceptions of AI. *Healthcare*, *11*(16), 2308. https://doi.org/10.3390/healthcare11162308
Shoaib, M. R., Wang, Z., Ahvanooey, M. T., & Zhao, J. (2023). *Deepfakes, misinformation, and frontier AI* intelligence ICCA Proceedings. https://doi.org/10.1109/ICCA59364.2023.10401723
Turner, S., & Critchlow, D. E. (2021). *Ethics and governance of AI*. SAGE Research Methods Cases. https://doi.org/10.4135/9781529733271

2 Comprehending Training Data

2.1 BASIS OF ARTIFICIAL INTELLIGENCE

ML and AI systems are trained on data; that's where they get their ability to spot patterns and make predictions (McDuff et al., 2023). The quality and scope of that data directly shape what the algorithm can do (Aroyo et al., 2021).

2.1.1 Definition of Training Data

Training data refers to the inputs and their corresponding outputs or labels that an AI model learns from. The model uses these examples to recognize patterns and, over time, produce its own predictions. Data quality matters here more than volume. A representative dataset helps the model generalize to situations it has not encountered before, but biased or low-quality data will push it toward unreliable outputs. What an AI model knows, and where it fails, traces back to what it was trained on (Aroyo et al., 2021).

Training data are the basis for the accuracy of an AI model, and to develop algorithms that perform optimally, diverse and high-quality training datasets are essential. The development of an AI model incorporates a difficult, time-consuming, and resource-intensive process of collecting, categorizing, and organizing data (McDuff et al., 2023; Aroyo et al., 2021). Although training data are critical to the success of AI, the sophisticated algorithms used in AI surpass the collection and refinement of training data as the "mundane" aspects of AI. Knowing that data is the most effective means of enhancing AI model performance has led to the emergence of the "data-centric AI" movement, which emphasizes the collaborative effort between AI developers and data users to continue filtering and iterating training data throughout the development of AI systems (McDuff et al., 2023; Aroyo et al., 2021) (Figure 2.1).

Training data are vital for AI, as they provide the necessary examples and information for ML models to function properly. To build trustworthy and credible AI systems, it is necessary to safeguard that the training data are of high quality, diverse, and representative (Aroyo et al., 2021; McDuff et al., 2023).

2.1.2 Categories of Training Data: Structured and Unstructured

There are two main types of training datasets: structured and unstructured datasets.

DOI: 10.1201/9781003679974-2

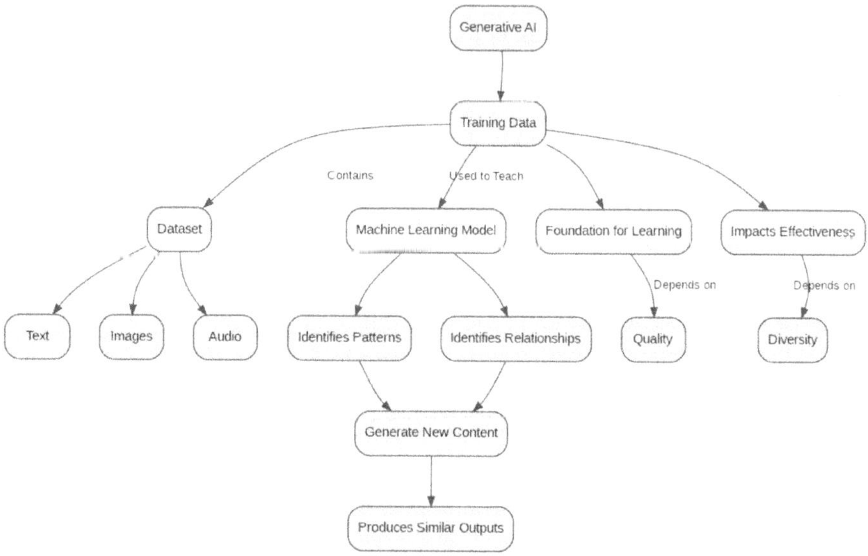

FIGURE 2.1 Training data: The cornerstone of generative AI.

Structured data are methodically organized and presented in a clearly defined table. Examples include databases, spreadsheets, and similar formats. Data stored in this manner typically consist of rows and columns. This system enables users to easily query and discover the information required for analysis. Applications that create structured data include customer relationship management systems and enterprise resource planning systems.

Unstructured data is the converse of structured data and consists of many data types: text, images, audio files, video files, etc. The contrast between structured and unstructured data is the structure (schema) acquired by the user or application to organize the information being entered into the system. Because of the lack of associated structure, it makes it harder for analysts to gain useful insights and perform analyses on such unstructured data.

Unstructured data can be built from various sources, including social media sites, websites, and devices with sensors. Structured data can be straightforwardly analyzed using traditional methods such as SQL queries; however, with the growing volume, variety, and velocity of unstructured data, innovative approaches have been developed to help organizations manage its volume as they continue to grow. Unstructured data are often mammoth and complicated, and there are numerous formats without a set of standards to identify what is considered valuable. A further type of data that falls somewhere in between is semi-structured data, which is why it can be challenging to distinguish between structured and unstructured data.

The term "semi-structured data" refers to data that has a certain level of organizational structure (such as metadata) that makes it easier to analyze than completely unstructured forms of data. Organizations that want to effectively leverage both structured and unstructured datasets for AI applications employ multiple methods, including data preprocessing, feature extraction, and advanced analytical techniques. While conventional techniques have enabled organizations to proficiently analyze structured datasets, the progress of big data has also led to the development of newer approaches that can handle the increasing volume, variety, and speed associated with unstructured datasets.

2.2 THE SIGNIFICANCE OF QUALITY IN TRAINING DATA

2.2.1 Data Quality: The Foundation of AI Precision

Data used for training AI systems must signify the anticipated outcome of the trained model through accuracy, completeness, and relevance (McDuff et al., 2023). The training data immensely influences the accuracy of an AI system. Any questions or inconsistencies in the training data lower the quality of the model and, as a result, the reliability of the AI models that come from it (Chen et al., 2023). As stated above, it is critical that training datasets accurately reflect all real-world situations that the trained AI system is likely to encounter. McDuff et al. (2023) state that, for AI systems to accurately predict outcomes based on the data supplied during training, the training dataset must be sufficient in size and representativeness to generalize the experiences of end users.

The quality of the training and validation data is essential for the clinical validation of AI/ML-based medical diagnostics (Chen et al., 2023). The clinical adoption of AI is based on the judgment of those developing the algorithms, leaving much ambiguity as to how generalizable the training datasets and validation systems are for various healthcare scenarios (Chen et al., 2023). An AI system is only as good as its training data. Too narrow or too small a dataset, and the model struggles to produce results that hold up in real-world use. While AI can improve the accuracy of diagnostics in many situations, the presence of a supervising medical professional remains essential, though (McDuff et al., 2023; Chen et al., 2023).

2.2.2 The Influence of Data Volume and Heterogeneity

How well an AI algorithm performs comes down largely to the size and variety of its training data. A model that only sees narrow or homogeneous examples won't generalize; a clean, representative dataset beats a massive but lopsided one every time.

What the model learns is shaped by what it observes and how accurate those observations are. Feed it poor or unrepresentative data and the output will reflect that: biased predictions, blind spots, gaps where the real-world complexity should be. Get the data right, though, and AI becomes genuinely useful, particularly in specialized diagnostic work, where it can catch things human reviewers might miss.

Data is the bottleneck. Not algorithms, not compute. Data. Collecting it is expensive, organizing it is complicated, and sharing it runs into privacy rules, technical silos, and a general lack of incentive (Celi et al., 2022). Healthcare records are scattered across clinics and hospitals that rarely talk to each other and pulling them into

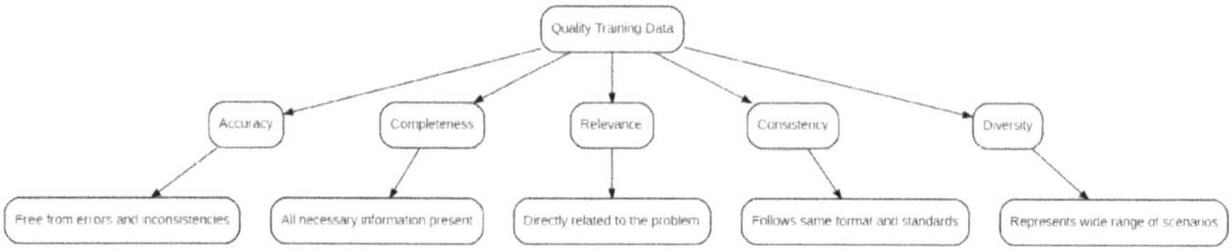

FIGURE 2.2 Critical Elements of Quality Training Data

something usable is a grind. When a team builds a model using data from one site or a narrow slice of patients, it tends to fall apart the moment it's deployed somewhere else (Davenport & Glaser, 2022; Chang, 2022). The demographic and geographic gaps in those datasets can widen the inequalities that healthcare AI is meant to address.

There's been a push toward spending more time on the data itself, curating it, expanding it, making it more representative, rather than obsessing over model architecture alone (Celi et al., 2022; McDuff et al., 2023). That sounds right in principle. In practice, though, diverse high-quality datasets are still rare. Privacy restrictions, limited availability, and thin funding keep it that way (McDuff et al., 2023). Without better data, models trained on narrow populations will keep producing results that don't generalize.

None of this is unsolvable, but the fix starts with the data, not the model. Get the training set right. Make it look like the patients it's supposed to help. The diagnostics follow. That starts with researchers and industry partners collaborating on data quality before worrying about model design (Davenport & Glaser, 2022; Chang, 2022). None of these works, though, without also confronting the biases already embedded in existing datasets. It means building pipelines that combine data from multiple sources while keeping patient information secure and being upfront about what the data still cannot capture.

2.3 THE NEGATIVE ASPECT: PREJUDICE IN TRAINING DATA

2.3.1 Comprehending Bias: Its Infiltration into AI

Bias is prejudice, a leaning for or against someone or something that lacks fair justification. Biases can be explicit (you know them) or implicit (you don't). Implicit and explicit biases create altered perspectives and affect decision-making, relationships with others, and outcomes. Bias can come from several sources in the AI world, including the data used to train ML models, the algorithms being implemented, and how these models are ultimately interpreted by people in creating AI and using it (Ferrara, 2023). ML models learn and mimic the patterns of bias in their training data. As a reflection of human thoughts, GenAI is susceptible to yielding biased results. To correctly address the issue of AI bias, we must first recognize the difference between explicit and implicit bias, since they influence AI systems in distinct ways.

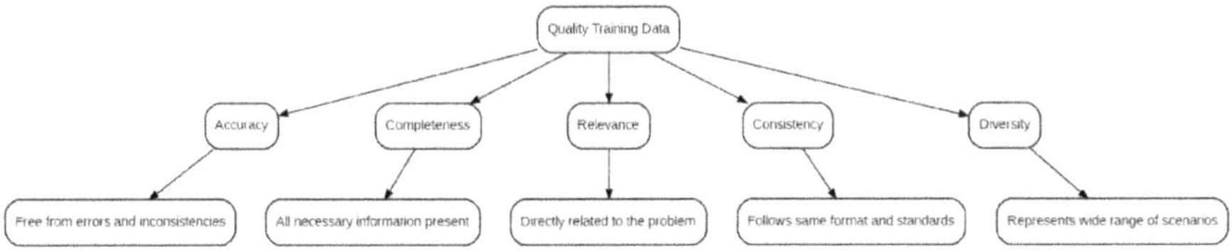

FIGURE 2.3 Comprehending bias in AI systems.

Explicit bias is when designers are aware of and want to support certain groups of people. An example of this is the company's AI-based recruiting program Amazon, which encouraged the selection of male job candidates over female ones by basing the selection on a dataset of primarily male resumes.

Implicit bias is more dangerous than explicit bias because it acts below our conscious level of awareness and, therefore, can affect the decision-making process in an insidious way. Implicit bias, even when not directly observed, can shape our perception of decisions about our behavior toward others. Thus, many studies have examined different forms of implicit bias. Examples include letters of recommendation for academic or professional employment (Figure 2.3).

Social stereotypes can adversely influence decision-making without being intentionally aware of them; this type of implicit bias is a risk associated with AI. AI systems utilize the biases of society to create their outputs, and there are several examples of implicit bias within various types of AI, including DALL·E. When prompted with "leader," DALL·E generated an image of a man. When prompted with "female leader," it produced Cleopatra. That gap comes straight from the training data. This kind of thing is common. Training datasets are often assembled by small, demographically similar teams, and their blind spots get carried into the model. Bias can creep in at any point, during data collection, preparation, or labeling—and without varied data sources, the model will just reproduce whatever skew is already there.

A liver disease prediction model, for example, misdiagnosed female patients at twice the rate of male patients because women were underrepresented in its training data. These are not edge cases. If problems like this keep showing up, evaluation must be baked into the development process, not bolted on at the end as a one-off audit, and good intentions are not enough. You need diverse data. You need people actively looking for bias during development, not after. Especially the kind of bias that doesn't announce itself in a summary table.

2.3.2 Prevalent Forms of Bias in AI Training Data

Selection bias creeps in when training data leaves out parts of the population. Facial recognition is the go-to example here. The datasets behind these systems skew lighter, so they perform noticeably worse on people with darker skin tones (Mehrabi et al., 2019). Sampling bias is a related problem, though the mechanism is slightly different: the data collected over-represents certain groups while underrepresenting others. The effects are similar. The model learns a version of reality that doesn't match the full picture. A recruiting algorithm trained on hiring data that is mostly male will, unsurprisingly, lean toward selecting men.

Measurement bias is less about who is in the data and more about how the data is recorded. Some healthcare AI models, for example, use socioeconomic status as a proxy for health status. That conflation warps the model's picture of what marginalized patients need (Ferrara, 2023).

Labeling bias occurs when the subjective opinions of human annotators or data labelers are introduced into the process of creating a data-labeling set. For instance, annotators may introduce their opinions of a sentiment into a sentiment analysis model, thus creating an output that closely resembles their opinions or backgrounds. The manifestation of historically formed stereotypes or societal discrepancies within data used to create AI systems constitutes historical bias. Over time, many AI systems have perpetuated biased patterns, which can be demonstrated with loan approvals using AI, where they may favor select groups of people based solely on financial data that has biased historical roots (Lepri et al., 2017).

Aggregated bias occurs when different types of people are combined into one model without considering how they vary individually. This will create poor predictions for all types of people. For example, an AI model in healthcare created using an accumulation of data does not consider the differences between male and female patients or between young and old patients.

Exclusion bias occurs when specific groups are intentionally or unintentionally left out of the training data; thus, the performance for these underrepresented populations will suffer consequently. An example of this would be language models built on data that exist for only certain dialects or languages.

2.4 PRACTICAL IMPLICATIONS: CASE STUDIES OF BIASED ARTIFICIAL INTELLIGENCE

2.4.1 Discriminatory Algorithms in Recruitment

A major example of bias within an AI system is Amazon's recruitment technology, as it was reported that this system favored male applicants over female applicants. The recruitment AI had been trained by analyzing applicant resumes submitted over 10 years to Amazon; this resulted in the AI reflecting Amazon's recruitment history of hiring more men than women for technical roles. AI's ability to learn from these types of trends means that a candidate's resume containing the word "women's," for example, would receive a lower score compared to male candidates with the same qualifications. Amazon afterward stopped using it and it serves as an example of the importance of AI being transparent and equitable.

2.4.2 Racial Prejudice in Facial Recognition Technology

Facial recognition has a racial bias problem, and it's not subtle. Research from the MIT Media Lab found that these algorithms misidentified roughly 34% of darker-skinned individuals, compared to just 1% of lighter-skinned ones. The reason is almost boring in how predictable it is: the training databases are full of lighter-skinned faces, so the models never learned to perform equally across skin tones. That's not a theoretical concern. People have been falsely accused because of flawed matches, and public trust in law enforcement tools built on this technology has eroded as a result.

2.4.3 Gender Bias in AI-Driven Virtual Assistants

Ask a virtual assistant the same question as a man and as a woman, and you'll often get different answers. Ask about job titles or leadership roles, and the responses tend to default to traditional gender assumptions. The more these tools are embedded in daily life, the more that matters—left unchecked, they quietly reinforce the stereotypes they were trained on.

2.5 ADDRESSING AND ALLEVIATING BIAS IN TRAINING DATA

2.5.1 Methods for Identifying Bias in Data

2.5.1.1 Statistical Tests

Spotting data bias requires looking at whether each protected group is represented well enough in the dataset for the model to learn from. The test is practical; if the trained model cannot pick up meaningful patterns for a given group, that group is underrepresented regardless of how the numbers look on paper. To assess whether an adequate representation of protected groups exists, AI practitioners typically employ one or more statistical test methods, including a chi-square test, z-test, one-way ANOVA, and two-way ANOVA, depending on the outcome goal variable in question and the protected groups being assessed. An example of this type of evaluation can be drawn from a railway station facial recognition system that was implemented for security. In this instance, for the model to learn effectively from the data that were presented to it, the training dataset must include enough images of protected group members to produce an equivalent false-negative rate for the protected group, relative to the total number of images contained in the comprehensive population dataset. If an adequate representation does not exist, the model's performance will suffer, and the protected group will be less accurately represented.

The quality of the data associated with a protected group, in addition to the quality in relation to the larger population, also needs to be examined. An imbalance in the quality of the data will create serious problems for the protected group's model and ultimately have a severe effect on the model results. Camera settings have historically been set for light-skinned individuals, producing lower-quality images for darker-skinned individuals in facial recognition databases. Therefore, this poor-quality representation of data introduced bias into the model, which may ultimately skew the model's results.

2.5.1.2 Data Evaluations

We must conduct a complete dataset audit to thoroughly analyze how datasets were created, the methods used in their creation, and any biases that may have influenced the process. One perfect example of this is when we conducted a dataset audit of the Correctional Offender Management Profiling for Alternative Sanctions (COMPAS) algorithm, which predicted the likelihood of re-offending (recidivating). Auditing of the dataset used to build the COMPAS algorithm found evidence of racial bias in that Black offenders were, on average, assigned a higher risk for being a recidivist compared to White offenders when controlling for the same types of criminal histories. Without regular audits of the data, biases that lead to unfair outcomes can go unnoticed until the damage is already done.

2.5.1.3 Assessment of Model Performance

One practical way to detect bias is to test AI systems across different demographic groups and compare the results. The IBM DeepFace project makes the case plainly. When MIT's Media Lab tested the system in 2019, it misidentified darker-skinned women about 34% of the time. For lighter-skinned men, it was under 1%. That gap doesn't come from nowhere. The model was trained on faces that looked a certain way, and it shows.

2.5.1.4 Visualization Instruments

Visualization makes bias harder to wave away. When ProPublica used heat maps to show how the COMPAS algorithm scored different racial groups, the disparities were obvious in seconds. A table of numbers might technically say the same thing, but nobody reacts to a table the way they react to a heat map.

Catching bias takes more than one angle, though. Statistical analysis can flag uneven distributions. Data audits can tell you whether historical biases have worked their way into the dataset. Outcome tracking across populations catches the problems that only surface once the model is making predictions. No single method gets everything, which is partly why visualization matters so much. It makes the inconsistencies concrete enough that people do something about them (Srinivasan & Chander, 2021).

2.5.2 Approaches for Acquiring More Representative Data

The simplest fix is also the most obvious: collect better data. Broaden the sources. Pull in a wider range of demographics, cultural backgrounds, and perspectives than most datasets currently bother with. That's not always practical, though. Oversampling can help fill in the gaps by increasing data points for underrepresented groups (Srinivasan & Chander, 2021), and GANs can generate synthetic data where real patient data is either unavailable or too sensitive to use (Srinivasan & Chander, 2021; Chinta et al., 2024). Public datasets built with fairness criteria are useful too, especially for teams that don't have the resources to build representative datasets from scratch (Srinivasan & Chander, 2021; Harbi et al., 2023; Chinta et al., 2024).

2.5.2.1 Varied Procurement

If the training data only comes from the usual sources, it's going to reflect the usual demographics. Google ran into this with natural language processing. Their models were underserving marginalized populations because those languages and speech patterns weren't in the data. So, they partnered with community organizations to build linguistically diverse datasets from the ground up. By working with community organizations, Google assembled a dataset that captured how different ethnic groups speak, not just how existing corpora said they did.

2.5.2.2 Proactive Sampling

Oversampling is one way to correct an imbalanced dataset by boosting the representation of underserved groups. The need for it is not hypothetical. Stanford researchers found that training data behind healthcare risk prediction algorithms came overwhelmingly from white participants, so the models performed poorly for other racial and ethnic groups. Researchers responded by building an expanded dataset that incorporated Black and Hispanic patient data through systematic reviews. With that data in place, the same algorithms should produce more reliable predictions for populations they previously got wrong.

2.5.2.3 Generation of Synthetic Data

The use of synthetic data provides additional datasets with more variety and protects people's privacy. NVIDIA's efforts to use Generative Adversarial Networks (GAN) to synthetically produce the images needed to train its facial recognition systems serve as a prime example. To eliminate the potential for bias in the facial recognition system, NVIDIA increased the variety of images in its dataset by creating very high-quality images of the same quality as naturally taken photographs under many different lighting conditions and perspectives.

2.5.2.4 Datasets Available to the Public

Using free datasets tested for demographic diversity and representativeness is the first step in developing more inclusive artificial intelligence models. The UCI Machine Learning Repository contains several datasets that have been tested for demographic diversity, allowing researchers and developers to access high-quality datasets for their training needs. Fairness researchers keep coming back to the Adult Income Dataset because it has the right variables for the job: race, sex, education level. You can test whether an algorithm treats different groups the same way. That's harder than it sounds with most datasets, which is partly why benchmarks like this one matter. They give developers a concrete way to find bias in their models before it ships.

2.5.3 The Significance of Human Oversight in AI Development

Bias doesn't get caught by one type of person. You need data scientists, ethicists, and domain experts working together from the start, not reviewing each other's work after the fact. IBM learned about this building Watson. They put technologists, ethicists, and social scientists in the same room to audit the model, and having that mix of perspectives meant problems got caught that any single group would have missed. The model ended up performing more equitably in healthcare and employment contexts because of it (Barclay & Abramson, 2021). Microsoft landed in a similar place, building out an ethical AI framework that incorporates bias checks into every stage of development rather than tacking them on at the end.

But none of this holds still. Social values shift. A model that looked fair at launch can drift as the world changes around it, so data collection and validation must be ongoing, not a box you tick once. Bringing community members and end users into the process helps too. Development teams get trapped inside their own assumptions. Outside voices tend to see what they can't (Brundage et al., 2020) (Figure 2.4).

The more AI gets involved in decisions that affect real people, the less room there is to be sloppy about how it works. Accuracy matters, sure. But a model that gets the right answer and can't show its reasoning isn't trustworthy. Neither is one that runs without any real human check on what it's doing. Transparency and oversight need to be there from day one. Not retrofitted before launch because someone remembered there's a compliance box to tick (Petkovic, 2022; Brundage et al., 2020; Barclay & Abramson, 2021; Blau et al., 2024).

2.6 THE FUTURE OF TRAINING DATA: ETHICAL AND INCLUSIVE ARTIFICIAL INTELLIGENCE

2.6.1 Advancing Ethical Data Collection Practices

The bigger the AI market gets, the harder it becomes to treat ethical data collection as something you'll deal with later (Nasir et al., 2023). Consent and privacy are at

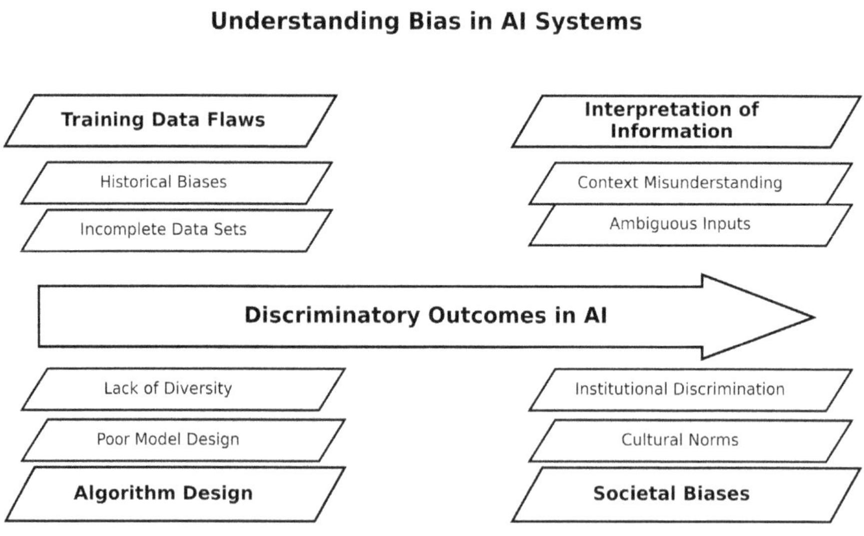

FIGURE 2.4 Addressing and mitigating bias in training data.

the center of this, and some governments have started spelling out expectations. The UK's Data Ethics Framework, for example, lays out how organizations should handle ethical questions when collecting and using data, and how to weigh innovation against public trust.

Privacy can't be an afterthought. Researchers have been saying for years that it needs to be designed into AI systems from the beginning (D'Aquin et al., 2018; Gaur and Gaur, 2024b; Karimian et al., 2022). There are technical tools for this: differential privacy, homomorphic encryption, federated learning. They make it possible to use sensitive data while limiting exposure. But without international legal and ethical standards that keep up with the technology, the tools only go so far.

Some companies aren't waiting. Spotify already tells users how their personal data feeds into recommendations. At a practical level, though, this kind of thing must go further: anonymizing data, building privacy into the design process, auditing regularly for problems that might otherwise go unnoticed.

Healthcare makes all of this more urgent. Frameworks covering transparency, accountability, and human oversight are out there, but they're only worth something if the organizations using them treat the commitments as binding. Too often they read more like mission statements than operating procedures.

2.6.2 The Importance of Transparency and Accountability

If people can't understand how an AI system works, they won't trust it. That's not a branding problem. It's a structural one. Some of the big tech companies have started publishing AI principles, pledging to reduce bias, be accountable to users, and use AI for social good. How much of that holds up when it cuts into revenue is an open question. Legislators seem to think it won't, which is why several are drafting laws that would force companies to disclose how their systems were built and take responsibility for what those systems do. On the technical side, transparency is more specific than it sounds. It means the system can tell you what it's capable of, where its limits are, and how it arrived at a given decision.

Explainable AI (XAI) methods are designed to do exactly this, making model reasoning interpretable enough that users have a real basis for trust rather than just a company's word for it. However, simply providing access to technical information on how an AI system works may not be sufficient to explain the underlying logic or justification for decisions made by the AI system. A better method would be to focus on creating AI systems that can provide understandable justifications for the data used to justify decision-making (Chaudhary et al., 2025; Doshi-Velez et al., 2017; Gaur, 2024; Gaur and Gaur, 2024a; Radanliev et al., 2024; Roche et al., 2022).

In addition, the UK House of Lords distinguished the varying degrees to which the transparency of an AI system can facilitate understanding of the rationale behind specific decisions. The protection of the integrity of the scientific and research community is another key factor in improving the transparency and accountability of AI in the age of generative AI. For instance, as AI systems develop to generate research findings, the attribution of findings must occur with equal accuracy, replicability of studies, and potential bias of the research generated by AI systems. AI is changing how research is done, but that does not mean the scientific community gets to abandon the standards that make research credible. The challenge is adapting to new tools without letting rigor slip in the process.

2.6.3 Imagining an Inclusive AI Future

AI is going to touch nearly every part of how society operates. That alone is reason enough to pay attention to who is building it and who gets left out of the conversation. The Diversity in AI initiative mentors people from marginalized communities into the AI industry. The logic is simple: if the teams building these systems all come from the same background, the blind spots are baked in before anyone writes a line of code. The AI for Good Global Summit, run by the International Telecommunication Union, works at a different scale, pulling stakeholders from across industries to push for ethical and inclusive development practices. This kind of collaboration matters. Not in a "we should all work together" way, but in the specific sense that researchers, developers, civil society groups, and policymakers working from shared commitments to human rights and non-discrimination are how vague principles turn into enforceable standards (Gibbons, 2021; Shams et al., 2023). Team composition matters for a more basic reason too. People with different lived experiences brought different assumptions about what fairness looks like. A homogeneous team will walk past problems in data or model behavior that someone with a different background would flag immediately. And when the communities most likely to be affected by a system are involved in building it, the trust that follows isn't performative. It's earned.

REFERENCES

Aroyo, L., Lease, M., Paritosh, P., & Schaekermann, M. (2021). *Data excellence for AI: Why should you care?* arXiv. https://doi.org/10.48550/arxiv.2111.10391

Barclay, I., & Abramson, W. (2021). *Identifying roles, requirements and responsibilities in trustworthy AI systems.* arXiv. https://doi.org/10.48550/arxiv.2106.08258

Blau, W., Cerf, V. G., Enriquez, J., Francisco, J. S., Gasser, U., Gray, M. L., … Witherell, M. S. (2024). Protecting scientific integrity in an age of generative AI. *Proceedings of the National Academy of Sciences, 121*(22). https://doi.org/10.1073/pnas.2407886121

Brundage, M., Avin, S., Wang, J., Belfield, H., Krueger, G., Hadfield, G. K., … Anderljung, M. (2020). *Towards trustworthy AI development: Mechanisms for supporting verifiable claims.* arXiv. https://doi.org/10.48550/arxiv.2004.07213

Celi, L. A., Cellini, J., Charpignon, M., Dee, E. C., Dernoncourt, F., Eber, R., … Yao, J. S. (2022). Sources of bias in artificial intelligence that perpetuate healthcare disparities: A global review. *PLoS Digital Health, 1*(3), e0000022. https://doi.org/10.1371/journal.pdig.0000022

Chang, E. Y. (2022). *Knowledge-guided data-centric AI in healthcare: Progress, shortcomings, and future directions.* arXiv. https://doi.org/10.48550/arxiv.2212

Chaudhary, M., Gaur, L., Chakrabarti, A., Singh, G., Jones, P., & Kraus, S. (2025). An integrated model to evaluate transparency in predicting employee churn using explainable artificial intelligence. *Journal of Innovation & Knowledge, 10*(3), 100700. https://doi.org/10.1016/j.jik.2025.100700

Chen, F., Hu, Y., & Simonetti, A. (2023). *Practical statistical considerations for the clinical validation of AI/ML-enabled medical diagnostic devices*. arXiv. https://doi.org/10.48550/arxiv.2303.05399

Chinta, S. V., Wang, Z., Yin, Z., Hoang, N., González, M., Quy, T. L., & Zhang, W. (2024). *FairAIED: Navigating fairness, bias, and ethics in educational AI applications*. arXiv. https://doi.org/10.48550/arxiv.2407.18745

D'Aquin, M., Troullinou, P., O'Connor, N. E., Cullen, A., Faller, G., & Holden, L. (2018). Towards an "ethics by design" methodology for AI research projects. In *Proceedings of the 2018 AAAI/ACM Conference on AI, Ethics, and Society* (pp. 54–61). https://doi.org/10.1145/3278721.3278765

Davenport, T. H., & Glaser, J. (2022). Factors governing the adoption of artificial intelligence in healthcare providers. *NPJ Digital Medicine, 5*, Article 170. https://doi.org/10.1007/s44250-022-00004-8

Doshi-Velez, F., Kortz, M., Budish, R., Bavitz, C., Gershman, S., O'Brien, D. P., … Wood, A. (2017). *Accountability of AI under the law: The role of explanation*. arXiv. https://doi.org/10.48550/arxiv.1711.01134

Ferrara, E. (2023). *Fairness and bias in artificial intelligence: A brief survey of sources, impacts, and mitigation strategies*. arXiv. https://doi.org/10.48550/arxiv.2304.07683

Gaur, L. (2024). From algorithms to ethics: XAI's impact on e-commerce. In L. Gaur & A. Abraham (Eds.), *Role of explainable artificial intelligence in e-commerce* (pp. 165–190). Springer. https://doi.org/10.1007/978-3-031-55615-9_8

Gaur, L., & Gaur, D. (2024a). ALS monitoring using explainable AI. In L. Gaur, A. Abraham, & R. Ajith (Eds.), *AI and neuro-degenerative diseases* (Vol. 1131). Springer. https://doi.org/10.1007/978-3-031-53148-4_5

Gaur, L., & Gaur, D. (2024b). Ethical considerations: Case scenarios. In L. Gaur, A. Abraham, & R. Ajith (Eds.), *AI and neuro-degenerative diseases* (Vol. 1131). Springer. https://doi.org/10.1007/978-3-031-53148-4_10

Gibbons, E. (2021). Towards a more equal world: The human rights approach to extending the benefits of artificial intelligence. *IEEE Technology and Society Magazine, 40*(1), 25–30. https://doi.org/10.1109/MTS.2021.3056295

Harbi, S. H. A., Tidjon, L. N., & Khomh, F. (2023). *Responsible design patterns for machine learning pipelines*. arXiv. https://doi.org/10.48550/arxiv.2306.01788

Karimian, G., Petelos, E., & Evers, S. (2022). The ethical issues of the application of artificial intelligence in healthcare: A systematic scoping review. *AI and Ethics, 2*(4), 539–551. https://doi.org/10.1007/s43681-021-00131-7

Lepri, B., Oliver, N., Letouzé, E., Pentland, A., & Vinck, P. (2017). Fair, transparent, and accountable algorithmic decision-making processes. *Philosophy & Technology, 31*(4), 611–627. https://doi.org/10.1007/s13347-017-0279-x

McDuff, D., Curran, T., & Kadambi, A. (2023). *Synthetic data in healthcare*. arXiv. https://doi.org/10.48550/arxiv.2304.03243

Mehrabi, N., Morstatter, F., Saxena, N., Lerman, K., & Galstyan, A. (2019). *A survey on bias and fairness in machine learning*. arXiv. https://doi.org/10.48550/arxiv.1908.09635

Nasir, S., Khan, R. A., & Bai, S. (2023). *Ethical framework for harnessing the power of AI in healthcare and beyond*. arXiv. https://doi.org/10.48550/arxiv.2309.00064

Petkovic, D. (2022). *It is not "accuracy vs. explainability"—We need both for trustworthy AI systems*. arXiv. https://doi.org/10.48550/arxiv.2212.11136

Radanliev, P., Santos, O., Brandon-Jones, A., & Joinson, A. (2024). Ethics and responsible AI deployment. *Frontiers in Artificial Intelligence, 7*, Article 1377011. https://doi.org/10.3389/frai.2024.1377011

Roche, C., Wall, P. J., & Lewis, D. (2022). Ethics and diversity in artificial intelligence policies, strategies, and initiatives. *AI and Ethics, 3*(4), 1095–1115. https://doi.org/10.1007/s43681-022-00218-9

Shams, R. A., Zowghi, D., & Bano, M. (2023). *Challenges and solutions in AI for all.* arXiv. https://doi.org/10.48550/arxiv.2307.10600

Srinivasan, R., & Chander, A. (2021). Biases in AI systems. *Communications of the ACM, 64*(8), 44–49. https://doi.org/10.1145/3464903

3 Strategies for Mitigating Bias in AI Development

3.1 METHODS FOR GENERATING EQUITABLE AND REPRESENTATIVE TRAINING DATA

3.1.1 Data Augmentation: Improving Diversity in Training Datasets

For ML and AI systems, the richness and consistency of the training sets are two major factors affecting their overall performance and generalization in the real-world scenarios. However, in most day-to-day situations, obtaining adequate information from a range of sources to develop models is challenging. To address this issue, data augmentation techniques have been developed as effective solutions (Mumuni et al., 2024). Data augmentation produces new training sets based on previously collected sets and uses various transformations of the current datasets. Oversampling creates copies of smaller classes until their sizes are equal, undersampling reduces the number of instances in larger classes to achieve balance, and synthetic data generation produces new, representative instances based on the original datasets (Figure 3.1).

Data augmentation is a technique that can considerably increase the diversity and representativeness of training sets, thus creating more robust models that generalize effectively to unseen data. When using augmentations to supply models with additional quantities and types of training examples, it creates a larger range of potential examples available for training a classifier, thus allowing better feature-based representations of the training data to be created and more generalized models. Text augmentations include but are not limited to random synonym substitutions, random insertions, random switches, and back-translations that create many new and varied text samples while maintaining the meaning of the text (Shorten et al., 2021). Many studies have examined the use of synthetic methods for augmentations to generate additional training images in the field of computer vision. The following types of synthetic methods for augmenting images in computer vision include but are not limited to random crop, random flip, random rotation, random scale, and creating new, realistic imagery using generative adversarial networks (Ding et al., 2022; Mumuni et al., 2024). Data augmentation has been shown to improve the performance and generalization of deep learning-based models in a variety of domains including but not limited to computer vision. The focus of this chapter is to examine the languages and graphs as described by Ding et al. (2022). Data augmentation techniques may help to solve the limitations of small and imbalanced datasets by enhancing the diversity and representativeness of training sets, thereby producing stronger and

DOI: 10.1201/9781003679974-3

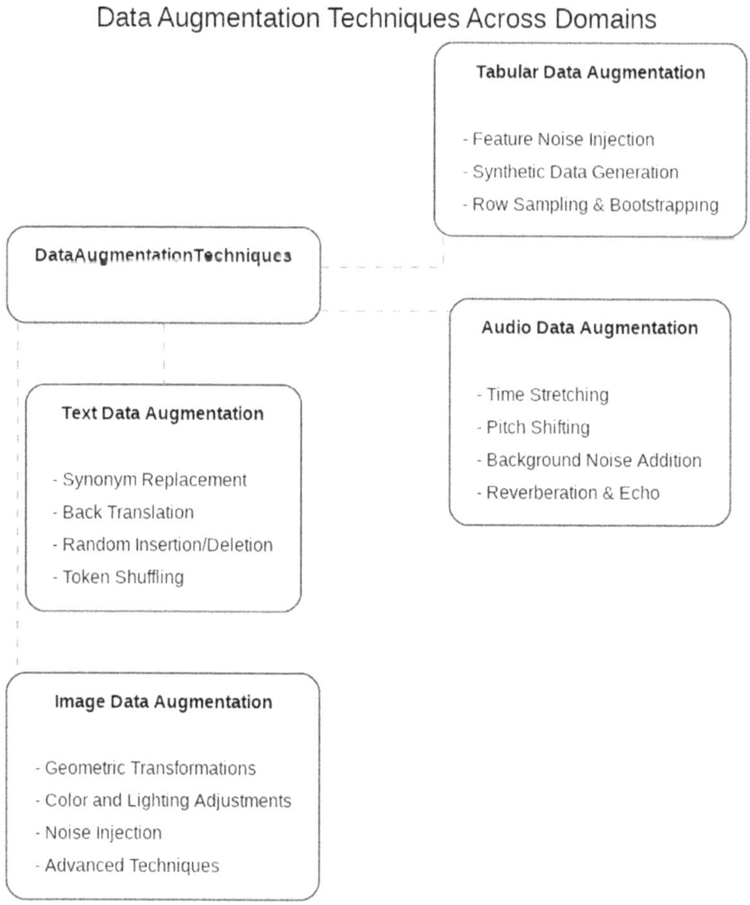

FIGURE 3.1 Techniques for data augmentation across various domains.

better-performing machine learning models (Ding et al., 2022; Mumuni et al., 2024; Chen et al., 2021). Table 3.1 summarizes various data augmentation techniques for different data types.

3.1.2 Compiling Inclusive Datasets: Optimal Practices

Having representatives of all demographics in an inclusive dataset is increasingly important when using ML and AI to make decisions based on data. Datasets that do not have sufficient diversity or have inherent bias may create algorithms that do not work well with specific demographics, contributing to the continued inequalities that exist in our society. To resolve this issue, researchers have identified optimal methods for curating inclusive datasets. An important aspect of the creation of an inclusive dataset is the ability to utilize several sources of data collection. Reaching out to and actively seeking individuals from disenfranchised or underrepresented groups

TABLE 3.1
Various Data Augmentation Techniques for Different Data Types

Category	Techniques	Description	Examples
Image data augmentation	Geometric Transformations	The design introduces spatial variations while preserving the key features.	Rotation, Scaling, Translation, Shearing, Flipping
	Color Augmentations	The system modifies the color properties to increase diversity.	Brightness adjustments, Contrast variations, Saturation changes, Hue modifications
	Noise Injection	Adds noise to simulate real-world distortions.	Gaussian noise, salt-and-pepper noise, blur (Gaussian, motion blur)
	Cutout and Mix-up	Introduces occlusions or blends images to improve generalization.	Cutout (random masking), Mix-up (weighted blending of images)
Text data augmentation	Synonym Replacement	The system replaces words with synonyms to generate variations.	Using WordNet, Word2Vec
	Random Deletion	The system randomly removes words while preserving their meaning.	"The quick brown fox" → "Quick brown fox"
	Back Translation	The system translates text to another language and back again to create paraphrases.	English → French → English
	Sentence Shuffling	The system changes word/sentence order while retaining semantics.	"AI is evolving quickly." → "Fast AI is evolving."
	Word Embedding Augmentation	The system replaces words with contextually similar embeddings.	"Happy" → "Joyful"
Audio data augmentation	Pitch Shifting	It changes pitch without affecting speed.	Increasing/decreasing vocal pitch

(Continued)

TABLE 3.1 *(Continued)*
Various Data Augmentation Techniques for Different Data Types

	Time Stretching	Alters audio speed without modifying pitch.	Slowing/speeding up speech
	Background Noise Addition	Injects noise to simulate real environments.	Crowd noise, white noise
	Reverberation and Echo	Mimics the acoustic effects of different spaces.	Concert hall reverb, room echo
	SpecAugment	Masks portions of spectrograms to force model learning.	Frequency masking, time masking
Tabular data augmentation	Synthetic Data Generation	Create synthetic samples to balance datasets.	SMOTE, GANs
	Feature Perturbation	Adds small noise to numerical features.	Jittering, Gaussian noise
	Interpolation and Extrapolation	The system generates new samples by combining the existing data points.	Linear interpolation between records

will assist in ensuring that your performed analysis will reflect most individuals within the area under study (i.e., your final dataset will incorporate those individuals for an AI-based program). Additionally, you should have an established plan in place to collect the data in a manner that is ethical, preserves the privacy of individual participants, provides the chance for informed consent to be obtained from the participants, and minimizes the risk of psychological injury to the participants.

As previously stated, it's important for developers of AI tools in the healthcare field to create datasets that represent the diversity of the patient population; however, like any tool, AI cannot be biased if the creators have created the datasets in a way that accurately reflects their target demographic(s). If a physician or an engineer (technologist) does not know about the existence of certain individuals/communities—as may happen with limited numbers of other individuals/communities included in the dataset—then that physician's or technologist's developed algorithms could contribute to generating further disparities in healthcare delivery (Arora et al., 2023). Current literature on AI applications has produced an identified need for standards related to healthcare datasets used for AI applications, and as a result, addressing the issue known as "Health Data Poverty" is necessary. "Health Data Poverty" describes underrepresented individuals/communities in health data, thus not having equivalent access to the benefits of health data for enhanced data utilization via advanced methodologies from AI/machine learning (Arora et al., 2023). Through careful evaluation of the methodology used to collect the health data, researchers will develop ways to mitigate possible biases within the dataset created. To accomplish this goal, researchers should assess various factors, including the sociodemographic characteristics of the person(s) who will collect the data (data collectors), the setting in which the data will be collected, and the potential for self-selection bias. The computing industry may use various professions' experiences related to developing diversity initiatives to reduce inequities in educational and employment practices (law, health) for developing their own diversity initiatives. As technologies evolve and are employed as tools for making decisions, creating inclusive health datasets is one way computing does its part to level the playing field of using data and AI technology justly and equitably. Developing an inclusive health dataset that employs diverse sources, utilizes ethical data collection methods, and incorporates the lessons of other related professions will lead to researchers incorporating a more inclusive representation of diverse communities and populations into the United States (Kuhlman et al., 2020; Arora et al., 2023).

3.1.3 The Function of Synthetic Data in Bias Mitigation

Machine learning models are now being used widely enough that people have noticed the many problems with machine learning about unfairness and discrimination historically associated with Machine Learning Model Use (MLMU). As a possible solution, synthetic data could be used as a supplement to existing datasets to help fill gaps that exist in the training of ML models by ensuring that underrepresented populations such as historically disadvantaged and underrepresented groups are included in the training of ML models. Synthetic data consist of artificially generated datasets that retain many of the features of real-world datasets but do not contain any actual identifiable information. This offers numerous advantages, such as protecting the identities of individuals, allowing greater access to data for researchers, and reducing many of the inevitable sources of bias in many real-world datasets. Researchers and developers may build more accurate and inclusive training datasets by generating synthetic data that are representative of the spectrum of diversity of the target market they hope to reach (Marwala et al., 2023).

However, synthetic data have several inherent dangers and challenges. One major concern is the increased risk associated with the use of synthetic data to train machine learning models: many individuals may have an unreasonable level of confidence in models trained on synthetic datasets. Whitney and Norman (2024) indicate that while using synthetic datasets can enhance the diversity of training data and improve the overall representation of underrepresented populations (thereby boosting the performance of machine learning models), it may inadvertently create a false sense of security for trained users, as synthetic datasets might not capture the full complexity and richness of real-world data; consequently, the "real-world" performance of machine learning models trained on synthetic data may not accurately represent their true performance. In addition, synthetic data may create a series of consent and data compliance issues because individuals are not directly involved in generating synthetic data, and they have no direct control over the use of their data; therefore, concerns exist regarding whether synthetic datasets generated in this manner are compliant with all relevant ethical and legal frameworks, specifically those regulations governing and limiting data collection and data utilization. To address these difficulties, sufficient and extensive procedures need to be applied to the generation, validation, and implementation of synthetic datasets (Figure 3.2).

There is confidence that the algorithms employed for producing synthetic data produce high-quality, fair, and unbiased results that will not discriminate against specific demographic groups, and that the synthetic datasets created will comply with applicable legal regulations, and that they will be appropriately monitored and regulated to ensure their ethical use.

3.2 BIAS MITIGATION IMPLEMENTATION: EXEMPLARY CASES FROM GENERATIVE AI INITIATIVES

3.2.1 Mitigating Gender Bias in AI-Generated Content

Researchers have shown that artificial intelligence systems are inheriting and amplifying the biases of humankind, especially related to facial recognition technology. AI facial recognition systems tend to represent male faces more accurately than female, and there are significant disparities between races where the facial recognition accuracy differs substantially as a function of race. Due to the presence of bias in healthcare systems using AI-based computer-assisted diagnosis, which will increase the need for programs to appropriately address AI-based bias, instances of bias have surfaced in healthcare, particularly when utilizing AI-generated diagnoses (Larrazabal et al., 2020). One of the major accomplishments of the project was the successful implementation of a large-scale initiative to mitigate gender bias within generative AI. A major goal of the project was to identify patterns of gender bias

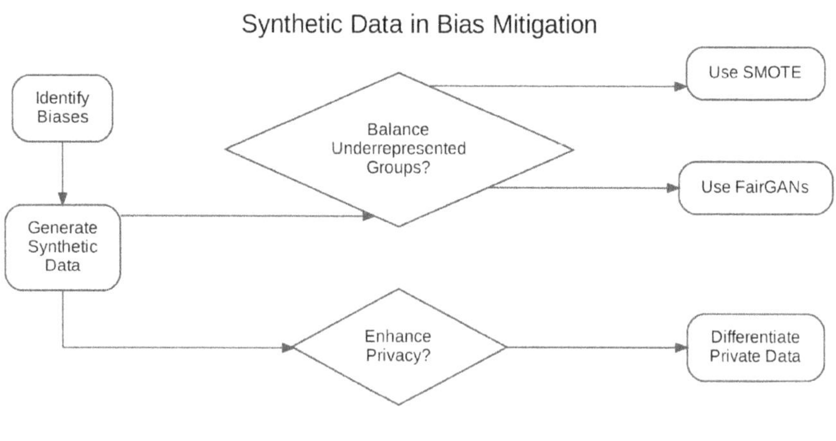

FIGURE 3.2 Illustration of the challenges and considerations when using synthetic data to address bias.

within various AI generators and develop methods for reducing these biases. The project was successful at identifying instances where female and African American individuals are severely underrepresented as compared to their male counterparts. In addition to establishing methods to combat gender bias, the project team adopted several methodological approaches. These approaches included using debiased training data, creating specific loss functions to promote fairness during training, and altering the architecture and complexity of their AI models (Zhou et al., 2024). Based upon the positive results from the experiences and methodologies of the project team, improving generative AI models has proven to be possible. In addition to demonstrating potential for future improvement; by strategically selecting their training data and providing clear debiasing objectives, the project team has significantly reduced the evidential representation of gender bias within their originally developed generative AI model. The output of their generative AI model produced gender representation on a far more equal basis and displayed many more visible manifestations of emotion and diversity in physical characteristics among the images generated than has historically been the case among images produced exhibiting various forms of adverse stereotyping. Ultimately, the project team's achievement of reducing gender bias in their generative AI image output has markedly increased the collective understanding of gender bias in generative AI, as well as establishing foundational support for the exploration of new innovative methodologies and methodological frameworks to address these issues in the future (Larrazabal et al., 2020; Zhou et al., 2024).

3.2.2 Addressing Racial Bias in AI-Driven Decision-Making

AI has generated considerable interest in recent years because of its increased use in nearly every sector and its increasing capabilities. However, a major area of concern, related to the advent of AI, has been its ability (or inability) to deliver equitable results among individuals based on race and other human characteristics. To begin addressing this growing concern, university teams conducting research on bias in AI have provided recommendations for building AI systems that produce more equitable results across all societal groups while also identifying ways to reduce the potential for bias in AI systems. Specifically, researchers identified many ways that AI systems can be biased, including (1) the training data used to construct the AI systems; (2) the algorithms used to make classification decisions; and (3) the biases of developers creating AI systems. Researchers at several universities developed an extensive methodological approach to minimizing bias and delivering more equitable outcomes that incorporated (a) addressing the technical aspects of the AI system; (b) addressing social justice principles when developing the algorithms; and (c) establishing strict governance policies regarding the data and models created by the AI systems. Research teams performed an in-depth analysis of the training data and determined potential bias in the representation of demographic groups in the training dataset, particularly minority groups. Additionally, to mitigate the historical bias often present in traditional datasets, AI researchers focused on acquiring and utilizing a variety of kinds of additional data sources. Researchers also developed algorithms with techniques to reduce bias, including (but not limited to) adversarial debiasing and causal models. These techniques were developed to mitigate the adverse effects of sensitive attributes (e.g., race) on the AI system's performance. Researchers did extensive evaluation of how to promote diversity and inclusion in the AI research and engineering teams developing the AI systems. By employing diverse teams of individuals on the AI research and engineering teams, researchers were able to identify potential examples of racial bias in AI systems. The results produced by the AI systems developed in this study were outstanding and provided the researchers with confidence that the AI systems produced by the researchers are providing "significantly more equitable" outcomes across various demographic groups. The success achieved by the research teams conducting this study and the quality of the resulting AI systems demonstrate the need for developing a comprehensive strategy to develop AI systems that capture both the technical components of the AI systems as well as the social and ethical aspects of the systems.

3.2.3 Guaranteeing Equity in AI-Driven Healthcare Solutions

Advanced AI technologies can now enhance many areas of patient care and patient outcomes through improved clinical workflow management and patient care improvements in new ways, with artificial intelligence in healthcare being rapidly expanded globally. It will therefore become increasingly important to ensure that the development and implementation of AI-based technologies in providing healthcare services will provide equitable access to all patient populations. An example of a collaborative effort aimed at reducing any bias that may occur in the use of AI in delivering healthcare is an initiative being carried out by the University of Chicago Medicine and members of the Diversity and Equity Committee, as cited by Rajkomar et al. (2018). By working closely together, members from the Center for Healthcare Delivery Science and Innovation (Data Science) and members from the Diversity and Equity Committee were able to identify potential inequities and develop a broad checklist for use during the design of machine learning models designed to promote equity (Rajkomar et al., 2018). Following the implementation of this proactive strategy to promote equity in machine learning, the members of this team were able to re-evaluate their historical biases and refine their methodology in order to develop machine learning models for use in their health systems that were more representative of the populations treated by their health systems and more accurately predicted the healthcare needs of those populations due to the racial, ethnic, and socioeconomic attributes of the populations they served. The attempt to mitigate bias in the algorithms used to determine access to healthcare services for various groups in the population is the most significant challenge to developing equitable AI solutions to deliver healthcare to consumers that operate within the framework of equitable access. The literature indicates the potential for algorithmic bias to occur during the development and implementation stages of AI; however, it is usually attributed to the data from which the algorithms were developed. In addition to the data, there are also multiple factors creating algorithmic bias, such as there not being diverse input and/or perspectives represented during the development of the AI solution.

3.3 OPTIMAL STRATEGIES AND SUGGESTIONS FOR BIAS REDUCTION

3.3.1 Incorporating Bias Mitigation into the AI Development Lifecycle

Concerns about potential discrimination caused by the increased use of artificial intelligence (AI) and discrimination associated with jobs or work and civil rights violations have arisen due to the increase in AI. The development of AI and the stages of its lifecycle should be conducted in a manner that is orderly to identify and remove biases as best as possible. Developing some form of strategy to eliminate systematic bias is important for everyone developing AI applications and systems to make sure that no biases are built into the applications or systems.

3.3.1.1 Data Acquisition and Organization

Data will immediately affect trained AI model bias; these data sources must have appropriate collection and curation protocols, including (but not limited to) the following: review data collection sources and address whether there exists sufficient diversity and inclusiveness within the dataset and remove any prior bias from those datasets (Leavy et al, 2020; Srinivasan & Chander, 2021; Ferrara, 2023).

3.3.1.2 Algorithm Design

There are opportunities for algorithmic bias to be integrated into an AI's algorithms prior to those algorithms being created. To identify and eliminate any possible algorithmic biases that an AI may have, explicit fairness constraints should be established in the algorithm's design phase, the application of debiasing methodology should be undertaken in the design of the algorithm, and adequate testing and evaluation processes should be put into place to identify and eliminate any potential sources of algorithmic bias (Leavy et al., 2020; Srinivasan & Chander, 2021; Ferrara, 2023).

3.3.1.3 Model Development and Evaluation

The bias mitigation strategies might also introduce bias into how the training methods are defined and the criteria used to assess performance. It is, therefore, recommended to use representative data; utilize fairness-sensitive training methods; create and implement thorough evaluation methods that incorporate numerous aspects of equity and bias to train the AI models.

3.3.1.4 Implementation and Monitoring

The ongoing evaluation and tracking of AI technologies should occur post-deployment. Post-deployment assessments and tracking of AI systems should employ and promote ecosystem-wide accountability and governance processes by providing continuous stakeholder engagement to ensure fair access and ethical operation of AI technologies.

3.3.2 Cooperative and Interdisciplinary Methodologies

Many aspects of artificial intelligence (AI) technology are advancing at a rapid pace; however, most recently, an area that has received growing interest crosses into an area of discussion surrounding what is referred to as bias. The sources of bias in AI can originate from several different things: such as the various datasets being used to conduct training, the different types of algorithms being used, and also the individual biases of developers that engineer these systems (Srinivasan & Chander, 2021; Bateni et al., 2022; Ferrara, 2023). Many different stakeholders need to work in concert to do everything possible to keep bias out of AI systems, as well as develop systems with accountability and fairness. For there to be successful and ethical development of AI systems, data scientists, ethicists, domain experts, as well as other individuals who have knowledge and expertise in this area, all need to work together to identify and address the sources of bias in AI systems. The most prevalent cause of bias in AI is the datasets that researchers used to train models. Researchers have pointed out that increasing the quality and diversity of the datasets they use to train models will help to reduce the amount of bias that is perpetuated throughout these systems and society. AI developers also need to be aware of the inherent biases that may become present in the algorithms they develop. For this reason, algorithm developers need to be cognizant of the possibility of bias and should continue to develop algorithms with the principles of equity and impartiality (Ferrara, 2023; Srinivasan & Chander, 2021; Ferrara, 2023) in mind. Ethicists are key players in the design and development of new AI systems, providing valuable insight into the ethical implications surrounding different aspects of AI systems, and recommending that AI systems be developed with respect to the prevailing values and norms in society. Domain experts with extensive experience using AI systems are key participants in identifying and eliminating sources of bias from the systems prior to their deployment. By collaborating across different disciplines, researchers and practitioners will have more opportunities to create and develop AI systems that are more responsible than traditional methods and ethical systems through which they can reduce bias and enhance fairness.

3.3.3 Ongoing Surveillance and Feedback Mechanisms

The emergence of artificial intelligence (AI) systems across all areas of life creates a need for ongoing monitoring and feedback mechanisms to ensure ethical responsibility in the deployment and use of AI systems (London, 2024). AI systems will impact how we recruit new employees, deliver services, and provide healthcare. Due to the data-driven nature of AI systems, they can be complex; therefore, they have the potential to perpetuate and/or worsen bias using AI systems, which can lead to significant social and ethical issues (Golbin et al., 2020). A major challenge in the development of AI systems has been the elimination of bias from many sources (Ferrara, 2023; i.e., through training data, algorithms, and decision-making processes), and it is crucial to have a system in place for ongoing monitoring and feedback so that bias can be recognized and corrected as it develops.

An ongoing monitoring process also ensures that all AI systems continue to be assessed for effectiveness and fairness after they have been deployed. Some examples of how this ongoing monitoring process can be applied include periodic audits, bias assessments, tracking the unintended effects of AI systems, and assessing the differential impact of AI systems on various demographic groups. Continuous monitoring allows organizations to eliminate developing biases or other problems as soon as they are identified; thus, the organization will remain committed to ensuring that their systems are being developed in a fair and ethically aligned manner to the original purpose of design.

The feedback loop will allow organizations to utilize the ongoing monitoring data to enhance the AI system over time. When problems are discovered, the submitted data can facilitate the rapid modification of AI models, training data, or decision-making processes to resolve the identified bias or problems. This iterative cycle of monitoring and identifying problems allows the organization to build long-term trust in the AI system (Ferrara, 2023; Srinivasan & Chander, 2021). As responsible AI continues to grow, the integration of feedback and ongoing monitoring will also become more relevant. By being proactive to address fairness and bias in AI technologies, organizations can maximize the benefit of AI technologies while minimizing existing inequities and the creation of new inequities (Kvasny et al., 2019; Ferrara, 2023; Srinivasan & Chander, 2021; Santosh and Gaur, 2021; Zwick and Encarnação, 2020).

3.4 THE PROSPECTS OF BIAS MITIGATION IN ARTIFICIAL INTELLIGENCE

3.4.1 Novel Techniques and Innovations

With the continued rise of AI systems in daily life, there is growing anxiety about the use and understanding of bias within these systems.

Based on several studies, there are multiple potential points within an AI system where bias can arise. Sources of bias may be as varied as the data used to train the model, the algorithms employed to create and operate the models, and the way in which individuals interpret the resultant output from the AI models. Thus, various methods have been recommended to combat bias, including improvement of data quality and creation of algorithms that have been designed to eliminate bias explicitly, as well as the application of AI ethical principles throughout the entire development lifecycle of an AI model.

Recently developed methods for removing bias use state-of-the-art machine learning algorithms, which can be used to identify and remove bias from an AI model. Commonly referred to as fairness-aware learning algorithms, these algorithms strive to create a fair outcome from an AI system with respect to demographic groups or attributes.

Research conducted by Srinivasan and Chander (2021) has demonstrated that using adversarial debiasing is a practical method for the identification and removal of bias from a primary AI model by using an additional or auxiliary AI model that is pure or free of bias. A second approach is to incorporate fairness constraints directly into the optimization process of an AI model to accomplish comparable levels of accuracy for predictive capabilities across demographic groups (Ferrara, 2023).

While the advancement of methods to build better algorithms is important, many Ethical Guidelines and Principles are being developed by governing bodies such as the IEEE and OECD to combat bias and discrimination. These often include recommendations for the fair and responsible design and use of AI systems, along with an emphasis on the necessity of transparency, accountability, and human oversight of the AI development process to reduce the risks associated with bias and discrimination on a global scale.

With the increasing presence of AI systems in all aspects of our society, as well as the growing need for effective methodologies to reduce bias in AI systems, researchers and practitioners alike must utilize the innovative techniques of fairness-aware learning and the integration of AI ethics throughout the entire lifecycle of development in order to ensure an unbiased and equitable AI system for everyone, according to Srinivasan and Chander (2021).

3.4.2 The Function of Policy and Regulation

The acceleration of AI technology has brought forward serious questions regarding biases and how it's being amplified in the lives of populations that have historically been marginalized (Bateni et al., 2022). To be able to create fair and inclusive opportunities through ethical design and use of AI systems, it is imperative for regulators and policymakers to create regulatory guidelines and standards.

One primary source of bias in AI comes from the data used to create AI systems. The data used to create these technologies are often reflective of the societal biases existing at the time of collection and have insufficient diverse representation to develop models that can reduce or eliminate inequities between groups receiving healthcare. Therefore, it will be important for governments and the public sector to work with AI developers to consider the development of data standardization when gathering data for model creation and encourage a diverse and inclusive system for collecting that data. Policymakers may need to implement laws requiring that all individuals from underrepresented populations be represented in the data used to develop training datasets or provide the ability for technologies to employ auditing methodologies to identify any existing biases (Kvasny et al., 2019). Regulatory frameworks and minimum requirements should be made available to AI developers to provide guidance and hold them accountable for ethical and/or fair use of their systems in conjunction with laws regulating the use of AI technologies. Policymakers must work with experts from multiple disciplines (e.g., computer science, social justice, and data governance) to find comprehensive solutions to the challenge of bias within AI technology. Because the circumstances surrounding bias in AI will need different viewpoints when developing ways to eliminate bias, such as technical solution(s), social justice initiative(s), and data governance, it is critical that organizations involved in mitigating bias in AI work collaboratively together to establish consistent means for supporting the ethical and equitable advancement of AI technology (Leavy et al., 2020). The complexity of addressing bias in AI is multidimensional and collaborative because the challenge of bias is closely connected with many other aspects of society (e.g., systemic inequity and historical discrimination; Leavy et al.,

2020). Nonetheless, it is very important that the establishment of regulations that address bias and its implications for vulnerable communities be created.

The creation of a more equitable and inclusive future for AI technology and its development can only occur through collaboratively working with a variety of stakeholders (e.g., policymakers and regulators) and defining how to address bias across disciplines (Srinivasan & Chander, 2021; Ferrara, 2023; Shams et al., 2023; Leavy et al., 2020).

3.4.3 Establishing a Bias-Free AI Future

With advances in AI technologies happening rapidly, it is necessary for those who are developing and creating AI solutions to ensure that they are minimizing bias and allowing equal access to AI and AI-based solutions, as well as creating AI and AI-based solutions that can be used for the benefit of everyone. According to Srinivasan and Chander (2021) and Ferrara (2023), the three major sources of bias in AI are (1) the training data used to build the AI model, (2) the algorithm used to build the AI model, and (3) the personal biases of the individual or individuals developing the AI model. Therefore, to develop an AI system that is free of bias, a critical first step toward that goal is to create an environment that is more diverse and inclusive when it comes to developing AI and AI-based solutions. By bringing in perspectives and experiences from a variety of people (especially from those who have not been equally represented), there is less chance that AI will be developed with bias. Additionally, creating a more diverse and inclusive environment will help identify and/or eliminate potential bias and will provide a greater opportunity for AI and AI-based solutions to have a more accurate representation of the needs and experiences of the group(s) of people for whom AI is being developed (Chaudhary et al., 2025; Gaur, 2024; Gaur and Gaur, 2024a, 2024b).

Developing diverse teams is one way to reduce bias in AI. In addition, the continual process of defining, identifying, measuring, and removing bias in AI will need to be employed. Furthermore, a clear structure and methodology for the identification and removal of bias throughout the entire AI lifecycle (from data collection to model deployment) will be required. AI systems are becoming more integrated into our daily lives; therefore, it is increasingly important that the systems be developed from a foundation of fairness and equity. By developing AI solutions with a focus on removing bias and developing inclusive, transparent, and accountable practices, organizations can help ensure that AI technologies serve all users fairly.

REFERENCES

Arora, A., Alderman, J., Palmer, J., Ganapathi, S., Laws, E., McCradden, M. D., Oakden-Rayner, L., Pfohl, S., Ghassemi, M., McKay, F., Treanor, D., Rostamzadeh, N., Mateen, B. A., Gath, J., Adebajo, A. O., Kuku, S., Matin, R., Heller, K., Sapey, E., … Liu, X. (2023). This article discusses the importance of standards for health datasets in artificial intelligence-based applications. *Nature Medicine, 29*(11), 2929–2938. https://doi.org/10.1038/s41591-023-02608-w

Bateni, A., Chan, M., & Eitel-Porter, R. (2022). *AI fairness: From principles to practice*. arXiv. https://doi.org/10.48550/arxiv.2207.0983

Chen, L., Dong, J., & Zhou, H. (2021). *Class-balanced underwater object detection dataset generated using class-wise style augmentation*. arXiv. https://doi.org/10.48550/arxiv.2101.07959

Chaudhary, M., Gaur, L., Chakrabarti, A., Singh, G., Jones, P., & Kraus, S. (2025). An integrated model to evaluate transparency in predicting employee churn using explainable artificial intelligence. *Journal of Innovation & Knowledge, 10*(3), 100700. https://doi.org/10.1016/j.jik.2025.100700

Ding, K., Xu, Z., Tong, H., & Liu, H. (2022). *Data augmentation for deep graph learning: A survey*. arXiv. https://doi.org/10.48550/arxiv.2202.08235

Ferrara, E. (2023). Fairness and bias in artificial intelligence: A brief survey of sources, impacts, and mitigation strategies. *Science, 6*(1), Article 3. https://doi.org/10.3390/sci6010003

Golbin, I., Rao, A. S., Hadjarian, A., & Krittman, D. (2020). Responsible AI: A primer for the legal community. In *Proceedings of the IEEE International Conference on Big Data* (pp. 5017–5026). https://doi.org/10.1109/BigData50022.2020.9377738

Gaur, L. (2024). From algorithms to ethics: XAI's impact on e-commerce. In L. Gaur & A. Abraham (Eds.), *Role of explainable artificial intelligence in e-commerce* (Vol. 1094). Springer. https://doi.org/10.1007/978-3-031-55615-9_8

Gaur, L., & Gaur, D. (2024a). Amyotrophic lateral sclerosis (ALS) monitoring using explainable AI. In L. Gaur, A. Abraham, & R. Ajith (Eds.), *AI and neurodegenerative diseases* (Vol. 1131). Springer. https://doi.org/10.1007/978-3-031-53148-4_5

Gaur, L., & Gaur, D. (2024b). Ethical considerations: Case scenarios. In L. Gaur, A. Abraham, & R. Ajith (Eds.), *AI and neurodegenerative diseases* (Vol. 1131). Springer. https://doi.org/10.1007/978-3-031-53148-4_10

Kuhlman, C., Jackson, L., & Chunara, R. (2020). *No computation without representation: Avoiding data and algorithm biases through diversity*. arXiv. https://doi.org/10.48550/arxiv.2002.11836

Kvasny, L., Payton, F. C., & Neupane, B. (2019). Algorithmic equity in the hiring of underrepresented IT job candidates. *Online Information Review, 44*(2), 383–395. https://doi.org/10.1108/OIR-10-2018-0334

Larrazabal, A. J., Nieto, N., Peterson, V., Milone, D. H., & Ferrante, E. (2020). Gender imbalance in medical imaging datasets produces biased classifiers for computer-aided diagnosis. *Proceedings of the National Academy of Sciences, 117*(23), 12592–12594. https://doi.org/10.1073/pnas.1919012117

Leavy, S., O'Sullivan, B., & Siapera, E. (2020). *Data, power and bias in artificial intelligence*. arXiv. https://doi.org/10.48550/arxiv.2008.07341

London, A. J. (2024). *Accountability for responsible AI practices: Ethical responsibilities of senior leadership*. SSRN. https://doi.org/10.2139/ssrn.473688

Marwala, T., Fournier-Tombs, É., & Stinckwich, S. (2023). *The use of synthetic data to train AI models: Opportunities and risks for sustainable development*. arXiv. https://doi.org/10.48550/arxiv.2309.00652

Mumuni, A., Mumuni, F., & Gerrar, N. K. (2024). A survey of synthetic data augmentation methods in computer vision. *Neural Computing and Applications*. https://doi.org/10.1007/s11633-022-1411-7

Rajkomar, A., Hardt, M., Howell, M., Corrado, G. S., & Chin, M. H. (2018). Ensuring fairness in machine learning to advance health equity. *Annals of Internal Medicine, 169*(12), 866–872. https://doi.org/10.7326/M18-199

Santosh, K., & Gaur, L. (2021). AI solutions to public health issues. In *Artificial intelligence and machine learning in public healthcare.* Springer. https://doi.org/10.1007/978-981-16-6768-8_3

Shams, R. A., Zowghi, D., & Bano, M. (2023). *Challenges and solutions in AI for all.* arXiv. https://doi.org/10.48550/arxiv.2307.10600

Shorten, C., Khoshgoftaar, T. M., & Furht, B. (2021). Text data augmentation for deep learning. *Journal of Big Data, 8*(1), 1–34. https://doi.org/10.1186/s40537-021-00492-0

Srinivasan, R., & Chander, A. (2021). Biases in AI systems. *Communications of the ACM, 64*(8), 44–49. https://doi.org/10.1145/3464903

Whitney, C. D., & Norman, J. (2024). Real risks of fake data: Synthetic data, diversity-washing and consent circumvention. In *Proceedings of the ACM Conference on Fairness, Accountability, and Transparency.* https://doi.org/10.1145/3630106.3659002

Zhou, M., Abhishek, V., Derdenger, T., Kim, J., & Srinivasan, K. (2024). *Bias in generative AI.* arXiv. https://doi.org/10.48550/arxiv.2403.02726

Zwick, D., & Encarnação, J. M. (2020). Algorithmic governance and the automation of moral decisions. *Journal of Business Ethics, 51*(4), 355–372. https://doi.org/10.1108/JBS-09-2019-0185

4 Techniques for Ethical Calibration of AI Models

4.1 INTRODUCTION

4.1.1 Definition of Calibration in AI

The process of calibrating AI models means that the outputs from an AI system are amended with respect to the true/actual probability values associated with the result. Hence, it is appropriate to calibrate the AI predictions or determine whether they are correct by gauging the likelihood of the underlying outcome given the AI's predicted outcome(s), which represents the true probability of occurrence. Calibration is crucial for several reasons. First, calibration decreases the probability of an AI model producing results that contain biases or distortions arising from insufficient calibration (Blau et al., 2024). Biases in terms of training data, algorithm design, or model assumptions can lead to systematic overestimations or underestimations of probabilities or values. Calibration allows for the detection and correction of these biases, resulting in better and more accurate outputs from an AI model.

The second reason is that calibration allows for the trustworthiness of AI-assisted decision-making. Humans often rely on the values or probabilities generated by AI systems when making important decisions. However, if an AI model has inadequate calibration, its output may lead humans to make incorrect decisions and/or result in unexpected consequences (Blau et al., 2024). Given the above problem, researchers have proposed several methods for performing calibration, both through post-processing techniques and training methods, to improve human users' self-confidence in AI systems and better support the rational use of AI recommendations (Ma et al., 2024).

Calibration is critical for ensuring an adequate level of transparency regarding errors in data and establishing a level of responsibility for these errors. By developing comprehensive protocols to validate the accuracy and reliability of AI outputs and documenting the processes used to build and test these systems, a multilayered accountability structure will be enabled. In sensitive fields such as healthcare, both users and providers of AI systems must understand their limits and the need for ongoing assessment and monitoring.

4.1.2 Calibration and Ethics: An Essential Relationship

The rapid development of AI has resulted in the emergence of a new factor in AI ethics: the calibration of AI models. Intermediate sectors, such as healthcare and

 DOI: 10.1201/9781003679974-4

banking, now use more AI systems, making the need for fair and unbiased results from these systems even more urgent and necessary (Siebert et al., 2021). The process of calibrating an AI system involves aligning its decisions with ethical standards and societal expectations. By calibrating AI systems, researchers and developers can facilitate transparency, fairness, and accountability in AI, which are essential traits of responsible and trustworthy AI. The principal ethical objective of calibration is to eliminate biases in AI outcomes. Like all technologies, AI systems are affected by the biases of the data on which they are trained, which can lead to inconsistent and unreliable results for specific populations. Researchers have investigated many ways to increase the fairness of AI systems, including data debiasing, algorithmic bias mitigation, and post-processing adjustment (Pfohl et al., 2020). These techniques aim to ensure that AI decisions do not exhibit discriminatory patterns but rather promote equity across different populations.

In addition to the technological aspect, calibrating AI systems also has a more comprehensive sociotechnical perspective. Responsible AI development is built on understanding how the use of AI affects society, such as civil rights, job displacement, and amplification of existing disparities (Horvitz, 2017). Owing to the increasing use of AI in important decision-making processes, the need for robust calibration processes is becoming increasingly clear. Continued oversight, community inclusion, and a multidisciplinary approach are necessary to ensure that AI is developed and used in accordance with ethical standards and societal expectations (Arora et al., 2023; Gaur, 2024; Gaur and Gaur, 2024a, 2024b; Gaur and Sahoo, 2022).

4.2 THE FUNCTION OF CALIBRATION IN ADVANCING ETHICAL AI

4.2.1 Equity via Calibration: Its Significance

As AI models are increasingly involved in decision-making, the topic of fairness has garnered much interest among researchers (Kim et al., 2023). Researchers have reported many obvious forms of bias embedded within AI models that can manifest as biases in facial recognition and rankings of different systems. Calibration has gained attention for minimizing biases while providing an overall fairer system (Mujtaba & Mahapatra, 2019). The calibration process ensures that different demographic groups can view the results generated by an AI model equally and without bias. This is primarily because many AI algorithms rely on information provided by humans, which may contain biases stemming from the methods used to create this data. Model calibration allows researchers to ensure "within-group fairness," meaning that all individuals from one group are treated fairly, and "between-group fairness," meaning that all individuals from different groups are treated fairly and equitably (Kim et al., 2023) (Figure 4.1).

Calibrating AI systems for fairness is an important aspect of ensuring that they are fair across multiple demographic groups. Calibration helps create impartial AI systems that provide equal consideration to all individuals, particularly those with different backgrounds, and allows researchers to develop models that address fairness within and between demographic groups, as indicated by Kim et al. (2023).

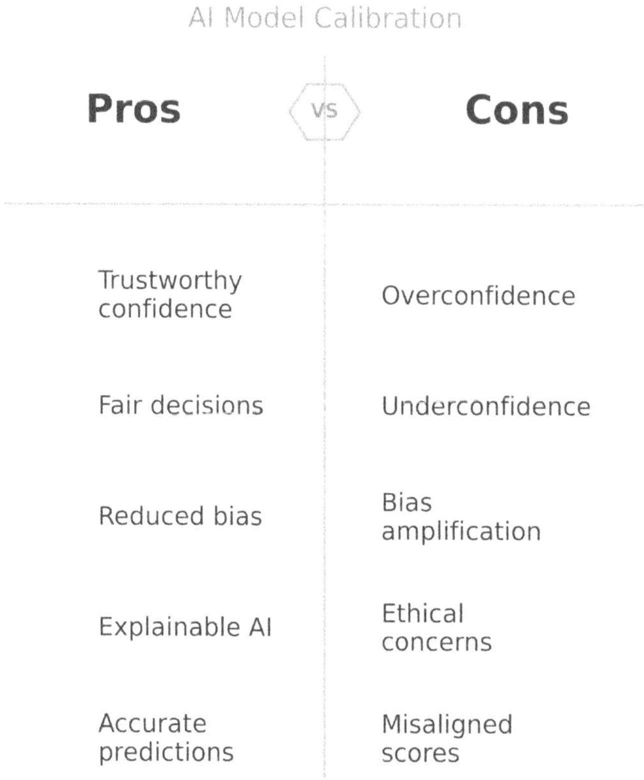

FIGURE 4.1 Advantages and disadvantages of AI model calibration.

When we calibrate the AI models used for decision-making, we create more equitable AI models. The authors of several studies related to the effect of calibration on fairness across different domains emphasize the importance of considering the social context in which AI is used and of understanding how the calibration of AI can lead to health disparities and socio-economic inequities, as outlined in Pfohl et al. (2020). Researchers and practitioners developing AI technologies and systems should not underestimate the importance of creating fair AI through calibration and achieving the same level of prediction and decision-making accuracy for all population groups. Therefore, it is important for researchers and practitioners to develop AI systems to take steps to ensure that they produce ethical and inclusive AI systems through their calibration processes (Figure 4.2).

4.2.2 Mitigating Bias via Efficient Calibration

We must address the inherent bias in AI systems as they become more prevalent. The model bias within AI systems can create unequal and unethical results, which can have a large impact on the individuals and society in which it exists. Calibration of

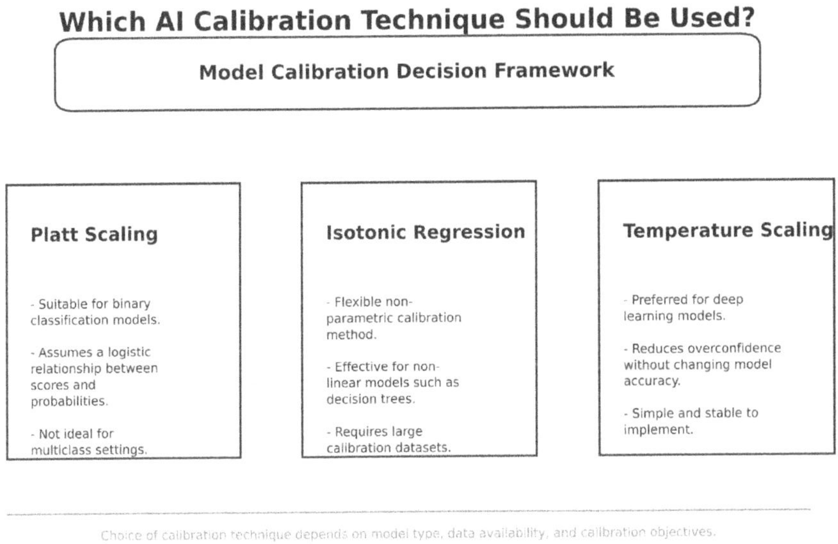

FIGURE 4.2 Guaranteeing ethical AI via calibration.

AI models can help reduce or eliminate bias; therefore, the calibration process ideally creates ethical and trustworthy AI systems.

Bias can arise from the data used to train the system, the algorithms used to build the AI system, and the biases of the AI system's creator (Bateni et al., 2022). The steps to reduce bias include creating fairness-aware algorithms, removing bias from training data, and correcting learned models. Leavy et al. (2020) claimed that an increasing number of researchers believe that bias is embedded in data created by human activity and that no data is neutral. Proper calibration of AI models can assist in reducing the impact of bias and, therefore, help ensure that the output of the model reflects what was intended by the modeler. Proper calibration results from a careful analysis of the training data, the methodologies used to create the models, and modifications to the model parameters aimed at reducing the bias. The presence of diverse and representative training data is a primary factor in the effective calibration of AI models. Bias can arise if the sample dataset cannot provide an adequate representation of the full diversity and variety of individuals and situations that a model will face after deployment. The use of multiple forms of data enables a model to capture different perspectives and experiences, which reduces the likelihood of bias. The algorithms employed for model training play a crucial role in achieving effective calibration. Researchers have suggested several methods to reduce bias at the algorithmic level, including improving data quality and developing fair algorithms (Ferrara, 2023). A diverse and inclusive team that participates in the development of AI systems is essential for successful creation. A diverse team can better identify and mitigate bias during development and deployment.

4.3 TECHNIQUES FOR CALIBRATING AI MODELS

4.3.1 Post-Processing Calibration Methods

Calibrating models are an integral part of ML and presents a means to improve the trustworthiness and interpretability of the model outputs. Model calibration consists of using post-processing methods, such as Platt scaling or isotonic regression, to enhance and calibrate model predictions after their original training (Bussmann et al., 2020). Platt scaling is a common post-processing method that converts the raw output of a model into an accurate probability estimate. In Platt scaling, a logistic regression model transforms raw output into a probability (Dheur & Taieb, 2024). Isotonic regression takes nonparametric data and fits a monotonic transformation function to relate the calibrated probability back to the raw outputs. These techniques can be used with any type of model, including linear regression, classification trees, and neural networks, to provide a better understanding and reliability of each individual model's output, thus improving interpretability. Selecting an appropriate scaling method for a model can greatly impact its classification performance (Amorim et al., 2022). When conducting a classification activity, proper scaling should be performed so that features that are spread further apart numerically are not overshadowed by features that are at closer numerical ranges, which skews the overall classification by giving it a lower weight than it needs. As noted earlier, model calibration methods can support increased interpretability and reliability through explainable AI (XAI) in the financial technology (Fintech) and risk management (RM) industries. Therefore, calibrating the output of a model using these methods results in more accurate and interpreted projections that meet the financial industry's requirements of transparency and accountability (Bussmann et al., 2020) (Figure 4.3).

Post-processing calibration techniques have only recently been introduced for use with neural networks (NN) in regression. They can be used to retain calibration while increasing the prediction accuracy of an NN using post-processing methods. This is beneficial if one is looking for a dependable, reliable, and accurately calibrated forecast.

4.3.2 Calibration Throughout Model Training

Owing to the need for dependable and credible outcomes from ML models used in critical applications (medical diagnosis, financial decisions, and autonomous systems), the calibration of ML models is becoming increasingly important. Essentially, the traditional training of a model focuses exclusively on optimizing measures such as accuracy and F1 score, which do not include the explicit calibration of the predictions generated by the model (Figure 4.4).

Calibration establishes an alignment between the predictions of a model's (algorithm's) probability distribution and the actual underlying probabilities of the target variables. There are many cases in which the output of a model requires proper calibration because an uncalibrated prediction leads to poor decisions and potentially

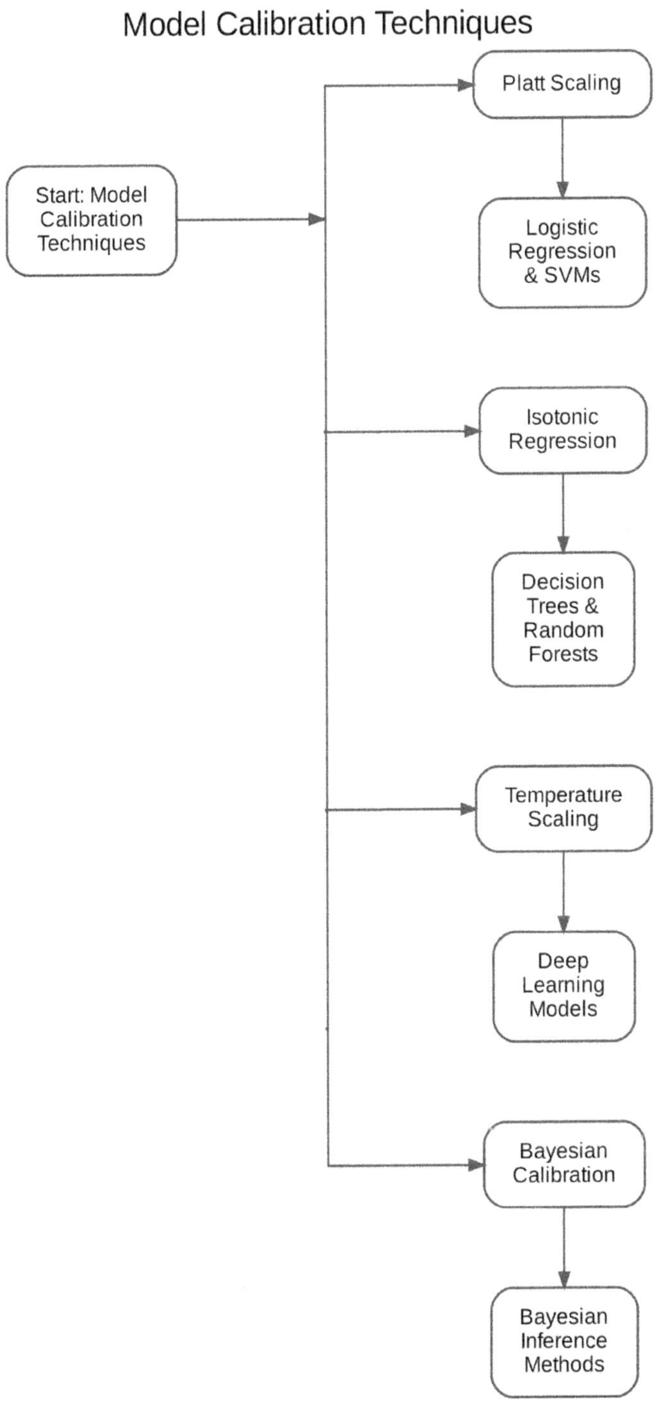

FIGURE 4.3 Which AI calibration technique should be employed.

FIGURE 4.4 Diverse techniques for model calibration.

harmful results. Recent research has focused on ways to integrate calibration into model training by using loss functions that encourage the model to produce calibrated outputs. One promising method is the use of imprecise Bayesian neural networks, which extend the concept of a Bayesian neural network to provide a better and more reliable representation of the uncertainty of the model's predictions (Caprio et al., 2023). Uncertainty indicates the reliability of the predictions made by the model and helps decide whether to seek more information or involve a human in the decision-making process. The uncertainty quantification will enable the identification of situations in which the model has low confidence in its predictions; thus, the resulting predictions are more reliable and lead to better decisions (Ding et al., 2019; Sicking et al., 2022).

4.3.3 Calibration Measurement: Metrics and Instruments

Calibration is critical for evaluating the trustworthiness and reliability of ML models. This allows us to determine how well a given model's (predicted) probability corresponds to the actual (true) probability of each possible outcome. To evaluate the calibration of an ML model, a wide variety of evaluation criteria have been created, with each criterion having its own strengths. The most widely used evaluation criterion for ML model calibration is the Expected Calibration Error (ECE). The ECE measures the average difference between the predicted probability of a given outcome by an ML model and the true probability of that same outcome, thereby providing an overall measure of the calibration of an ML model across its entire range of predicted probabilities. However, the ECE is often influenced by outliers or artifacts within the training data and, therefore, may not accurately represent localized fluctuations in the calibration of an ML model (Figure 4.5).

The Brier score measures how closely a binary outcome prediction matches, in a numerical way, with how confidently the algorithm predicts the outcome. Although the Brier score provides an understanding of how close a model's predicted probabilities are to its actual outputs, it does not offer a direct connection with the notion of calibration (Hossin & Sulaiman, 2015). Previously, various forms and methods for improving model calibration assessments have been developed. Both the ECE and Brier scores can be obtained through free libraries, such as Scikit-learn and TensorFlow Probability, although there are also more advanced methods for the visual representation of the features of calibration, such as reliability diagrams and calibration curves. Evaluating the performance of a model's calibration in the case of a shift in the underlying data is important for practitioners using models that rely on multiple sources of information. This evaluation revealed the capability of the model to continue providing reliable uncertainty estimates in the face of different input distributions. Evaluating a model's calibration in the context of multiple distributions will help practitioners determine when the model continues to provide reliable uncertainty estimates. For instance, when practitioners use different techniques to evaluate a model's calibration and subsequently apply those techniques to determine when the model will provide reliable uncertainty estimates, they will be equipped with the necessary tools and methods for evaluating and deploying the model (Ma et al., 2024; Tygert, 2020; Ovadia et al., 2019; Hayes, 2003).

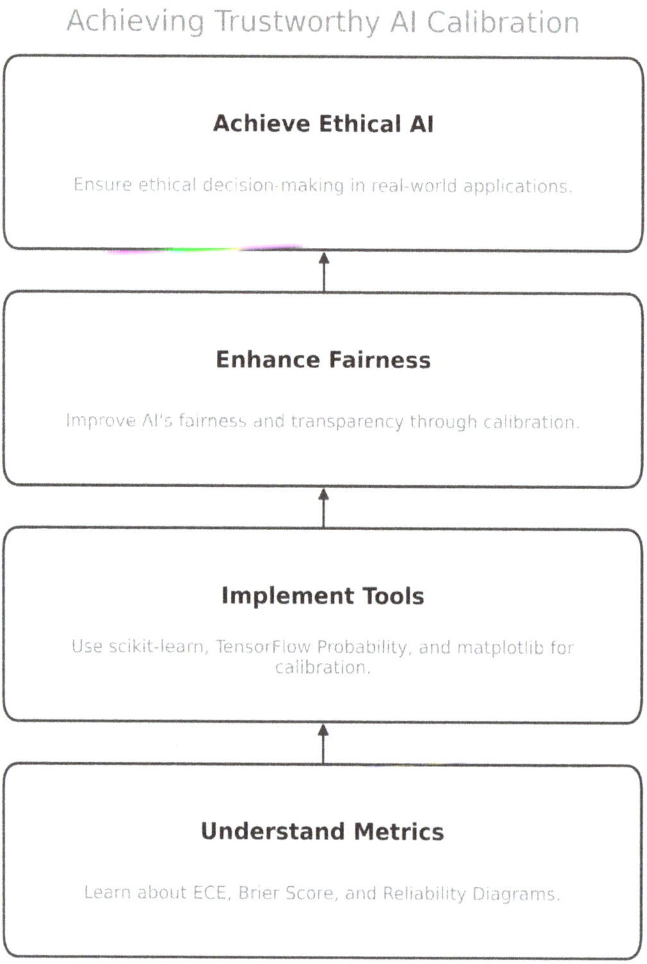

FIGURE 4.5 Overview of calibration metrics.

4.4 CHALLENGES IN ATTAINING NEUTRALITY AND EQUITY IN CALIBRATION

4.4.1 The Compromise Between Precision and Fairness

Most ML models focus on maximizing forecast accuracy, which leads to a loss of fairness across various demographic groups. Using only optimal performance metrics to develop ML models can lead to a model that strongly favors a given demographic's predicted outcomes and results in an adversarial relationship with health equity (Rajkomar et al., 2018). People are concerned that ML algorithms will replicate the existing biases in the data on which they were trained. This can result from insufficient diversity within the training sample or because of human annotator-used characteristics that have established bias(es) throughout the annotation history (Liu & Luo, 2021). The predictions of ML models may negatively impact demographic groups because of potentially embedded biases, even if the overall accuracy (FC) of the models is high. In response to this challenge, researchers have proposed methods for developing an ML model that explicitly maximizes fairness measures alongside fairness criteria (FC) (Liu & Luo, 2021) and employed debiasing algorithms and techniques to reduce bias in training data (Gianfrancesco et al., 2018). Consequently, both researchers and practitioners must balance the relative trade-off between achieving optimal levels of FC and achieving levels of fairness that adequately fit their respective applications. Within the healthcare field, these trade-offs have major implications, as biased or poorly written ML models exacerbate existing disparities in access to and health outcome(s). For example, an ML model may fail to identify rare disorders in individuals who are members of Historically Underrepresented (HUR) groups or allocate scarce resources in a manner that is harmful to communities. Thus, researchers have emphasized the importance of proactively considering equity and justice throughout the entire lifecycle of ML model development. This includes proper curation of training data, validation of the model using diverse subgroups, and continuous monitoring for unintended bias(es) after deploying the model. By prioritizing equity alongside optimal FC, ML has the potential to significantly enhance healthcare delivery and health outcomes for individuals; however, this can only be accomplished if ML is appropriately written and implemented with a strong commitment to equity.

4.4.2 Calibration in Imbalanced Datasets

The model cannot make reliable predictions with unbalanced datasets (those with large differences in the number of instances of each group or class). When using unbalanced datasets with ML algorithms, the model's objective is most often to maximize the overall accuracy. In doing so, the models do not produce reliable or trustworthy predictions regarding the minority class. Consequently, overconfidence in the predictions of the minority class occurs, resulting in biased predictions that could have devastating results in real-world applications, such as medical disease diagnosis and fraud detection. Many approaches are currently being explored to address the challenges of unbalanced datasets. Some common approaches include oversampling the minority class, undersampling the majority class, or using a combination of both (Kim & Hwang, 2022). Although these resampling techniques attempt to improve the classification performance, they do not always result in well-calibrated models. Recent studies have evaluated the effects of various resampling methods on model calibration for unbalanced datasets. The findings suggest that oversampling has the potential to improve the overall classification performance; however, it may introduce overconfidence in the predictions of the minority class, especially when SMOTE-like methods are applied. Conversely, undersampling methods (e.g., random undersampling) generally produce better-calibrated models but typically do so at the expense of overall classification performance (More, 2016).

To address the calibration problems associated with unbalanced datasets, researchers have developed new calibration methods tailored to the needs of these datasets. Examples include class-wise temperature scaling and isotonic regression conditional on class. The purpose of these new methods is to adjust the predicted output probabilities of a model to better reflect the actual probabilities of the target classes. The adjustment of prediction probabilities improves the model calibration while simultaneously preserving the original classification performance.

4.4.3 The Complexity of Multidimensional Fairness

This study aimed to investigate the challenges presented by multiple meanings and measurements associated with multidimensional fairness and the resultant consequences of calibration attempts. The desire to achieve multidimensional fairness is complicated by the multiplicity of meanings associated with "fairness" within these different dimensions. This multiplicity leads to confusion regarding which variables to use and how to weigh them to measure fairness. Consequently, many fairness evaluations are based on group-level comparisons, such as comparing the mean outcomes associated with different demographic populations within the context of fair hiring practices. However, this approach presents challenges, as different demographic groups experience different characteristics, and the choice of demographic group, as well as the weight of different characteristic variables, can significantly affect the determination of whether an evaluation of fairness is accurate. Therefore, the choice of demographic groups and the weights associated with their respective characteristics will result in either false positives or false negatives when evaluating fairness (Garg et al., 2020). The trade-off between increasing fairness for one group while decreasing it for another is especially evident when evaluating fairness for marginalized groups (Chohlas-Wood et al., 2023). Algorithms and AI systems have gained popularity in many areas of decision-making, where serious ramifications may occur (Garg et al., 2020). For example, while algorithms may improve the efficiency of decision-making and create more equitable outcomes, there is also a risk of entrenched and perhaps exacerbated inequities if the underlying fairness problems associated with their development are not addressed.

4.5 CASE STUDIES: CALIBRATION IN ACTION

4.5.1 Calibrating AI for Fair Lending Decisions

The emergence of AI has transformed the financial sector. AI-based solutions have a growing influence in the lending and credit rating industries. In tandem with this rise in influence is the rising concern regarding fairness and bias reduction in these technologies (Maple et al., 2023). Our study provides insight into how calibration methods were applied to ensure fairness with respect to the AI models used in credit scoring and loan decisions and how biases against certain demographic groups were removed (Kozodoi et al., 2021; Maple et al., 2023). ML models trained on historical loan data often express existing societal bias; therefore, when lenders approve loans based on these models, it may result in a disproportionate rejection of certain demographic groups from receiving loans, or those demographic groups will receive higher interest rates than others. In response to this trend, researchers have developed several classes of fairness-aware algorithms to calibrate AI-modeled decisions and correct for bias.

4.5.2 Calibration in Healthcare: Ensuring Equitable Outcomes

The use of AI in the healthcare industry has changed how we deliver care and has opened new possibilities for improved patient outcomes. However, as we continue to use AI-based solutions in healthcare, it will be critical for these systems to be calibrated to achieve equitable results for all patients, regardless of demographic background (Sezgin, 2023; Johnson et al., 2020; Harry, 2023; Varnosfaderani & Forouzanfar, 2024). Calibrating AI-powered healthcare systems to mitigate bias and promote fairness is a key element in accomplishing this (Harry, 2023). Life course analysis is essential; the assessment of how algorithms impact different populations over the life course is incredibly important for researchers, especially in the healthcare field, since incorrect, partial, or biased predictions can significantly impact patient well-being and health outcomes (Zou & Schiebinger, 2021). A case study from the University of Chicago Medicine illustrates the importance of calibrating AI systems to ensure equity. Through collaboration between data scientists at the University of Chicago Medicine and representatives from the Diversity and Equity Committee, processes for reducing access-related bias when developing ML models were researched and implemented in this study. By developing a local checklist that included an examination of equity concerns as part of creating and implementing ML models, the team was able to proactively address equity concerns and ensure that the benefits of their AI tools were available to as many diverse patient groups as possible.

4.5.3 Addressing Bias in AI-Powered Hiring Tools Through Calibration

Rapid advances in AI technology have transformed hiring and recruitment processes in multiple industries. Businesses are increasingly utilizing AI-based systems to accelerate their hiring efforts, hoping that these systems will eliminate or reduce the amount of human bias involved (Chen, 2023). However, recent research indicates that AI-based hiring tools may continue to perpetuate existing biases, leading to unfair hiring practices (Chen, 2023; Mujtaba & Mahapatra, 2024). To combat this problem, researchers have been investigating possible strategies to calibrate AI models for use in hiring to minimize bias and provide more equitable evaluations of candidates from different backgrounds. Examples of these calibration techniques include scrutinizing the training data used to develop AI models. Humans may have created training data that could potentially contain inherent societal biases. Therefore, by detecting and removing such bias from the training data, it will allow for the AI models to develop and make unbiased employment decisions in the future (Mujtaba & Mahapatra, 2024). Another important step in calibrating AI hiring tools is developing and applying fairness metrics, which will provide an organization with a means to measure how fairly or equitably the model produces its outputs. Fairness metrics help organizations recognize instances of disparate treatment or impact created by their models across candidate groups owing to demographic differences.

Beyond ensuring data quality and incorporating fairness metrics, researchers have examined the importance of utilizing other techniques to eliminate bias from the filter process in AI models through adversarial debiasing. Adopting various calibration techniques helps organizations reduce bias in their AI-powered hiring solutions while creating a more inclusive and equitable recruitment ecosystem.

4.6 FUTURE DIRECTIONS: ADVANCING CALIBRATION FOR ETHICAL AI

4.6.1 Emerging Techniques and Innovations in Calibration

The increasing demand for accurate model calibration in the field of AI has also led to the need for equal access to knowledge and expertise in AI development. Consequently, new algorithms have been developed by researchers to address these issues and provide future researchers with new methods to enhance the fairness of AI models (Beutel et al., 2019; Mujtaba & Mahapatra, 2019).

Beutel et al. (2019) proposed a method for training AI models to enhance fairness metrics during the development process. This method allows researchers to create a framework to effectively implement fairness principles while considering the challenges associated with this implementation and how these principles will ultimately be measured during the AI model development process. In addition to developing a framework to implement fairness principles, the authors introduced the concept of within-group fairness and how it can be used to enhance between-group fairness. This concept is based on creating mathematical definitions for within-group fairness, as well as creating learning algorithms that can balance both within-group fairness and between-group fairness at the same time without sacrificing model performance. The authors provide an example of future advancements in this area with the introduction of a casual conversation dataset. The causal conversations dataset provides an overview of how multiple top-performing AI systems treat people from different backgrounds. This dataset revealed that AI models trained on datasets that were not evenly distributed across subgroups experienced a significant amount of bias, which caused them to perform poorly when applied in real-life situations. Therefore, this finding emphasizes the importance of developing equitable and inclusive AI systems.

4.6.2 The Role of AI Governance in Calibration

The increased integration of AI into everyday life has increased the importance of developing adequate governance frameworks and policies to support the calibration process in recent years. Having a strong governance structure to support the responsible use of AI is essential to ensure that AI is used ethically (Gill et al., 2022). AI calibration is the process of fine-tuning AI systems to achieve optimal performance.

To achieve this, good governance structures that follow the rules of fairness, openness, and responsibility are required. Without appropriate governance structures, the calibration of AI systems may result in unintended biases, violations of privacy, and other ethical issues with potentially significant consequences. Modern AI systems are built on a data-centric framework, which requires the operationalization of all governance requirements with respect to data. Therefore, the calibration process requires an examination of not only the technical components of the AI system but also the quality, origin, and ethics of the data used to train and improve AI systems. In addition, a multiple-layered governance approach to AI integrated with ethical principles, regulatory guidelines, and policies at the organizational level can support society's values of AI calibration and legal requirements (Gasser & Almeida, 2017). As the use of AI grows rapidly, the legal field must assist in providing guidance and interpretation of responsible AI development and use. Creating a comprehensive governance framework and policy for AI will help organizations navigate the unfamiliar precinct of AI calibration, minimize risk, and gain maximum benefit from these disruptive technologies (Gasser & Almeida, 2017; Gill et al., 2022; Golbin et al., 2020; London, 2024; Santosh and Gaur, 2021; Zhou et al., 2024; Zwick and Encarnação, 2020).

4.6.3 Toward a Future of Fair and Neutral AI Models

With the increasing reliance on AI worldwide to make decisions that have a direct impact on our lives, it is critical that the design of these models is based on an approach that incorporates fairness and neutrality in the training data. Historically, the development of many AI models has been plagued by bias and unfairness resulting from bias in the data used to train these models. The results from these biased models can have negative real-world consequences, such as discrimination against specific classes of people within a company's recruitment process or other high-stakes decision-making scenarios (Leavy et al., 2020; Mujtaba & Mahapatra, 2019). Researchers are now starting to devise new methods and technologies that can be utilized to mitigate such biases through the development of fairness-aware ML algorithms and the creation of tools that may allow the interpretation of "black-box" models (Mujtaba & Mahapatra, 2019; Leavy et al., 2020). However, there is a progressively popular belief that it may be impossible to realize true objectivity within AI because the data used to train these models reflect human bias (Leavy et al., 2020). This demands a reevaluation of the entire AI development process. To this end, the development process must encompass multiple perspectives and provide further transparency and accountability for both the foundational data and the model being created.

REFERENCES

Amorim, L., Cavalcanti, G. D. C., & Cruz, R. M. O. (2022). The choice of scaling technique is important for classification performance. *Applied Soft Computing, 133*, 109924. https://doi.org/10.1016/j.asoc.2022.109924

Arora, A., Alderman, J., Palmer, J., Ganapathi, S., Laws, E., McCradden, M. D., Oakden-Rayner, L., Pfohl, S., Ghassemi, M., McKay, F., Treanor, D., Rostamzadeh, N., Mateen, B. A., Gath, J., Adebajo, A. O., Kuku, S., Matin, R., Heller, K., Sapey, E., … Liu, X. (2023). The value of standards for health datasets in AI-based applications. *Nature Medicine, 29*(11), 2929–2938. https://doi.org/10.1038/s41591-023-02608-w

Bateni, A., Chan, M., & Eitel-Porter, R. (2022). *AI fairness: From principles to practice.* arXiv. https://doi.org/10.48550/arxiv.2207.09833

Beutel, A., Chen, J., Doshi, T., Qian, H., Woodruff, A., Luu, C., Kreitmann, P., Bischof, J., & H., E. (2019). *Putting fairness principles into practice: Challenges, metrics, and improvements.* arXiv. https://doi.org/10.48550/arxiv.1901.04562

Blau, W., Cerf, V. G., Enriquez, J., Francisco, J. S., Gasser, U., Gray, M. L., Greaves, M. F., Grosz, B. J., Jamieson, K. H., Haug, G. H., Hennessy, J. L., Horvitz, E., Kaiser, D., London, A. J., Lovell-Badge, R., McNutt, M., Minow, M., Mitchell, T. M., Ness, S., … Witherell, M. S. (2024). Protecting scientific integrity in an age of generative AI. *Proceedings of the National Academy of Sciences, 121*(22), e2407886121. https://doi.org/10.1073/pnas.2407886121

Bussmann, N., Giudici, P., Marinelli, D., & Papenbrock, J. (2020). Explainable AI in fintech risk management. *Frontiers in AI, 3*, 26. https://doi.org/10.3389/frai.2020.00026

Caprio, M., Dutta, S., Jang, K. J., Lin, V., Ivanov, R., Sokolsky, O., & Lee, I. (2023). *Imprecise Bayesian neural networks.* arXiv. https://doi.org/10.48550/arxiv.2302.09656

Chen, Z. (2023). The article discusses ethics and discrimination in AI-enabled recruitment practices. *Humanities and Social Sciences Communications, 10*(1). https://doi.org/10.1057/s41599-023-02079-x

Chohlas-Wood, A., Coots, M., Goel, S., & Nyarko, J. (2023). Designing equitable algorithms. *Nature Reviews Methods Primers, 3*(7), 601–610. https://doi.org/10.1038/s43588-023-00485-4

Dheur, V., & Taieb, S. B. (2024). *Probabilistic calibration by design for neural network regression.* arXiv. https://doi.org/10.48550/arxiv.2403.11964

Ding, Y., Liu, J., Xiong, J., & Shi, Y. (2019). *Evaluation of neural network uncertainty estimation with application to resource-constrained platforms.* arXiv. http://dblp.uni-trier.de/db/journals/corr/corr1903.html#abs-1903-02050

Ferrara, E. (2023). Fairness and bias in AI: A brief survey of sources, impacts, and mitigation strategies. *Science, 6*(1), Article 3. https://doi.org/10.3390/sci6010003

Garg, P., Villasenor, J., & Foggo, V. (2020). Fairness metrics: A comparative analysis. In *Proceedings of the IEEE International Conference on Big Data* (pp. xx–xx). https://doi.org/10.1109/BigData50022.2020.9378025

Gasser, U., & Almeida, V. (2017). A layered model for AI governance. *IEEE Internet Computing, 21*(6), 58–62. https://doi.org/10.1109/MIC.2017.4180835

Gaur, L. (2024). From algorithms to ethics: XAI's impact on e-commerce. In L. Gaur & A. Abraham (Eds.), *Role of explainable AI in e-commerce* (Vol. 1094). Springer. https://doi.org/10.1007/978-3-031-55615-9_8

Gaur, L., & Gaur, D. (2024a). Amyotrophic lateral sclerosis (ALS) monitoring using explainable AI. In L. Gaur, A. Abraham, & R. Ajith (Eds.), *AI and neurodegenerative diseases* (Vol. 1131). Springer. https://doi.org/10.1007/978-3-031-53148-4_5

Gaur, L., & Gaur, D. (2024b). Ethical considerations: Case scenarios. In L. Gaur, A. Abraham, & R. Ajith (Eds.), *AI and neurodegenerative diseases* (Vol. 1131). Springer. https://doi.org/10.1007/978-3-031-53148-4_10

Gaur, L., & Sahoo, B. M. (2022). Explainable AI in ITS: Ethical concerns. In A. Adadi & A. Bouhoute (Eds.), *Explainable AI for intelligent transportation systems.* Springer. https://doi.org/10.1007/978-3-031-09644-0_5

Gill, N., Mathur, A., & Conde, M. V. (2022). *A brief overview of AI governance for responsible ML systems.* arXiv. https://doi.org/10.48550/arxiv.2211.13130

Gianfrancesco, M., Tamang, S., Yazdany, J., & Schmajuk, G. (2018). Potential biases in ML algorithms using electronic health record data. *JAMA Internal Medicine, 178*(11), 1544. https://doi.org/10.1001/jamainternmed.2018.3763

Golbin, I., Rao, A. S., Hadjarian, A., & Krittman, D. (2020). Responsible AI: A primer for the legal community. In *Proceedings of the IEEE International Conference on Big Data* (pp. xx–xx). https://doi.org/10.1109/BigData50022.2020.9377738

Harry, A. (2023). The future of medicine: Harnessing the power of AI for revolutionizing healthcare. *International Journal of Medical and Dental Science and Applications, 2*(1), 36–47. https://doi.org/10.47709/ijmdsa.v2i1.2395

Hayes, J. L. (2003). Calibration and maintenance of test and measuring equipment. In R. A. Meyers (Ed.), *Encyclopedia of analytical chemistry.* Wiley. https://doi.org/10.1002/3527600434.eap048

Horvitz, E. (2017). AI, people, and society. *Science, 357*(6346), 7. https://doi.org/10.1126/science.aao2466

Hossin, M., & Sulaiman, M. N. (2015). A review on evaluation metrics for data classification evaluations. *International Journal of Data Mining & Knowledge Management Process, 5*(2), 1–11. https://doi.org/10.5121/ijdkp.2015.5201

Johnson, K. B., Wei, W., Weeraratne, D., Frisse, M. E., Misulis, K. E., Rhee, K., Zhao, J., & Snowdon, J. (2020). Precision medicine, AI, and the future of personalized health care. *Clinical and Translational Science, 14*(1), 86–93. https://doi.org/10.1111/cts.12884

Kim, M., & Hwang, K. (2022). An empirical evaluation of sampling methods for the classification of imbalanced data. *PLOS ONE, 17*(7), e0271260. https://doi.org/10.1371/journal.pone.0271260

Kim, S., Yu, K., & Kim, Y. (2023). *Within-group fairness: A guidance for more sound between-group fairness.* arXiv. https://doi.org/10.48550/arxiv.2301.08375

Kozodoi, N., Jacob, J., & Lessmann, S. (2021). Fairness in credit scoring: Assessment, implementation and profit implications. *European Journal of Operational Research, 297*(3), 1083–1094. https://doi.org/10.1016/j.ejor.2021.06.023

Leavy, S., O'Sullivan, B., & Siapera, E. (2020). *Data, power and bias in AI.* arXiv. https://doi.org/10.48550/arxiv.2008.07341

Liu, S., & Luo, Y. (2021). *Assessing social determinants-related performance bias of ML models: A case of hyperchloremia prediction in ICU population.* arXiv. https://doi.org/10.48550/arxiv.2111.09507

London, A. J. (2024). *Accountability for responsible AI practices: Ethical responsibilities of senior leadership.* SSRN. https://doi.org/10.2139/ssrn.4736880

Ma, X., Wang, X., Ying, L., Shi, C., Yin, M., & Ma, X. (2024). *"Are you really sure?" Understanding the effects of human self-confidence calibration in AI-assisted decision making.* arXiv. https://doi.org/10.48550/arxiv.2403.09552

Maple, C., Szpruch, Ł., Epiphaniou, G., Staykova, K., Singh, S. B., Penwarden, W., Wen, Y., Wang, Z., Hariharan, J., & Avramović, P. (2023). *The AI revolution: Opportunities and challenges for the finance sector.* arXiv. https://doi.org/10.48550/arxiv.2308.16538

More, A. (2016). *Survey of resampling techniques for improving classification performance in unbalanced datasets.* arXiv. https://doi.org/10.48550/arxiv.1608.06048

Mujtaba, D. F., & Mahapatra, N. R. (2019). Ethical considerations in AI-based recruitment. In *Proceedings of the IEEE International Symposium on Technology and Society (ISTAS).* https://doi.org/10.1109/ISTAS48451.2019.8937920

Mujtaba D. F., Mahapatra N. R. (2024). *Fairness in AI-driven recruitment: Challenges, metrics, methods, and future directions.* arXiv. https://doi.org/10.48550/arxiv.2405.19699

Ovadia, Y., Fertig, E., Ren, J., Nado, Z., Sculley, D., Nowozin, S., Dillon, J. V., Lakshminarayanan, B., & Snoek, J. (2019). *Can you trust your model's uncertainty? Evaluating predictive uncertainty under dataset shift.* arXiv. https://doi.org/10.48550/arxiv.1906.02530

Pfohl, S., Foryciarz, A., & Shah, N. H. (2020). An empirical characterization of fair ML for clinical risk prediction. *Journal of Biomedical Informatics, 113*, 103621. https://doi.org/10.1016/j.jbi.2020.103621

Rajkomar, A., Hardt, M., Howell, M., Corrado, G. S., & Chin, M. H. (2018). Ensuring fairness in ML to advance health equity. *Annals of Internal Medicine, 169*(12), 866–872. https://doi.org/10.7326/M18-1990

Santosh, K., & Gaur, L. (2021). AI solutions to public health issues. In K. C. Santosh & L. Gaur (Eds.), *AI and ML in public healthcare.* Springer. https://doi.org/10.1007/978-981-16-6768-8_3

Sezgin, E. (2023). AI in healthcare: Complementing, not replacing, doctors and healthcare providers. *Digital Health, 9.* https://doi.org/10.1177/20552076231186520

Siebert, L. C., Lupetti, M. L., Aizenberg, E., Beckers, N., Zgonnikov, A., Veluwenkamp, H., Abbink, D. A., Giaccardi, E., Houben, G., Jonker, C. M., van den Hoven, J., Förster, D., & Lagendijk, R. L. (2021). *Meaningful human control over AI systems: Beyond talking the talk.* arXiv. http://arxiv.org/pdf/2112.01298.pdf

Sicking, J., Akila, M., Schneider, J., Hüger, F., Schlicht, P., Wirtz, T., & Wrobel, S. (2022). *Tailored uncertainty estimation for deep learning systems.* arXiv. https://doi.org/10.48550/arxiv.2204.13963

Tygert, M. (2020). *Plots of the cumulative differences between observed and expected values of ordered Bernoulli variates.* arXiv. https://doi.org/10.48550/arxiv.2006.02504

Varnosfaderani, S. M., & Forouzanfar, M. (2024). The role of AI in hospitals and clinics: Transforming healthcare in the 21st century. *Bioengineering, 11*(4), 337. https://doi.org/10.3390/bioengineering11040337

Zhou, M., Abhishek, V., Derdenger, T., Kim, J., & Srinivasan, K. (2024). *Bias in generative AI.* arXiv. https://doi.org/10.48550/arxiv.2403.02726

Zou, J., & Schiebinger, L. (2021). Ensuring that biomedical AI benefits diverse populations. *EBioMedicine, 67*, 103358. https://doi.org/10.1016/j.ebiom.2021.103358

Zwick, D., & Encarnação, J. M. (2020). Algorithmic governance and the automation of moral decisions. *Journal of Business Ethics, 51*(4), 355–372. https://doi.org/10.1108/JBS-09-2019-0185

5 Addressing Privacy Challenges in Generative AI

5.1 INTRODUCTION: THE CONVERGENCE OF PRIVACY AND GENERATIVE AI

5.1.1 Defining Privacy within the Framework of AI

The combination of advanced digital technology and progressive growth in data generation and digital communications has made privacy far more complex and integrated into a larger number of concepts than ever. All industrial sectors have embraced new AI technologies, necessitating governmental, business, and consumer recognition of privacy (Wu & Liu, (2023). Privacy represents one of the largest components of the AI landscape. Consumers are demanding standardized transparency about how their data is collected and used, in addition to protecting their private information. Consumers are increasingly struggling to understand core concepts of privacy and how data is collected for these new and evolving AI systems, as well as experiencing a dramatic and relativistic increase in the amount of time that data remains on the internet. It is necessary to establish laws to govern how companies and governments collect, use, and disclose consumer data considering existing privacy and data protection standards (Huang, 2023). There has already been considerable discussion of the intersection of AI and data privacy in an industrial setting, through advocacy groups, and in academic circles. Despite a generally accepted understanding that AI provides a substantial number of benefits, the protection of data privacy must remain the focal point for all stakeholders. Medical imaging is one rapidly evolving area using new AI-based technologies that presents a unique opportunity for key stakeholders to identify how they will utilize and acquire data, demonstrating that there is a considerable amount of uncertainty regarding the protection of personal privacy (Kaissis et al., 2020). Given the opportunity to improve the future regulations of AI data, it is in the best interests of key stakeholders to examine existing legislative frameworks regarding privacy and data protection. Currently, an urgent focus is on developing a comprehensive, consistent, and legal framework to balance the advantages of AI with the need to protect consumers' privacy.

5.1.2 The Importance of Privacy in GenAI

The newly developed branches of GenAI have brought forth many unique characteristics, which are continuing to raise great privacy concerns across multiple

DOI: 10.1201/9781003679974-5

industries: from content creators to those working with AI-based solutions to solve daily problems (Epstein et al., 2023). The main danger regarding GenAI is that the data used to train these models could be misused. GenAI systems are made up of huge amounts of data; most of the data comes from user-generated content, which means it includes personal information about the user itself and sensitive information. Therefore, the GenAI produced content resembles the original data; therefore, it has the potential to infringe on an individual's right to privacy (Epstein et al., 2023). The ethical implications of infringing upon an individual's privacy using GenAI are frightening. Because these AI systems can produce extremely high quality, lively, and almost indistinguishable content such as text, audio, and images, this immoral use of the GenAI systems will be possible to perpetrate, such as committing fraud, impersonating a person or criminal, or disseminating false information (Baldassarre et al., 2023). Another concern regarding the complexity of these AI systems is their ability to create, either by accident or on purpose, bias or error during the training process, making it very difficult to identify the instances and correct them when there are problems with the AI model. There is an increasing number of companies using GenAI systems in sensitive markets, such as healthcare and financial services; therefore, there is an increased need to recognize and address privacy violations and unintended consequences (Baldassarre et al., 2023). Privacy issues created using GenAI require a unified effort from researchers, governmental authorities, and industry participants (Baldassarre et al., 2023). This unification process involves establishing ethical and all-inclusive practices for protecting individual privacy throughout the various stages of GenAI (Kadaruddin, 2023; Baldassarre et al., 2023; Chu et al., 2020) (Figure 5.1).

5.2 IDENTIFYING PRIVACY RISKS IN DATA COLLECTION AND UTILIZATION

5.2.1 Data Collection: The Initial Point of Risk

Communications, human interaction, and the methods we use to communicate are dependent upon the availability and widespread use of a vast array of data, collected from numerous sources, via the Internet and the services/technologies that utilize that data. The rise in data collection and the amount of data collected is creating issues related to the privacy of individuals (Cate et al., 2012; Stopczynski, et al. 2014; Nabbosa & Kaar, 2020). There is certainly an increasing level of concern regarding the use of personal information by others, by individuals concerning their data collection, and the subsequent misuse, exploitation, and/or unlawful use of the data collected from the individual, and there has resulted an increased level of concern regarding the use of the information to which the individual has been subjected and/or had access. The general population and researchers have also experienced an increase in feelings of insecurity with respect to the data collected from them as a result of individuals being concerned about individuals being unauthorized to access data through the commission of unlawful acts including the unlawful gaining of access to data, breaching of data, capturing sensitive data without the knowledge or consent of

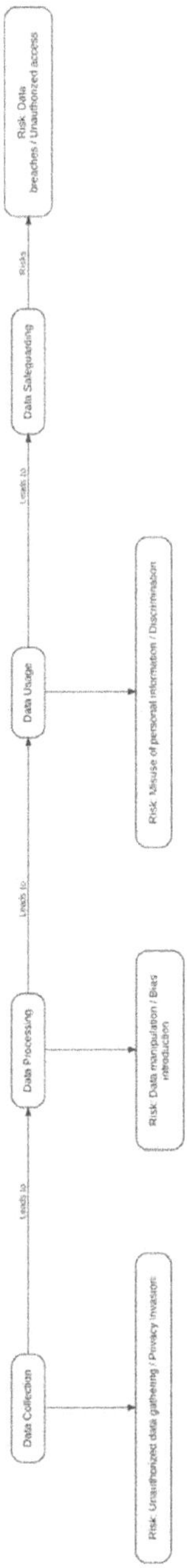

FIGURE 5.1 The importance of privacy in GenAI.

the individual, and whatever has been collected without the knowledge and/or consent of the individuals has been unfairly treated, including unfair practices that have been executed against them in terms of the collection and/or use of their data. Stopczynski et al. (2014) report that the emotion or feeling that one does not have control over the way their data is collected and/or how it will be used contributes to the feeling of lack of power of individuals for protecting their data from being used by the entities collecting their data without the consent of the individual (Liu, 2020).

The possibility of obtaining confidential information without consent is a significant concern for researchers. Although the data collected and stored are the property of an entity and thus managed properly in compliance with laws and regulations, there is still the potential for the data to be compromised or exposed, which may unintentionally disclose sensitive personal information about individuals to the public without their knowledge or consent (Aïmeur & Lafond, 2013). Additionally, the Internet allows companies and governments to obtain a wide variety of new forms of sensitive personal data, such as clickstream and location data, which are outside the traditional transaction data scope, increasing the potential for consumer privacy violations (Milne and Culnan, 2004). Consumers often have no idea how or why companies obtain their sensitive personal information and often feel powerless to stop them. While some individuals choose to disclose sensitive personal information despite being fully aware of the risks and consequences of doing so, most consumers do not envision how they would continue to perform daily tasks without corporations or governments collecting their data (Liu, 2020). To combat the potential privacy loss from collecting sensitive personal information, organizations should adopt and implement policies and practices that ensure that they are open and transparent about how they collect user information and about the security and safeguarding of their data. Companies should provide users with clear and comprehensive privacy notices outlining how their information will be used and protected prior to and at the time of collecting information from users. Additionally, companies should (1) limit the amount of sensitive personal information they collect, (2) implement excellent security practices to safeguard data, and (3) provide users with the ability to access, correct, or delete their data as needed (Stopczynski et al., 2014; Liu, 2020; Milne and Culnan, 2004). Data-gathering activities give rise to extremely complex privacy-related issues that require a strategic and comprehensive approach to address. By providing consumers with information on both the potential advantages and disadvantages associated with providing sensitive personal information to a third party, helping users to become more aware of their personal information, equipping them with the tools necessary to control their information, and implementing a strong set of data security policies and procedures, organizations can build trust and reduce the risk of harm to consumers (Barhamgi et al., 2018; Sheung, 2015; Casadesus-Masanell & Hervas-Drane, 2020; Milne and Culnan, 2004).

5.2.2 Data Utilization in AI: Harmonizing Innovation and Privacy

There are many sectors in which AI has made extreme advancements, owing to the massive amounts of data used to train AI models. The advent of fast-moving technological advancements has raised serious issues regarding personal privacy as these systems are trained on a wealth of technological advancement data; much of it has some level of privacy (Lepri et al., 2021). Training AI models requires a significant amount of data because these data enable AI systems to identify patterns, create predictions, and provide information and services. Because much of this data contains sensitive and private information about individuals, it poses a significant privacy and security risk. One concern with using data to train AI models is the risk of re-identifying anonymized data. In the past, individuals could protect their privacy using conventional anonymization methods; however, as AI technology advances and the amount of data grows, successfully anonymizing data has become more challenging. Therefore, there is increased concern among individuals that their personal information can be re-identified based on information that is supposed to be anonymized, thus putting sensitive information at risk and violating an individual's right to privacy. In addition, there is a tremendous concern regarding unintentional data leakage. AI systems contain immense amounts of data and are built on an intricate network of interconnected systems that provide many opportunities for accidental breaches and unauthorized access. To address these issues, academic and governmental leaders are calling for the development of new privacy-enhancing technologies and the establishment of stringent regulatory policies to ensure that people can protect their information while still benefiting from the development and implementation of new and innovative technologies utilizing AI.

5.2.3 The Function of Third-Party Data in Privacy Vulnerabilities

The use and storage of personal information in the digital age have become widespread. Third-party data sources have also created opportunities to acquire vast amounts of data collected by third parties and disseminated about users without their awareness or permission (Liu, 2020). The use of data in ways that are not intended or agreed upon by the individual can violate their privacy. Other problems are associated with the amount of information collected and the ease with which it can be aggregated. The rapid growth of online platforms within the public service arena has created this challenge and necessitated protective measures to prevent the same problems observed in the implementation of platform services in other areas of public service. Collectively aggregating and centralizing "Big Data" creates tremendous challenges to the protections offered to individuals using these aggregated resources, including providing data brokers with unprecedented levels of power and control over people to create the potential for prediction and manipulation (Rychwalska et al., 2021). Literature highlights ethical challenges related to data-driven innovation, particularly the "data trust deficit," and emphasizes the critical need to take prudent steps to mitigate this issue. A significant concern is that, given that no regulatory framework exists to accommodate developments in Big Data technologies, individuals are now vulnerable to increasingly invasive methods of collecting personal information. To summarize, working on the potential issues of using third-party data sources, as well as some of the associated problems of data-sharing, data aggregation, and the lack of control over how third-party data will be used, is a major issue to resolve. Solutions will require a collaborative effort from many with an interest in data-driven innovation to achieve some level of balance between the benefits of data-driven innovation and the privacy and freedom of the individual Christen et al. (2019), Bormida (2021), Liu (2020) and Rychwalska et al. (2021).

5.3 INDUSTRY BEST PRACTICES FOR PROTECTING USER PRIVACY

5.3.1 Privacy by Design: Incorporating Privacy into AI Development

A concern as AI technology advances is the safeguarding of people's private information. Privacy by Design embodies the necessity for confidentiality to be built into each element of AI; thus, when designing AI, activities occur with an awareness of privacy from the outset, making sure it is examined first; the intention being that any privacy issue will be existent when the basic purpose of the design lies with the specific privacy issue (Balboni & Mačėnaitė, 2013). A critical aspect of Privacy by Design is the minimization of entailed personal data; consequently, only the desired or necessary data will be collected, stored, or used by the AI system to fulfill its purpose. Therefore, the likelihood of unauthorized access or application of personal data will be reduced and additionally, maintain compliance with data protection laws and moral ramifications in relation to AI. In addition, the application of anonymization methods can provide further assurance to the individual, by converting their identifiable data into a format in which they cannot be identified (Romanou, 2017). When producing an AI application that typically contains and generates considerable sensitive, personal information about a person, the principles within Privacy by Design should also be considered when developing the application. By addressing any potential privacy issue(s) when considering the design phases of an AI, the organization has created an efficient, effective, and trustworthy AI system, which will respect individuals' privacy rights (Iezzi, 2020). New possibilities for privacy-preserving data science have arisen through developing new cryptographic techniques, e.g., homomorphic encryption. These techniques can be used to perform complex computations on encrypted data, allowing insights to be generated without the need to share sensitive private information underlying the data (Felzmann et al., 2020; Iezzi, 2020). Additionally, implementing Transparency by Design principles increases the ability to hold AI systems accountable while also providing a clearer understanding for users and stakeholders regarding how these technologies work and their implications for privacy (Felzmann et al., 2020).

5.3.2 Federated Learning: A Privacy-Conscious Method for Model Training

Federated learning is designed to provide a new way of training models for AI that reduces user concerns about the growing level of data privacy and centralization. Traditional machine learning practices involve the collection and storage of all data in one location for training purposes, whereas federated learning allows AI models to be trained on user data from multiple locations, thus providing users with greater privacy levels and reducing the need to collect and store data in a single, central location (Li et al., 2020). Federated learning works by training the AI model directly on the user's device and then sending only the model's updated information back to the primary storage location. This represents a significant change in the way model training occurs, as it balances user privacy concerns with the issues of data silos and availability/heterogeneity of data (i.e., data types and formats) across edge devices (Mothukuri et al., 2020; Data Sharing in the Age of Deep Learning, 2023). Additionally, federated learning has numerous advantages, particularly in relation to resolving the accessibility of centralized data, which has been an ongoing challenge in traditional machine learning. As indicated by Hasan (2023) and Mothukuri et al. (2020), certain sensitive information cannot be retained at a centralized location owing to accessibility requirements; however, federated learning addresses this problem by utilizing local data sources from edge devices. In addition, federated learning helps ensure the privacy of user data by prohibiting the transfer of sensitive data to a central server and instead utilizing asynchronous communication to transfer information regarding changes made to the AI model to a central server (Mothukuri et al., 2020; Hasan, 2023). The privacy-preserving features of federated learning open many possibilities for using AI in various applications, particularly in areas involving sensitive data and diverse environments. However, despite the positive contributions of federated learning to the ongoing evolution of user privacy protection, it still poses security and privacy risks. Researchers have proposed taxonomies for different attack types on federated learning systems, allowing for the identification of the types of attacks that have been identified; however, further research is necessary to develop enhanced threat modeling and security protocols (Jere et al., 2020). A challenge in developing and deploying a private federated learning system is balancing privacy and performance. Current approaches to improving user privacy in federated learning environments utilize technologies such as secure multiparty computation and differential privacy. However, techniques designed to improve the privacy of federated learning systems typically incur performance or efficiency costs and reduce the effectiveness of the AI model they are designed to enhance (Li et al., 2020). Academics are still undertaking the charge of reconciling these trade-offs both theoretically and empirically.

5.3.3 Differential Privacy: Protecting Personal Data

Machine learning models run the risk of leaking personal information from their datasets, allowing for attacks on individual privacy (Boenisch et al., 2023; Berrada et al., 2023; Truex et al., 2018; Kurakin et al., 2022). Several techniques have emerged that provide a standard approach to protect an individual's privacy by providing differential privacy in model training (Boenisch et al., 2023; Ziegler et al., 2022; Berrada et al., 2023). Differential privacy is a theoretical framework in which every data point can only marginally change the outcomes of the calculation, despite a potential adversary's added knowledge (Berrada et al., 2023; Ji et al., 2014; Ziegler et al., 2022). In machine learning, differential privacy provides a statistically insignificant change in the final output of models when adding or dropping a single record from the training data. Differential privacy uses noise introduced throughout the training process to achieve statistically insignificant changes in the model output because of adding or dropping records from the training dataset. Numerous studies have established that differential private training helps mitigate the risk of disclosing sensitive attributes, identifying individuals in the training dataset, or even reconstructing the training data (Berrada et al., 2023; Ziegler et al., 2022; Kurakin et al., 2022; Boenisch et al., 2023). In addition to providing a strong theoretical basis for privacy, the use of noise to achieve differentially private models can result in reduced utility owing to the inherent trade-off between privacy and accuracy. Current research is focused on reaching an optimal balance between these two competing factors using personalized privacy budgets and federated learning to allow the full potential of differentially private machine learning (Ziegler et al., 2022; Kurakin et al., 2022; Berrada et al., 2023; Boenisch et al., 2023). Recent studies have demonstrated that differential privacy can be successfully implemented across various machine learning tasks, such as healthcare and image classification. As the need to protect individuals' privacy becomes increasingly important, the benefits of creating and using differential privacy will continue to grow, supporting the ethical advancement and implementation of machine learning models.

5.3.4 Secure Multiparty Computation: Augmenting Data Security

Several data-intensive areas, such as healthcare, finance, and security, have witnessed an increase in the application of AI (AI) and Machine Learning (ML) to improve efficiency. The primary use of large AI models is to enable tasks such as disease diagnosis, financial forecasting, and other applications. Unfortunately, large AI models are often fragile and difficult to scale up. Research conducted by Zhang et al. (2024) found that decentralized systems provide a solution by spreading the burden of processing across multiple locations, thereby reducing the risk of failure through a single point of control. However, data and processes shared over multiple nodes may also be susceptible to unauthorized access, especially when the information is sensitive or constitutes Personal Identifiable Information (PII; Zhang et al., 2024). As such, Secure Multiparty Computation (MPC) is viewed as a reasonable way to solve the problems associated with the development of Shared AI models; that is, multiple parties can collectively train a Shared AI model without sharing their own raw data, thus protecting their privacy (Rieyan et al., 2023). In contrast, federated learning is a specific type of AI development in which several different entities can collectively train a common model without sharing raw data with each other. When doing so, each party shares only the result of its contribution to the model; therefore, all shared AI results are commonly known to all parties. These updates may include information about the effectiveness of each contribution to the Common Model; if not properly protected, they could reveal Sensitive Information (Li et al., 2020; Cheng et al., 2020). Researchers have sought to improve federated learning privacy by exploring ways to apply Secure Multiparty Computation (MPC) and Differential Privacy techniques together (Figure 5.2).

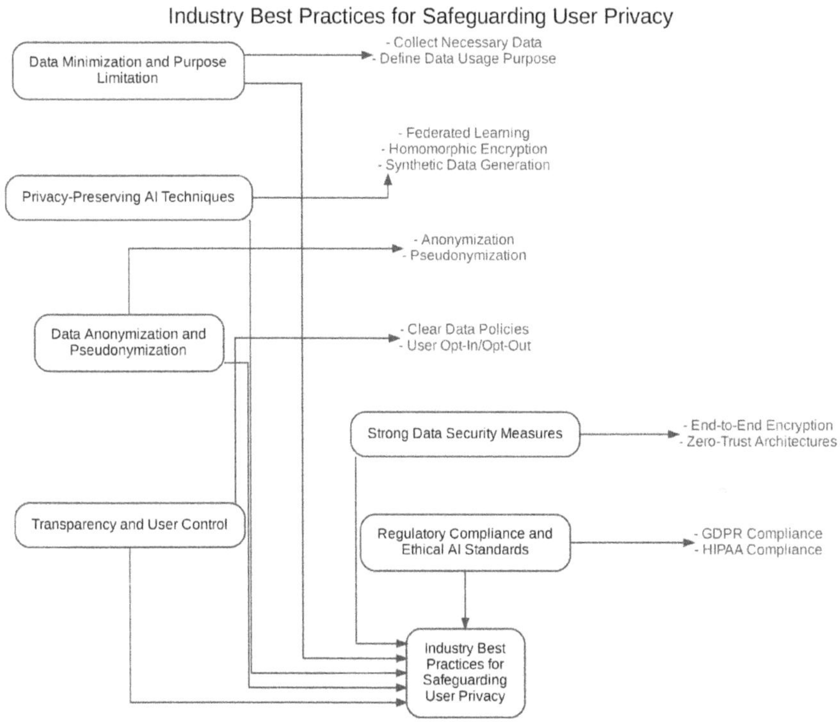

FIGURE 5.2 Optimal practices for protecting user privacy.

5.4 REAL-WORLD CASE STUDIES: PRIVACY-CENTRIC APPROACHES IN GENAI

5.4.1 Case Study: Privacy-First AI in Healthcare

Integrating GenAI into the rapidly growing healthcare industry is critical for elevating patient care and maximizing operational functions across multiple sectors. The following case study demonstrates how GenAI can be used in healthcare and how the use of privacy-preserving techniques and compliance with applicable regulations can help protect patient privacy. GenAI could transform the way healthcare professionals perform clinical engagements and work. With the advancement of GenAI, by 2023, it could assist healthcare providers by enabling them to analyze and integrate patient data (e.g., medical histories, imaging records, genetic data, and laboratory results) in one integrated view, regardless of the format or location of each form of data. According to Sun and Ortiz (2024), the widespread adoption of GenAI technologies in healthcare facilities has raised questions regarding privacy protection and the security of patient-related data. One of the primary challenges associated with the use of GenAI in healthcare is the possibility of data loss or exposure. Using de-identified datasets as source materials to construct GenAI models exposes the source of data to re-identification during the data gathering, cleaning, and processing phases of a study and, ultimately, could compromise the confidentiality and privacy of a patient's healthcare record. Despite anonymizing the data, researchers have found that genome sequencing can re-identify individuals. Consequently, there are privacy concerns associated with the use of GenAI in clinical practice (Chen & Esmaeilzadeh, 2024). Healthcare organizations have been proactive in developing privacy-preserving techniques to address these challenges. For instance, the differential privacy method instills uncertainty in the data, making it difficult to identify individual data points. Another method, federated learning, allows organizations or institutions to build GenAI models without the need to share raw patient data between multiple entities. Organizations or businesses that provide healthcare services are also required to comply with various laws and regulations regarding the collection and storage of patient data. Examples of such regulations include the Health Insurance Portability and Accountability Act (HIPAA) in the United States and the General Data Protection Regulation (GDPR) in Europe. Consequently, organizations and businesses must implement robust data protection protocols, such as secure data storage, stringent access controls, and comprehensive privacy policies (Sun & Ortiz, 2024; Chen & Esmaeilzadeh, 2024). While the potential for the application of GenAI technology in healthcare is significant, the proper and ethical application of GenAI requires a thorough approach to implementation. Healthcare providers must partner with researchers, policymakers, and technical experts to develop and implement effective privacy-preserving methodologies to maximize the benefits of GenAI while ensuring the highest levels of data protection and privacy for patients (Sun & Ortiz, 2024; Chen & Esmaeilzadeh, 2024; Kadaruddin, 2023; Al-antari, 2023).

5.4.2 Case Study: Privacy in AI-Enhanced Social Media Platforms

The intertwining of social media and AI technologies has cluttered privacy in the digital age. Both types of technologies are generally used by social media networks to generate content and provide recommendations for users, threatening to create a personalized experience for users while still protecting the way an individual experiences his/her privacy. For example, companies that operate social media networks, such as Facebook and Twitter, have been examining their methods of gathering, storing, and using data on their user bases, especially those who are using AI-related features and services. Through a review of research on how advertisers utilize AI to target customers, this paper highlights how the collection and use of user data pose a risk of data misuse, like what occurred with Cambridge Analytica when millions of Facebook accounts were misused for political purposes (Kietzmann et al., 2018). In response to the threat posed to user data and the risk of the misuse of AI to augment users' experiences, the researchers recommend that advertisers adapt their AI systems to comply with increasing legislative and regulatory restrictions regarding how user data are collected, used, and stored, and to convert these challenges into opportunities to enhance their customers' understanding and engagement with their brand. Another study on the ethical controversy of monitoring users through AI monitoring found that there are trade-offs between the advancement of technology and the privacy of individuals, using the example of Amazon. The authors of that article concluded that an integrated approach that supports the advancement of technology with an ethical and regulatory framework will enable businesses to take full advantage of the potential of AI while ensuring that their customers' privacy is protected (Bao et al., 2022).

5.4.3 Case Study: Privacy Protections in AI-Enhanced Financial Services

As GenAI (AI) technology evolves rapidly, the financial services industry has benefited from many advancements while creating increased concerns regarding the protection of individual financial data (IFD). Many financial institutions have developed proactive solutions to mitigate IFD privacy issues by implementing stringent protections for consumer IFD. The financial services industry has primarily benefited from digital transformation with the deployment of AI (AI) and machine learning (ML) technologies across multiple areas of the financial services industry, such as trading, risk management, and fraud detection. The "Black Box" of some AI models has raised significant concerns about transparency, interpretability, and the risks of unintended biases in decision-making processes regarding the use of AI for IFD privacy. Given these concerns, it is essential for financial institutions to prioritize the protection of consumer privacy associated with AI-driven services, including establishing privacy protections for any GenAI technology used in financial services.

5.5 THE FUTURE OF PRIVACY IN GENAI

5.5.1 Emerging Privacy-Preserving Techniques

As GenAI has developed rapidly, concerns regarding privacy have increased. Therefore, we need to develop privacy-preserving AI technologies in new and innovative ways to help mitigate these significant issues. While there are many approaches to building privacy-preserving AI technologies, some of the most common include using methods such as cryptography to protect sensitive data and using decentralized AI systems to increase privacy by decreasing the chance of centralized data breaches. Ethical data governance frameworks that promote values such as transparency, accountability, and user consent are also important for the development of privacy-preserving GenAI. AI technologies that preserve users' privacy will bring a number of benefits to help enhance existing educational uses of GenAI in the future. For example, using privacy-preserving AI to personalize how students learn and develop adaptive assessment methods while keeping students' data secure will lead to greater fairness in the use of algorithms (Gaur, 2024). Because of these many potential benefits from using privacy-preserving methodologies, the integration of these technologies into practice presents a number of complex challenges. Some challenges stem from issues related to data bias, the need for acceptance and interpretability of AI, and changes in how teachers work with AI to enhance education. As AI technologies proliferate and GenAI continues to evolve, both researchers and practitioners will need to focus on the study and development of privacy-preserving AI so that they can strive to address this growing dissatisfaction among educators who work with these technologies (Kim et al., 2024) (Figure 5.3).

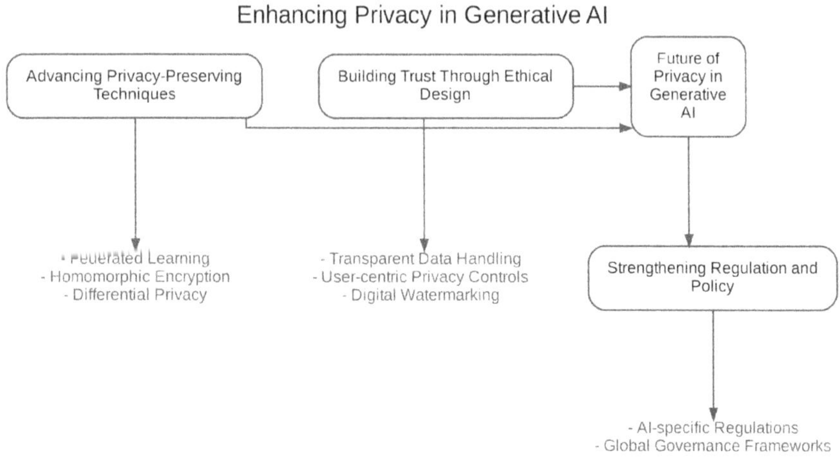

FIGURE 5.3 Enhancing privacy.

5.5.2 The Role of Regulation and Policy in Protecting Privacy

As AI rapidly advances, it is necessary to develop strict regulations and procedures to protect the privacy rights of individuals who use AI technology. The use of AI-enabled devices is becoming more prevalent in society while also providing an often-hunted balancing act for policymakers attempting to manage the innovative technologies and all the societal benefits they might provide. The General Data Protection Regulation (GDPR) established by the European Union (EU) represents an important move by the EU to establish a global standard for consumer data privacy through the creation of a regulatory framework for consumer data privacy. The interest and importance of the GDPR have caused many companies worldwide to re-evaluate their methods for collecting and processing consumer data and to do so in a transparent manner, thereby increasing accountability. Additionally, the California Consumer Privacy Act (CCPA) and China's Cybersecurity Act are other important legal frameworks that serve as an example of the necessity for effective consumer data protection legislation. For legislation to be created that is appropriate and effective in regulating AI technology, the legislation must provide protections for consumers and use other consumer protection strategies beyond simply protecting the privacy of the consumer's data through regulation of AI technologies. Many AI technologies can be used illegally by malicious actors (i.e., drones) and as such require legislative action that results in developing regulations that provide for comprehensive and robust regulation of AI technologies. To protect the public from the threat of malicious use of AI technology, legislators will have to take proactive steps to identify and mitigate the risks associated with the malicious use of AI technology through collaboration with AI developers and researchers. By doing so, legislation that regulates AI technologies must strike a balance between regulating AI technologies while at the same time limiting innovation or implementing unnecessary costs on the companies creating and selling AI products and services. As noted by one organization, "Regulatory agencies can develop bureaucratic processes that have the potential to limit the innovation and make it impossible to afford to innovate." Consequently, legislative leaders, industry leaders, and civil society organizations must create cooperative working relationships with one another to find ways to navigate the complexities of AI-related legislation and establish a regulatory framework for the responsible development and use of AI technology. Regulatory agencies and various legislative initiatives that are designed to protect the privacy of individuals will work collaboratively to foster the development of privacy laws for AI's use in the workplace. As AI technology continues to develop and evolve at a rapid pace, governments must proactively plan to safeguard the fundamental civil rights of individuals and remain vigilant to ensure people can realize their privacy rights Carter (2020) Kuner et al. (2018) Lauterbach (2019).

5.5.3 Establishing Trust in GenAI: The Way Ahead

There has been much recent development in GenAI across the spectrum of various businesses. Due to the rapid adoption of GenAI, there is an increased requirement for the development of trust in this area. Therefore, a government framework that focuses on making individuals accountable for their actions while developing policies surrounding transparency in GenAI will be a key part of developing and establishing trust in this area (Baldassarre et al., 2023; Avin et al., 2021). It is universally agreed upon that the impact of GenAI models will be vast across many different industries, with examples like ChatGPT illustrating this fact. GenAI will have an impact across the operations of educational institutions, healthcare systems, banks, and many other organizations (Baldassarre et al., 2023). GenAI is currently a topic of much discussion among educators due to the recent rise in its use in universities and colleges; thus requiring careful consideration of both the positive and negative potential challenges and opportunities associated with it as well as the development of guidelines for using this technology in an educational environment (Michel-Villarreal et al., 2023; Wu et al., 2024). The growing number of leading colleges, universities, and education associations resulting in the development of guidelines on how GenAI should be utilized shows that while there are ethical implications and concerns regarding the privacy risks associated with using GenAI, using this technology is necessary (Wu et al., 2024). As these institutions navigate the process of developing their own governance on GenAI, other educational institutions can benefit from their experiences. The development of transparent practices when establishing trust in GenAI is a key component in creating that trust. Teachers and universities should focus on developing design transparency for GenAI models by clarifying the algorithms and data used to train them. Regular audits of privacy practices and ongoing disclosure to stakeholders regarding privacy issues and the prosecution of data exploitation will further build trust in educational institutions using GenAI (Kadaruddin, 2023; Wu et al., 2024; DeFranco and Biersmith, 2024; Jiang et al., 2022). In addition, the effective engagement of people with a vested interest in the use of GenAI (GAI) to improve educational outcomes (i.e., students, parents, and educators) is critical to minimizing the chances of privacy-related concerns and directing the appropriate deployment of GAI in education. Creating opportunities for stakeholder dialogue and encouraging stakeholders' contributions to GAI in education allows educational institutions to develop and execute a more open, collaborative, and unified approach to GAI in education, thereby building equity and trust in these revolutionary technologies.

The continually changing face of education affords educational institutions the perfect opportunity to leverage GAI to provide students with the tools, resources, and support they need to learn in ways tailored to them and to enhance their total educational experience. However, this requires a comprehensive plan that prioritizes openness, privacy, and proactive stakeholder engagement.

REFERENCES

Aïmeur, E., & Lafond, M. (2013). The scourge of Internet personal data collection. In *Proceedings of the 2013 International Conference on Availability, Reliability, and Security (ARES)* (pp. 821–828). IEEE. https://doi.org/10.1109/ARES.2013.110

Al-Antari, M. A. (2023). AI for medical diagnostics—Existing and future AI technology. *Diagnostics, 13*(4), 688. https://doi.org/10.3390/diagnostics13040688

Avin, S., Belfield, H., Brundage, M., Krueger, G., Wang, J., Weller, A., Anderljung, M., Krawczuk, I., Krueger, D., Lebensold, J., Maharaj, T., & Zilberman (2021). Filling gaps in the trustworthy development of AI. *Science, 374*(6573), 1327–1329. https://doi.org/10.1126/science.abi7176

Balboni, P., & Mačėnaitė, M. (2013). Privacy by design and anonymization techniques in action: A case study of Ma3tch technology. *Computer Law & Security Review, 29*(4), 330–340. https://doi.org/10.1016/j.clsr.2013.05.005

Baldassarre, M. T., Caivano, D., Nieto, B. F., Gigante, D., & Ragone, A. (2023). The social impact of GenAI: An analysis of ChatGPT. https://doi.org/10.1145/3582515.3609555

Bao, Y., Li, W., Ye, Y., & Zhang, Q. (2022). Ethical disputes of AI surveillance: A case study of Amazon. https://doi.org/10.2991/aebmr.k.220307.220

Barhamgi, M., Perera, C., Ghédira, C., & Benslimane, D. (2018). User-centric privacy engineering for the Internet of things. *IT Professional, 5*(5), 47–57. https://doi.org/10.1109/mcc.2018.053711666

Berrada, L., De, S., Shen, J. H., Hayes, J., Stanforth, R., Stutz, D., Kohli, P., Smith, S., & Balle, B. (2023). *Unlocking accuracy and fairness in differentially private image classification.* arXiv Preprint. https://doi.org/10.48550/arxiv.2308.10888

Bormida, M. D. (2021). The big data world: Benefits, threats, and ethical challenges. In *Research in ethical issues in organizations* (pp. 71–91). Emerald Publishing. https://doi.org/10.1108/s2398-601820210000008007

Boenisch, F., Mühl, C., Dziedzic, A., Rinberg, R., & Papernot, N. (2023). *Have it your way: Individualized privacy assignment for DP-SGD.* arXiv Preprint. https://doi.org/10.48550/arxiv.2303.17046

Casadesus-Masanell, R., & Hervas-Drane, A. (2020). Strategies for managing the privacy landscape. *Long Range Planning, 53*(4), 101949. https://doi.org/10.1016/j.lrp.2019.101949

Cate, F. H., Dempsey, J. X., & Rubinstein, I. (2012). Systematic government access to private-sector data. *International Data Privacy Law, 2*(4), 195–199. https://doi.org/10.1093/idpl/ips027

Carter, D. (2020). Regulation and ethics in AI and machine learning technologies: Where are we now? Who is responsible? Can the information professional play a role? *Business Information Review, 37*(2), 60–68. https://doi.org/10.1177/0266382120923962

Chen, Y., & Esmaeilzadeh, P. (2024). GenAI in medical practice: In-depth exploration of privacy and security challenges. *Journal of Medical Internet Research, 26*, e53008. https://doi.org/10.2196/53008

Cheng, Y., Liu, Y., Chen, T., & Yang, Q. (2020). Federated learning for privacy-preserving AI. *Communications of the ACM, 63*(12), 33–36. https://doi.org/10.1145/3387107

Christen, M., Blumer, H., Hauser, C., & Huppenbauer, M. (2019). The ethics of big data applications in the consumer sector. In M. Christen, B. Gordijn, & M. Loi (Eds.), *The ethics of cybersecurity* (pp. 161–180). Springer. https://doi.org/10.1007/978-3-030-11821-1_10

Chu, L. C., Anandkumar, A., Shin, H. C., & Fishman, E. K. (2020). The potential dangers of AI for radiology and radiologists. *Journal of the American College of Radiology, 17*(10), 1309–1311. https://doi.org/10.1016/j.jacr.2020.04.010

Data sharing in the age of deep learning. (2023). *Nature Biotechnology, 41*(4), 433. https://doi.org/10.1038/s41587-023-01770-3

DeFranco, J. F., & Biersmith, L. (2024). *Assessing the state of AI policy.* arXiv Preprint. https://doi.org/10.48550/arxiv.2407.21717

Epstein, Z., Hertzmann, A., Akten, M., Farid, H., Fjeld, J., Frank, M. R., Groh, M., Herman, L., Leach, N., Mahari, R., Pentland, A., Russakovsky, O., Schroeder, H., & Smith, A. (2023). Art and the science of GenAI. *Science, 380*(6650), 1110–1111. https://doi.org/10.1126/science.adh4451

Felzmann, H., Fosch-Villaronga, E., Lutz, C., & Tamò-Larrieux, A. (2020). Towards transparency by design for AI. *Science and Engineering Ethics, 26*(6), 3333–3361. https://doi.org/10.1007/s11948-020-00276-4

Gaur, L. (2024). From algorithms to ethics: XAI's impact on e-commerce. In L. Gaur & A. Abraham (Eds.), *Role of explainable AI in e-commerce* (Studies in Computational Intelligence, Vol. 1094). Springer. https://doi.org/10.1007/978-3-031-55615-9_8

Hasan, J. (2023). *Security and privacy issues of federated learning.* arXiv Preprint. https://doi.org/10.48550/arxiv.2307.12181

Huang, L. (2023). Ethics of AI in education: Student privacy and data protection. *Science Insights Education Frontiers, 16*(2), 2577–2587. https://doi.org/10.15354/sief.23.re202

Iezzi, M. (2020). Practical privacy-preserving data science with homomorphic encryption: An overview. https://doi.org/10.1109/bigdata50022.2020.9377989

Jere, M., Farnan, T., & Koushanfar, F. (2020). A taxonomy of attacks on federated learning. *IEEE Security & Privacy, 19*(2), 20–28. https://doi.org/10.1109/msec.2020.3039941

Ji, Z., Lipton, Z. C., & Elkan, C. (2014). *Differential privacy and machine learning: A survey and review.* arXiv Preprint. https://doi.org/10.48550/arxiv.1412.7584

Jiang, H., Gao, Y., Sarwar, S., GarzaPerez, L., & Robin, M. H. (2022). Differential privacy in privacy-preserving big data and learning: Challenge and opportunity. In J. Li, P. Li, Z. Liu, X. Chen, & T. Li (Eds.), *Privacy-preserving big data and learning* (pp. 33–44). Springer. https://doi.org/10.1007/978-3-030-96057-5_3

Kadaruddin, K. (2023). Empowering education through GenAI: Innovative instructional strategies for tomorrow's learners. *International Journal of Business, Law, and Education, 4*(2), 618–625. https://doi.org/10.56442/ijble.v4i2.215

Kaissis, G., Makowski, M. R., Rückert, D., & Braren, R. (2020). Secure, privacy-preserving and federated machine learning in medical imaging. *Nature Machine Intelligence, 2*(6), 305–311. https://doi.org/10.1038/s42256-020-0186-1

Kietzmann, J., Paschen, J., & Treen, E. (2018). AI in advertising. *Journal of Advertising Research, 58*(3), 263–267. https://doi.org/10.2501/jar-2018-035

Kim, S., Roh, Y., Heo, G., & Whang, S. E. (2024). *PFGuard: A generative framework with privacy and fairness safeguards.* arXiv Preprint. https://doi.org/10.48550/arxiv.2410.02246

Kuner, C., Cate, F. H., Lynskey, O., Millard, C. J., Loideáin, N. N., & Svantesson, D. J. B. (2018). Expanding the AI-data protection debate. *International Data Privacy Law, 8*(4), 289–292. https://doi.org/10.1093/idpl/ipy024

Kurakin, A., Song, S., Chien, S., Geambasu, R., Terzis, A., & Thakurta, A. (2022). *Towards training at ImageNet scale with differential privacy*. arXiv Preprint. https://doi.org/10.48550/arxiv.2201.12328

Lauterbach, A. (2019). AI and policy: Quo vadis? *Digital Policy, Regulation and Governance, 21*(3), 238–263. https://doi.org/10.1108/dprg-09-2018-0054

Lepri, B., Oliver, N., & Pentland, A. (2021). Ethical machines: The human-centric use of AI. *iScience, 24*(3), 102249. https://doi.org/10.1016/j.isci.2021.102249

Li, T., Sahu, A. K., Talwalkar, A., & Smith, V. (2020). Federated learning: Challenges, methods, and future directions. *IEEE Signal Processing Magazine, 37*(3), 50–60. https://doi.org/10.1109/msp.2020.2975749

Liu, F. (2020). *A statistical overview on data privacy*. arXiv Preprint. https://doi.org/10.48550/arxiv.2007.00765

Łodzikowski, K., Foltz, P. W., & Behrens, J. T. (2024). *GenAI and its educational implications*. arXiv Preprint. https://doi.org/10.48550/arxiv.2401.08659

Michel-Villarreal, R., Vilalta-Perdomo, E. L., Salinas-Navarro, D. E., Thierry-Aguilera, R., & Gerardou, F. S. (2023). Challenges and opportunities of GenAI for higher education as explained by ChatGPT. *Education Sciences, 13*(9), 856. https://doi.org/10.3390/educsci13090856

Milne, G. R., & Culnan, M. J. (2004). Strategies for reducing online privacy risks: Why consumers read (or don't read) online privacy notices. *Journal of Interactive Marketing, 18*(3), 15–29. https://doi.org/10.1002/dir.20009

Mothukuri, V., Parizi, R. M., Pouriyeh, S., Huang, Y., Dehghantanha, A., & Srivastava, G. (2020). A survey on security and privacy of federated learning. *Future Generation Computer Systems, 115*, 619–640. https://doi.org/10.1016/j.future.2020.10.007

Nabbosa, V. L., & Kaar, C. (2020). Societal and ethical issues of digitalization. https://doi.org/10.1145/3437075.3437093

Rieyan, S. A., News, M. R. K., Rahman, A., Khan, S. A., Zaarif, S. T. J., Alam, M. G. R., Hassan, M. M., Ianni, M., & Fortino, G. (2023). An advanced data fabric architecture leveraging homomorphic encryption and federated learning. *Information Fusion, 102*, 102004. https://doi.org/10.1016/j.inffus.2023.102004

Romanou, A. (2017). The necessity of the implementation of privacy by design in sectors where data protection concerns arise. *Computer Law & Security Review, 34*(1), 99–110. https://doi.org/10.1016/j.clsr.2017.05.021

Rychwalska, A., Goodell, G., & Roszczyńska-Kurasińska, M. (2021). Data management for platform-mediated public services: Challenges and best practices. *Surveillance & Society, 19*(1), 22–36. https://doi.org/10.24908/ss.v19i1.13986

Sheung, C. T. (2015). How online privacy systems assure more customer satisfaction and trust? *[Journal name not provided], 3*(5). https://doi.org/10.4172/2162-6359.1000209

Stopczynski, A., Pietri, R., Pentland, A., Lazer, D., & Lehmann, S. (2014). *Privacy in sensor-driven human data collection: A guide for practitioners*. arXiv Preprint. https://doi.org/10.48550/arxiv.1403.5299

Sun, Y., & Ortíz, J. (2024). Rapid review of GenAI in smart medical applications. *International Journal of Computer Science and Information Technology, 3*(2), 80–93. https://doi.org/10.62051/ijcsit.v3n2.10

Truex, S., Baracaldo, N., Anwar, A., Steinke, T., Ludwig, H., Zhang, R., & Zhou, Y. (2018). *A hybrid approach to privacy-preserving federated learning*. arXiv Preprint. https://doi.org/10.48550/arxiv.1812.03224

Wu, C., Zhang, H., & Carroll, J. M. (2024). AI governance in higher education: Case studies of guidance at Big Ten universities. *Future Internet, 16*(10), 354. https://doi.org/10.3390/fi16100354

Wu, W., & Liu, S. (2023). *A comprehensive review and systematic analysis of AI regulation policies.* arXiv Preprint. https://doi.org/10.48550/arxiv.2307.12218

Zhang, H., Zhao, Y., Angione, C., Yang, H., Buban, J., Farhan, A., Johnston, F., & Colangelo, P. (2024). *Complete security and privacy for AI inference in decentralized systems.* arXiv Preprint. https://doi.org/10.48550/arxiv.2407.19401

Ziegler, J., Pfitzner, B., Schulz, H., Saalbach, A., & Arnrich, B. (2022). Defending against reconstruction attacks through differentially private federated learning for classification of heterogeneous chest X-ray data. *Sensors, 22*(14), 5195. https://doi.org/10.3390/s22145195

6 Ensuring Transparency and Accountability in AI Systems

6.1 OVERVIEW

As artificial intelligence (AI) continues to evolve, it presents new ethical challenges to society as it relates to transparency concerning AI systems and the responsibility associated with AI outputs. Due to the inherent lack of understanding associated with how machine learning (ML) works, there are severe questions as to the opaqueness of ML algorithms, how to convey the transparency of these systems, and what is necessary to provide for their accountability (Buijsman, 2023). Transparency in AI refers to the degree to which AI systems are transparent, both in how the algorithms function and how the organizations using the algorithms have made their decisions regarding the algorithms and data sources they used when developing their algorithms. Accountability in AI refers to the ability of individuals or organizations to be held accountable for their behaviors and/or decision-making that was associated with the use of AI systems (Figure 6.1).

The building of trust in new technologies and assurance that they comply with social standards and legal regulations requires transparency and accountability. Fjeld et al. (2020) noted that industries such as health care, financial services, and criminal justice require transparency and accountability because the consequences of AI-based decisions can affect people's lives for many years. For example, in the financial sector, people are raising concerns about discrimination and fairness due to the lack of transparency in AI-generated credit scoring models, and there are calls for creating AI credit scoring models that are more transparent and easier for consumers to understand (Reuters, 2024). There are many toolkits and frameworks to help address these issues. One approach is the idea of "designing for transparency," which advocates considering transparency in your AI solution during the AI development cycle instead of considering it afterwards (Ananny & Crawford, 2018). Another example is the creation of model cards and datasheets for data set projects to define a standard way of expressing AI models and data sets, improving the understanding and accountability of these systems (Mitchell et al., 2019). Even with these approaches, finding a way to achieve sufficient transparency and accountability in AI will remain a challenge. Achieving transparency and accountability requires technical solutions, organizational commitment, and governmental oversight. To accomplish this objective, it is critical to engage many types of

DOI: 10.1201/9781003679974-6

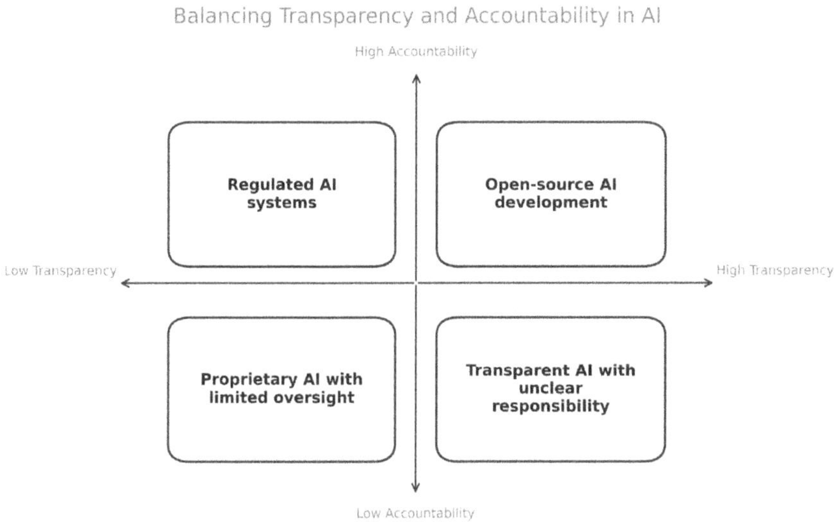

FIGURE 6.1 Balancing transparency and accountability in AI.

stakeholders, such as ethicists, lawyers, and end users, to create AI systems that operate efficiently and ethically (Morley et al., 2020). The purpose of this chapter is to discuss the need for transparency and accountability in the development and use of AI systems, describe current barriers to transparency and accountability within AI systems, and present best practices and examples of effectively providing transparency and accountability within AI systems. These added elements will provide a more complete understanding of developing responsible AI practices that comply with social values and inspire confidence from society.

6.2 COMPREHENDING TRANSPARENCY IN AI

Transparency can be defined as having complete knowledge of and access to all aspects of the algorithm and data behind AI, including the algorithms' method of processing that data to get to an artificial intelligence's conclusion or decision.

Stakeholders who build or use AI, such as developers, end-users, and regulatory authorities, should have access to sufficient information about AI systems to analyze, interpret, and evaluate their functionality. This will enable these groups to make informed choices regarding the reliability, equity, and ethical compliance of AI systems (Jobin et al., 2019). A critical aspect of AI transparency is algorithmic clarity. Algorithmic clarity refers to the level of access to and understanding of the computational logic and prediction algorithms that inform the AI model's predictions. Restricting access to the algorithmic processes used to create the model produces "black box" (or opaque) algorithms that cannot be interpreted. These algorithms create significant barriers to accountability and build mistrust, particularly in high-stakes areas such as healthcare and the justice system (Rudin, 2019). To create transparent algorithms, a detailed level of documentation and explanation is required, as well as the ability of third-party stakeholders, including end-users and regulatory authorities, to conduct audits to ensure that the computational methods remain unchanged. Another facet of transparency includes the data used by the AI model to train and validate itself. This is referred to as data transparency. Dataset transparency requires that all data used to train or validate AI models be clearly documented, with full disclosure of how the data were collected, the characteristics/attributes of the data, and so on. Datasets can often contain societal biases or lack balance, which, when left undetected or unreported, will perpetuate historical disparities through algorithmic-based decisions (Binns, 2018). The "Datasheets for Datasets" initiative promotes a standardized protocol for documenting datasets that includes relevant metadata, known limitations/constraints, and potential ethical issues with using that dataset so that stakeholders can properly assess if the dataset is appropriate for their applications (Gebru et al., 2021). When discussing transparency, it is important to weigh the various options for providing sufficiently detailed information on how AI systems make decisions. For example, Explainable AI (XAI), which includes SHAP values, LIME explanations, and counterfactual reasoning methods, are all AI-explaining tools developed to assist users in understanding how AI-produced individual forecasts and recommendations were created (Arrieta et al., 2020). All these exposition tools support the idea that transparency should enable non-technical stakeholders to verify, question, and evaluate the automated decisions made by AI systems (Figure 6.2).

The potential benefits of utilizing these transparency principles are beginning to emerge in regulatory products, product offerings, and implementations across various industries. For example, IBM Watson Health employs AI systems designed to provide medical professionals with clear and easy-to-understand explanations of how diagnostic suggestions are developed (Ahmad et al., 2018). Similarly, Google introduced a "Model Card" approach that involves providing structured and standardized disclosures about how AI models are created, their intended uses, performance,

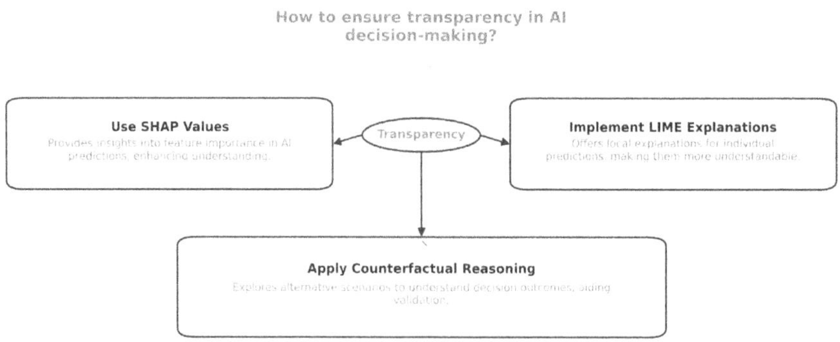

FIGURE 6.2 Approaches to providing transparency for AI decision-making.

ethical considerations, and limitations, thereby improving external evaluations of AI models and increasing stakeholder trust (Mitchell et al., 2019). There are many hurdles to achieving a truly transparent AI, even though these improvements will significantly contribute to increasing the transparency of AI. For example, protecting proprietary interests; being able to remain competitive; and the difficulty involved in building sophisticated neural networks are just some of the obstacles to achieving transparency in AI. This is why stakeholders need to think of transparency in AI as something that exists on a continuum rather than in a binary sense (existence/non-existence). In fact, users can expect that not all AI systems exist with the same degree of openness, interpretability, and/or disclosure, but rather that the degree to which AI exists in a transparent way is determined by a variety of factors including the context, the needs of each stakeholder, and/or regulatory requirements. To achieve complete transparency for AI, users must be provided with full access to algorithms and other technological resources; users must have access to clear documentation about the datasets used, and users must have clear and understandable documentation about the criteria and processes utilized by AI to reach decisions. Developers and users will be able to create responsible, fair, and accountable AI only through cooperative efforts to embed these principles of transparency in the entire AI lifecycle.

6.3 THE NECESSITY FOR ACCOUNTABILITY

Accountability in AI involves the systems and structures used by businesses and individuals to take responsibility for what the AI system does, decides, and causes to happen. The increased use of GenAI in critical and impactful fields (including healthcare, finance, and government) reinforces the importance of having clearly defined and enforceable accountability systems to reduce risks related to errors, bias, and ethics that are built into AI-generated decisions (Floridi et al., 2018). AI accountability has technical, organizational (or business), ethical, and legal dimensions.

Foundational to accountability are traceability tools, rigorous testing, and organized audit trails of actions and processes of AI (Ananny & Crawford, 2018). This means that accountability within organizations incorporates not only the technical oversight of the development of AI but also defining the roles and responsibilities of all stakeholders involved in the development process (Mittelstadt, 2019). Moral and fairness are connected to ethical accountability; therefore, ethical accountability requires that both developers and end users take steps to anticipate and mitigate any potentially negative consequences of the AI development and use. The prevalence of algorithmic bias in facial recognition systems, particularly those that are race and gender based, illustrates the need for a well-defined ethical accountability framework to protect vulnerable populations (Buolamwini & Gebru, 2018). These situations have drawn significant public attention and spurred calls for more thorough ethical regulation on the development and use of AI. Regulations and laws in many countries mandate the establishment of formalized frameworks for accountability. The European Union's possible AI Act is an example of a legislative initiative to create a framework of accountability through transparency, risk assessment, and mandates for auditing the development and use of high-risk AI products (Veale & Zuiderveen Borgesius, 2021). Legislative frameworks proposed in the United States, United Kingdom, and elsewhere demonstrate an interest in creating frameworks to ensure accountability for the protection of civil rights, privacy, and fairness in algorithmic decision-making (Barfield & Pagallo, 2020). Figure 6.3 illustrates the concept of accountability in AI, as elaborated by the author. For instance, IBM's AI Fairness 360 toolkit uses a combination of open-source tools and processes to provide a framework for assessing, recording, and mitigating bias in algorithms developed by third parties (Bellamy et al., 2019). Another example is Microsoft's Ethical AI Governance initiative, which uses established ethical review boards and processes to conduct rigorous assessments of ethical compliance as part of the development process (Microsoft, 2023). However, creating a comprehensive accountability model for GenAI systems remains a significant challenge. The complexity of AI frameworks often makes it difficult to identify who is responsible for the failure of an AI system or for unexpected results. Additionally, the tension between proprietary interests and the need for openness often leads to conflicts between competing interests regarding accountability and the potential for innovation (Kroll 2018). Therefore, a strong accountability framework is the foundation for ethical responsibility in AI development. To create ethically responsible AI, stakeholder groups must work together to develop a strategy that includes technical transparency, clear organizational accountability, proactive ethical engagement, and strong regulatory oversight. A consistent multidisciplinary approach will enable stakeholders to ensure that GenAI is accountable, trusted, and aligned with social values.

FIGURE 6.3 Establishing trustworthy AI with comprehensive accountability frameworks. Source: Authors.

6.4 PRINCIPAL OBSTACLES TO ATTAINING TRANSPARENCY AND ACCOUNTABILITY

GenAI recognizes the importance of accountability and transparency but faces many serious hurdles regarding its successful application. Many barriers to accountability stem from technological (algorithmic and architectural), organizational, or legal levels and hinder the development of consistently enforced and well-defined standards of accountability for AI systems.

6.4.1 Algorithmic Opacity and Complexity of AI Technology

One of the key barriers to achieving transparency is the extreme complexity and obscurity associated with advanced AI technologies, which are generally defined as the use of generative deep learning and/or neural networks to develop AI applications. Many advanced AI applications utilize millions or billions of parameters in their construction and operation, making it very difficult to specify with clarity and precision how they work internally (Lipton, 2018). This "black box" characteristic limits the understanding of how AI makes decisions, making it virtually impossible for key stakeholders (e.g., developers, regulators, and users) to easily identify the source of a particular outcome, thereby raising concerns about accountability (Rudin, 2019). Apart from lack of clarity, there are several existing models which assist users to interpret a complex algorithm such as SHAP or LIME; however, they function at best as a rough estimation of understanding and raise concerns about their final suitability when high stakes come into play (Arrieta et al., 2020).

6.4.2 Data Provenance and Inherent Bias

Lack of transparency with respect to AI systems is directly correlated with training data that make up both the content and the related metadata used to generate those AI systems; training data often replicate the systemic inequalities and discrimination of society as a whole; thus, by "baking in" these systemic inequalities and discrimination through the AI system's use of those same types of training data, the AI systems have the potential to perpetuate systemic injustice and inequality (Mehrabi et al., 2021). Providing evidence of the presence of systemic inequality and discrimination requires creating clear/complete/comprehensive metadata about how the dataset was created, how the data was originally collected (i.e., by whom), and how the data was processed after being collected (Gebru et al., 2021). The difficulty of this effort to create clear/complete/comprehensive metadata is compounded when a dataset involves any personal/private/sensitive data or is constrained in terms of personal privacy limitations.

6.4.3 Commercial and Competitive Dimensions

As businesses create and own unique forms of AI technology, they will likely experience an increased need for both transparency around their operations and a commitment to behaving ethically due to the high level of financial risk associated with these products. In most situations, companies will choose not to divulge or provide detailed descriptions of the algorithms or datasets that they utilized to create their proprietary products, citing reasons such as: "intellectual property," "business confidentiality," or "a competitive edge" (Whittaker et al., 2018) among others. Businesses face many ethical dilemmas as they balance the need for transparency with the need to protect their intellectual property and reputation, making it increasingly difficult to develop accountability measures.

6.4.4 Lack of Consensus and Benchmarks

Currently, there is no definitive global consensus on how to establish benchmarks to assess the transparency and accountability of AI technologies. The numerous and varied interpretations and meanings of the terms "transparency" and "accountability" based on institutional (e.g., industry, commercial, governmental) and regional (e.g., country) contexts have created disparate practices regarding how to enforce standards of accountability (Jobin et al., 2019). Without a set of common standards among the global AI community or any defined documentation practices, it will be difficult to adequately assess the accountability of AI applications and render meaningful evaluations regarding individual AI applications and their fitness in the larger context of the development of AI technologies. The rapid speed of technological development continues to outstrip the ability of government regulators to effectively enforce and develop standards. Many challenges are associated with developing standards and effective enforcement mechanisms that can address the unique attributes of AI-based decision-making as they evolve (Calo, 2017). The ongoing uncertainty regarding legal liability or responsibility resulting from AI-related injuries and damage continues to present a challenge to victims seeking recourse (Barfield & Pagallo, 2020). These issues will be compounded by the absence of any definitive jurisdictional guidelines, creating an environment of accountability voids where the developers or operators of AI systems will not have any ultimate responsibility or liability for their actions. As AI continues to grow in popularity and use, it has become clear that organizational characteristics, such as a lack of transparency and accountability, present additional barriers to establishing transparency and accountability in the use of AI. In addition, to develop effective methods for promoting transparency and accountability and to do so in a timely manner, organizations will need serious commitment to time, energy, investment, and possibly a re-evaluation of governance practices. Most organizations will likely be hesitant to utilize these practices unless they clearly understand the benefits to be gained and there is sufficient pressure from their consumers and regulatory authorities (Ananny & Crawford, 2018). Therefore, supporting transparency and accountability within organizations will require widespread reform of culture, procedures, and priorities. Implementing effective transparency and accountability for AI-related technologies and services presents complex and interrelated challenges. As a result, a multifaceted approach must be used to overcome these obstacles, including technological innovations, improvements to regulatory frameworks, engagement and collaboration of multiple stakeholders, and, ultimately, a wholesale organizational transformation. Only through the collaborative efforts of organizations from many different disciplines will the true benefits of transparency and accountability for the generative use of AI be realized.

6.5 STRATEGIES TO ENHANCE TRANSPARENCY

Transparent practices for GenAI applications should be implemented throughout all stages of AI development models using purpose-driven and methodical approaches. Solutions for promoting transparency in AI systems involve both the development of new technologies and the establishment of guidelines and standards governing their use in the workplace and public sector.

6.5.1 Frameworks for Transparency-by-Design

One of the basic approaches to ensuring that AI technology is transparent is to include it in the actual design and construction of the AI system; this is referred to as transparency-by-design (Floridi et al., 2018). With this methodology, measures are taken early in the lifecycle of AI technology to help determine algorithm selection, model complexity, data-gathering techniques, and user interface design. The transparency-by-design process requires the continuous involvement of stakeholders in the AI development process, with iterative evaluations and documented records throughout the AI system's lifecycle. These practices will significantly mitigate the risks of non-transparency (Winfield & Jirotka, 2018).

6.5.2 Standardized AI Documentation Instruments

Model cards and datasheets for datasets indicate clear improvements in terms of transparency, as they are forms of standardized documentation instruments designed specifically to improve transparency by providing an organized way for anyone to understand (1) the purpose, (2) limitations, (3) how it will be used, and (4) potential bias that may be present within an AI model (Mitchell et al., 2019), and (1) how to describe, (2) collect, (3) what they were collected for, and (4) ethical concerns (Gebru et al., 2021), respectively. The collateral from the creation of these standardization tools allows all parties to evaluate not only how well a specific AI will work but also allows for greater levels of accountability and trust among all parties.

6.5.3 Techniques for Explainability and Interpretability

Techniques for Explainable AI (XAI) provide essential transparency for complicated generative models. Techniques such as SHAP (SHapley Additive exPlanations) and LIME (Local Interpretable Model-agnostic Explanations) clarify and break down the "why" behind a given model's decisions by creating easy-to-understand cases of justification and an easy-to-follow set of simplified representations that demonstrate the reasoning of the model's underlying technology (Arrieta et al., 2020). As businesses create and own unique forms of AI technology, they will likely experience an increased need for both transparency around their operations and a commitment to behaving ethically due to the high level of financial risk associated with these products. In most situations, companies will choose not to divulge or provide detailed descriptions of the algorithms or datasets that they utilized to create their proprietary products, citing reasons such as: "intellectual property," "business confidentiality," or "a competitive edge" (Whittaker et al., 2018) among others.

6.5.4 Open Source and Collaborative AI Initiatives

The exposure of an algorithmic framework, training method, and code repositories through open-source methodologies increases the openness of a system. This has contributed to collaborative efforts, such as those of Google and OpenAI with their respective TensorFlow and GPT models, enabling outsiders to identify potential bias, error, or inaccuracy in their work. Additionally, when more individuals can view how these systems work, they become more likely to participate in and hold those systems accountable.

6.5.5 Transparency Requirements Driven by Regulatory and Policy Frameworks

Countries within the EU are creating a set of perceived behavioral expectations (i.e., expectations about how an entity should act) that will give entities a distinct incentive for complying with the transparency requirements of the regulation being created by the EU. For example, one of the regulatory initiatives in the EU is the proposed AI Act, which contains obligations on high-risk AI systems to meet defined requirements related to transparency, including conducting risk assessments, providing public access to documented information related to the AI system, and undergoing annual audits by third parties (Veale & Zuiderveen Borgesius, 2021). Proposed regulatory approaches are likely to provide similar regulatory frameworks that establish disclosure requirements, provide more understandable and consistent documentation as well as mandate third-party audits, thus institutionalizing transparency throughout diverse industries.

6.5.6 Autonomous Audits and External Evaluations

To check how well a business is open about its work, it is helpful to do regular third-party evaluations of their operations. By using unbiased auditors, organizations can have an impartial evaluation of their artificial intelligence (AI) systems and the data and methods they use to build algorithms. These audits are very useful in finding bias and problems that may not have been noticed by the organization's employees (Raji et al., 2020). The independent perspective of the auditor will also allow them to provide feedback on the organization so they can take corrective action with confidence in their product and service to customers and stakeholders. This is especially true for organizations in the financial services, governmental, and healthcare industries. Organizations that have an open culture typically practice the principle of transparency, and leaders must provide continual support to create a culture of transparency. Educational programs focusing on the need for ethical conduct and behaviors will also need to be implemented; an organization must have an incentive system connecting the organization's goals to its goals for transparency and accountability (Ananny & Crawford, 2018). Some examples of organizations that have intentionally developed a culture of transparency through structured processes and strategies within their direction are IBM and Microsoft (Bellamy et al., 2019; Microsoft, 2023). To foster a culture of transparency surrounding artificial intelligence, organizations will need to use many strategies at the same time, such as adopting best practices when developing AI, developing and using standardization documentation, using technology to create AI that is easily understood, and maintaining an effective culture of change. Collectively, these efforts will increase the transparency of AI and increase stakeholders' trust in their accountability as GenAI continues to expand.

6.6 MECHANISMS FOR ENSURING ACCOUNTABILITY

There is a need for a structured and holistic framework that can be used to hold GenAI accountable. A framework of this type will help define responsibilities, support a robust oversight process, facilitate the active enforcement of ethical standards, and create a trustworthy environment for developers. A strong accountability framework for GenAI includes the creation of an official governance framework for AI, an efficient auditing and reporting process, and an accurate documentation process during each phase of the AI lifecycle.

6.6.1 Ethics Review Boards and AI Governance Committees

To promote accountability for organizations that utilize artificial intelligence (AI), all organizations incorporating the use of AI should create either an ethical review board or an AI governance committee as part of their organizational infrastructure. The interdisciplinary approach of using these committees will be beneficial in overseeing the AI activities in the organization (including the authorization of AI system implementations), as well as evaluating the ethical compliance of these implementations and analyzing the data from the AI activities to determine the potential for bias or other negative unintended consequences. For example, at Microsoft, the AETHER Committee serves as an ethical review board in developing a systematic process to incorporate ethical considerations in the AI development process and provide oversight and monitoring of the AI implementation process.

6.6.2 Algorithmic Auditing and Impact Evaluations

To hold algorithmic systems accountable, it is essential to conduct thorough algorithmic audits with independent third-party teams or corporate compliance units performing an audit of AI algorithms and their related applications to identify and correct any biases, errors, or unintended social consequences (Raji et al., 2020). Impact assessments and Algorithmic Impact Assessments (AIAs) provide a framework for predicting the ethical, social, and legal impact of AI algorithms and systems and identifying the accountability gaps present in such systems before they are implemented (Reisman et al., 2018). Such assessments provide organizations with opportunities to develop proactive strategies for mitigating ethical risks.

6.6.3 Protocols for Documentation and Record-Keeping

For a healthcare system to be accountable, it is essential to maintain comprehensive and uniform records through thorough documentation, including but not limited to decision logs, development records, audit trails, and Model Cards (e.g., organized model reports), so that there is visible traceability and explicit attribution of who has made decisions in the healthcare system (Mitchell et al., 2019). The records should be used as the best practice for regulatory situations or public investigations to ensure effective oversight and accountability of the healthcare system.

6.6.4 Frameworks for Legal and Regulatory Compliance

Strong regulatory systems provide accountability. Regulations, such as the EU's anticipated AI Act and other sector-specific regulations, outline the responsibilities of both AI developers and AIDIs (AI Developers and Implementers) regarding their legal obligations and accountability. They also specify the legal consequences of non-compliance, how to ensure compliance, and how to dissuade AI developers and deployers from engaging in unethical conduct (Veale & Zuiderveen Borgesius, 2021).

6.6.5 Explicit Assignment of Responsibility and Liability

It is important to delegate responsibility clearly and transparently to the various stakeholders involved in AI implementation, including development, organizational ownership, deployment, oversight, and regulatory action. The more precise and well-defined the responsibilities assigned to each stakeholder, the stronger the mechanism to hold them accountable for any harm caused or unethical actions taken by AI systems (Yeung et al., 2019). Excellent communication and well-written legal documents, such as contracts, regulatory agreements, and internal company policy documents, allow both the developer and other stakeholders to reduce uncertainty regarding the responsibilities of each party while increasing the level of confidence of each party (including the public) in the performance of the AI system.

6.6.6 Transparency and Public Disclosure Systems

Access to public data regarding AI applications, such as AI registries and transparency portals, creates a level of accountability for the public. In turn, these increased levels of accountability allow for greater levels of oversight from the public as well as third-party verification of a collection of AIs, thus building trust among stakeholders in AI and ensuring that all parties comply with ethical standards (Whittaker et al.,

2018). Corporations such as Google and IBM have made data about their AI models and effectiveness assessments publicly available, promoting increased levels of accountability through greater community-based expectations or input regarding AI.

6.6.7 Feedback Mechanisms and Stakeholder Involvement

A continued strategy for achieving accountability is to incorporate stakeholder engagement and construct methodologies for gathering feedback. Regular engagement with stakeholders, such as end users, affected communities, civil society organizations, and independent experts, can help identify potential ethical "blind spots" that may otherwise go unnoticed. Additionally, they can provide an avenue for identifying deficiencies in the current accountability structure of AI systems. This interaction allows for the iterative improvement of AI systems (Jobin et al., 2019), while also allowing stakeholders to play an active role in improving their organizations by learning from their experiences and adapting to changing environments and conditions.

6.6.8 Whistleblower Safeguards and Reporting Mechanisms

Accountability can also be established through secure and confidential whistleblowing channels. Excellent whistleblower protection protects employees or external agencies reporting any violation of ethical behavior, algorithm bias, or ethical accounting practices from any fear of retaliation. Therefore, the presence of a viable whistleblower option serves as an incentive to proactively enforce the accountability measures established by an organization (West, 2018). Therefore, accountability in AI includes the following key components: governance oversight, systematic audits, written documentation, compliance with regulations, clearly defined responsibilities, public transparency, stakeholder engagement, and positive whistleblower provisions. Collectively, these components can support accountability at the system level, promote ethical practices, reduce risks, and increase public confidence in the application of GenAI in business.

6.7 CASE STUDIES ON TRANSPARENT AND ACCOUNTABLE AI

The investigation of real-life examples demonstrates how companies build transparency and accountability into GenAI systems. The following case studies highlight examples of best practices for promoting the development and use of responsible AI and offer suggestions on how to establish those practices. OpenAI's GPT series provides examples of transparency in AI model development. The GPT-3 and GPT-4 versions are open-source and come with comprehensive documentation detailing the models' capabilities, limitations, and potential biases. OpenAI has established a systematic approach to transparency by publicly sharing the methodologies it uses for "aligning" its models and the types of constraints it imposes to avoid or mitigate potential ethical concerns (Brown et al., 2020). OpenAI uses transparent dissemination of comprehensive documents and insights into its model's performance to build the trust of stakeholders, facilitate external scrutiny of its models by the public and stakeholders, and promote healthy public discourse regarding its models. In contrast to OpenAI, IBM Watson has taken a more proactive approach to transparency and accountability by offering a free-to-download, open-source AI Fairness 360 toolkit that provides developers with a means to identify, document, and address biases that may be present in AI systems. The AI Fairness 360 toolkit has clear frameworks to evaluate the fairness of algorithms and includes suggested best practices for developers to correct any potential bias in their AI models (Bellamy et al., 2019). IBM's proactive approach to transparency via these technologies supports an ethical and standardized approach to evaluating AI from both developer and stakeholder perspectives. Therefore, the AI Fairness 360 toolkit enhances the responsibility of developers to implement AI in various sectors, including finance, healthcare, and human resources. Google has developed initiatives to create ethical AI with Model Cards to provide standardized transparency for AI models. Model Cards provide standardized documentation of the intended application for an AI model, the performance metrics used to evaluate an AI model's performance, ethical considerations, and limitations; therefore, they allow for an external review process for stakeholders to access information about the use of the model (Mitchell et al., 2019). By developing the Model Card system and making it part of their beliefs about transparency, Google provides greater accountability by providing their stakeholders with information about the assumptions made in the training process, the methods used to train the model, and the social impact of the model thereby providing greater clarity and trust for users. Microsoft's Responsible AI framework provides support for their principles of openness and responsible AI governance by developing committees with multidisciplinary oversight (e.g., AETHER), supporting the development of a transparent documentation system for the use of AI, and developing ethical review processes to provide established oversight and the prospective identification of ethical and accountability concerns (Microsoft, 2023). Microsoft's efforts to institutionalize responsible AI demonstrate a pathway that organizations may utilize to incorporate accountability as part of their internal operations and external product implementations. The proposed EU AI Act provides both regulatory clarity and regulatory accountability for the utilization of AI. The proposed legislation includes mandates for specific requirements regarding transparency and accountability with high-risk AI systems (Veale & Zuiderveen Borgesius, 2021). Some of these mandates include public disclosure, independent audits, algorithmic impact assessments, and public registries, providing a comprehensive legal structure regarding ethical responsibility in AI. The Mozilla Foundation is providing resources (e.g. Mozilla AI Transparency Toolkit) to provide practical assistance in helping users to evaluate the ethical use and overall environmental impacts of AI; therefore, Mozilla's approach to AI emphasizes creating a collaborative environment through open-source technologies that support community-based efforts for AI accountability and lead to increased public participation in AI governance (Mozilla Foundation, 2023). ProPublica's exploration of the Correctional Offender Management Profiling for Alternative Sanctions (COMPAS) algorithm provides an example of how transparency can be used to hold AI accountable. ProPublica's exploration identified that

AI-based judicial sentencing algorithms are biased based on racial characteristics. Therefore, ProPublica advocates for the establishment of external oversight mechanisms so that independent accountability is established to identify and correct ethical failures with AI (Angwin et al., 2016). Thus, the above examples show different pathways to the achievement of transparency and accountability in the application of GenAI. Examples include establishing structured documentation (i.e., Model Card), developing open-source toolkits, undertaking regulatory oversight, and advocating for transparency and accountability demonstrate that developing and using AI in a responsible and transparent manner is both ethical and feasible.

6.8 THE SIGNIFICANCE OF MULTI-STAKEHOLDER COLLABORATION

To ensure the transparency and accountability of GenAI technology, collaboration among diverse stakeholders, such as engineers, ethicists, policymakers, civil society, academia, and end users, is required. The collaborative approach of bringing together diverse perspectives from multiple stakeholders can create more comprehensive and ethically robust AI systems to solve complex societal and ethical issues (Cath et al., 2018).

6.8.1 Multidisciplinary and Cross-Sector Collaboration

Multi-stakeholder collaboration results in the integration of knowledge from technical, ethical, social, and legal practices, thus creating a balanced perspective that is essential for achieving the highest level of transparency and accountability for AI inquiries. Interdisciplinary/multi-stakeholder partnerships, such as the Partnership on AI, demonstrate an effective model of how businesses, such as Google and Microsoft, academia, and civil society organizations can come together and share knowledge that will assist organizations in establishing a responsible AI framework through coordinated ethical guidelines, standards of transparency, and best practices for responsible AI use (Partnership on AI, 2023).

6.8.2 Collective Design and Participatory AI Development

Participatory design processes create opportunities for stakeholder groups, particularly those directly impacted by a proposed AI product or service, to engage in the design and development phase of the technology. Involving the end user in the early stages of AI development will enhance the organization's awareness of the importance of ensuring transparency and accountability to its end users in the development of AI, as well as helping to mitigate the risk of bias or unethical decisions in the design/development process (Costanza-Chock, 2020). Initiatives for community-driven AI technology solutions in healthcare and public wellness often require the active participation of both patients and healthcare professionals to design and develop systems that meet the needs of users and adhere to ethical principles and societal values.

6.8.3 International AI Governance Discussions

Many international governance discussions are taking place on multiple institutional platforms (e.g., UNESCO's worldwide draft of the ethical principles governing AI and the OECD's principle of AI). These platforms promote collaboration among various stakeholders globally, enabling the establishment of consensus-driven ethical standards, transparency protocols, and accountability, which inform a nation's regulatory framework and organizations worldwide (UNESCO, 2021; OECD, 2019). A global approach to ethical AI requires collaboration among public and private entities via a structured framework and channels for the exchange of best practices, an avenue for addressing transnational barriers to AI regulation, and developing and implementing an internationally applicable framework of standards for AI accountability and governance.

6.8.4 Partnerships Developing Ethical AI Through Cooperative Business Models

The combined efforts of actors across different sectors (e.g., corporations and governments) build toward a system that possesses two core characteristics: those characteristics are transparency and accountability within the creation and operation of AI entities. For example, AI4People is an ongoing initiative in Europe made up of public, corporate, academic, and civil society stakeholders collaborating to facilitate the development of ethical frameworks and best practice recommendations, which have impacted corporate and European Union level (EU) AI policy and development activities (Floridi et al., 2018). The output of these types of cooperative efforts facilitates comprehensive mutual accountability that requires both corporate and governmental actors to adhere to a framework of ethical principles in the manner of carrying out their activities regarding the development and implementation of AI products.

6.8.5 Civil Society and Advocacy Organizations

Civil society organizations provide substantial advocacy and monitoring of AI to ensure that the development of AI products is accomplished in an ethical manner and evaluate AI products according to their compliance with ethical standards and principles. The independent evaluations of the ethical and effective use of AI undertaken by civil society organizations such as AlgorithmWatch, the AI Now Institute, and the Mozilla Foundation facilitate raising public awareness regarding AI entities, as well as providing accountability to corporate and governmental actors through public examinations, publishing transparency reports, and advocating for ethical AI (Whittaker et al., 2018; AlgorithmWatch, 2023). These organizations serve as independent evaluators of organizations working in the field of AI and ensure strict adherence to accountability.

6.8.6 Academic Institutions and AI Literacy Programs

Educational institutions can enhance the transparency and accountability of AI by raising awareness of AI literacy among stakeholders. Institutions such as Stanford

University and MIT are raising awareness of AI and engaging with stakeholders through public outreach, policy discussions, and interdisciplinary research on the ethical, social, and technical dimensions of AI systems (Stanford HAI, 2023). AI literacy programs provide stakeholders with the confidence to evaluate AI ethically and contribute to the establishment of transparency and a more significant role in AI governance.

6.8.7 Independent Research and Think Tanks

Independent research and think tanks (Ada Lovelace Institute and Brookings Institution) provide critical insights and analytical expertise on issues regarding transparency and accountability in AI. These organizations engage in high-quality independent research and provide policymakers with recommendations based on their findings. The findings of independent research and policy recommendations help define best practices in the development and use of ethical AI, influence the creation of regulatory frameworks, and stimulate public discourse on ethical issues in AI (Ada Lovelace Institute, 2023; Brookings Institution, 2023). Multi-stakeholder collaborations are essential to bringing accountability and transparency into the development of AI. Collaborative models provide an integrated accountability framework that is required for the ethical/legitimate innovation of AI. By utilizing these types of collaborative models for the purpose of enhancing interdisciplinary collaboration, creating public participatory structures, establishing means of global dialogue, supporting public-private partnerships, providing oversight through civil society organizations, educating and increasing public awareness about AI through civil society organizations, and supporting independent research.

6.9 FUTURE PERSPECTIVES: CULTIVATING A CULTURE OF ETHICAL ACCOUNTABILITY

With GenAI becoming more prevalent throughout society, business, culture, and everyday life, it is apparent that building a culture of ethical responsibility is critical. To build an ethical culture, the stakeholders in the development and implementation of AI—organizations, education, regulatory bodies, and society—must collaborate and take intentional action to develop a culture of ethical responsibility. Each stakeholder in the development and implementation of AI must incorporate the concept of ethics into the daily operational activities of their organizations.

6.9.1 Integrating Ethics from the Beginning

All organizations that create AI products need to factor in ethical considerations early on and throughout the entire lifetime of the product. Organizations that create and deliver ethical AI products include ethical considerations from the initial design of the product through to the final use of the product. Organizations that have developed an "ethics-by-design" approach proactively assess their products and services against ethical criteria and establish mechanisms for ethical accountability at the organization level throughout the product development phase. By proactively addressing ethical considerations, organizations greatly reduce the likelihood of having any ethical violations and align more closely with society's expectations.

6.9.2 Commitment of Leadership and Governance of Organizations

For organizations to fulfill their ethical obligations, organizations must have a strong commitment from leadership and appropriate governance structures to promote, uphold, and demonstrate ethical values throughout the organization. Leadership must define and articulate ethics as a core value of their organization; actively communicate the ethical values of the organization to employees through transparent and well-documented governance processes; and adequately provide the necessary resources to ensure successful ethical oversight and compliance initiatives are in place. Leading organizations, such as Microsoft, Google, and IBM, have established their commitment to ethics by establishing internal ethical review teams, external oversight bodies, and ongoing transparent and ethical accountability systems. The importance of training, education, and literacy in AI cannot be overstated. As AI systems become more widely adopted across industries, employees, leaders, and stakeholders must understand both the capabilities and limitations of these technologies.

One way that educational institutions help create a culture of ethical accountability among their students is by providing students with AI literacy training modules as part of the curricula at both universities and businesses. These training modules help stakeholders gain an understanding of the skills needed to evaluate the effectiveness and ethical use of ethical principle-related ethical AI systems (Long & Magerko, 2020). A good example of institutions that have adopted an interdisciplinary approach to teaching students about AI ethics are MIT, Stanford, and Carnegie Mellon; they offer interdisciplinary approaches to educate future professionals on how to make ethical decisions concerning AI system design and implementation (Stanford HAI, 2023).

6.9.3 Encouragement of Ethical Behavior

Organizational frameworks for incentive structure must provide transparency and accountability to create a culture of ethical behavior. Organizations that provide incentives for ethical outcomes, such as performance evaluations, recognition programs, and benchmarks for ethics, will promote the development of a long-term culture of ethical behavior and increase accountability at all corporate levels (Hagendorff, 2020). Organizations that use ethical-related metrics to evaluate an employee's performance are demonstrating a commitment to ethical accountability and providing long-term opportunities to align with social norms.

6.9.4 Public Involvement and the Discussion of Ethical Issues

Public involvement in the discussion of ethical issues, as well as public participation, will create a culture of ethical accountability for all stakeholders involved in the creation and development of AI, ensuring that the development of AI is aligned with societal values and needs and public agreement. Community forums, participating in inclusive conversations about ethical dilemmas will lead to transparency and a mutual level of accountability among all involved parties (Costanza-Chok, 2020). Organizations that develop a system of inclusive and visible stakeholder engagement develop trust within the parties involved and create a richer view of society at large, as it relates to the AI development process.

6.9.5 Continuous Evaluation and Ongoing Improvement

For AI to be ethically accountable, there must be continuous evaluation of AI systems, instances of feedback from users or stakeholders, and continual cycles of development (product cycles). By implementing continual audits of ethicality, making public and open disclosures of ethical audit results, and implementing accountability systems, there will be activities that make ethical frameworks fluid, will predict new futurist trends in ethics, and will adjust to new types of ethical challenges (Raji et al., 2020). Through cyclical reviews of the ethical competency of an organization's practices, an organization can readily identify and correct ethical process deficiencies, as well as can meet ethical standards and social expectations.

6.9.6 Creation of Systems of Regulatory Guidelines and Legal Frameworks

The creation of a complete system of regulatory guidelines for AI is a requisite condition for clearly delineating the ethical responsibilities of AI developers and holding them accountable for unethical conduct; therefore, establishing a culture of ethical accountability in the development of AI. The establishment of common, precise, and well-defined legal frameworks (i.e., the EU AI Act) that require all AI developers to comply with a set of defined ethical standards and establish a basis for imposing punitive actions or sanctions on AI developers who are not ethical has a direct connection to improved accountability and compliance with ethical standards for AI across multiple industries and sectors (Veale & Zuiderveen Borgesius, 2021).

To develop a culture of ethical accountability within the field of GenAI it is important to include ethical considerations at every level of development, have a strong commitment to ethics and ethical behaviors from organizational leadership, provide periodic and continuous training and education to all parties involved, establish aligned organizational incentives that promote the use of ethical standards, and actively and continually involve the public during the development of AI. In addition, it is essential to implement mechanisms to continually provide for iterative review processes of ethical accountability and compliance. The overall adoption of these strategies will create a systemic commitment to transparency and accountability; thus, facilitating the creation of trust and responsible innovation during the development of GenAI.

REFERENCES

Ada Lovelace Institute. (2023). *Research themes and policy guidance*. https://www.adalovelaceinstitute.org/research/

Ahmad, M. A., Eckert, C., & Teredesai, A. (2018). Interpretable machine learning in healthcare. In *Proceedings of the 2018 ACM International Conference on Bioinformatics, Computational Biology, and Health Informatics* (pp. 559–560). ACM. https://doi.org/10.1145/3233547.3233667

AlgorithmWatch. (2023). *AI accountability and transparency initiatives*. https://algorithmwatch.org/en/projects/

Ananny, M., & Crawford, K. (2018). Seeing without knowing: Limitations of the transparency ideal and its application to algorithmic accountability. *New Media & Society, 20*(3), 973–989. https://doi.org/10.1177/1461444816676645

Angwin, J., Larson, J., Mattu, S., & Kirchner, L. (2016). *Machine bias*. ProPublica. https://www.propublica.org/article/machine-bias-risk-assessments-in-criminal-sentencing

Arrieta, A. B., Díaz-Rodríguez, N., Del Ser, J., Bennetot, A., Tabik, S., Barbado, A., … Herrera, F. (2020). Explainable AI (XAI): Concepts, taxonomies, opportunities, and challenges towards responsible AI. *Information Fusion, 58*, 82–115. https://doi.org/10.1016/j.inffus.2019.12.012

Barfield, W., & Pagallo, U. (2020). *Advanced introduction to law and AI*. Edward Elgar Publishing. https://doi.org/10.4337/9781789905137

Bellamy, R. K., Dey, K., Hind, M., Hoffman, S. C., Houde, S., Kannan, K., … Zhang, Y. (2019). AI Fairness 360: An extensible toolkit for detecting and mitigating algorithmic bias. *IBM Journal of Research and Development, 63*(4/5), 1–15. https://doi.org/10.1147/JRD.2019.2942287

Binns, R. (2018). Fairness in machine learning: Lessons from political philosophy. In *Proceedings of the 2018 Conference on Fairness, Accountability, and Transparency* (pp. 149–159). ACM. https://doi.org/10.1145/3287560.3287576

Brookings Institution. (2023). *AI and emerging technology policy research*. https://www.brookings.edu/topic/artificial-intelligence/

Brown, T. B., Mann, B., Ryder, N., Subbiah, M., Kaplan, J., Dhariwal, P., … Amodei, D. (2020). Language models are few-shot learners. *Advances in Neural Information Processing Systems (NeurIPS), 33*, 1877–1901. https://arxiv.org/abs/2005.14165

Buijsman, S. (2023). Transparency for AI systems: A value-based approach. *Ethics and Information Technology, 25*(1), 1–14. https://doi.org/10.1007/s10676-023-09654-z

Buolamwini, J., & Gebru, T. (2018). Gender shades: Intersectional accuracy disparities in commercial gender classification. In *Proceedings of the Conference on Fairness, Accountability, and Transparency* (pp. 77–91). ACM. https://doi.org/10.1145/3287560.3287596

Calo, R. (2017). AI policy: A primer and roadmap. *UC Davis Law Review, 51*(2), 399–435. https://lawreview.law.ucdavis.edu/issues/51/2/Symposium/51-2_Calo.pdf

Cath, C., Wachter, S., Mittelstadt, B., Taddeo, M., & Floridi, L. (2018). AI and the good society: The US, EU, and UK approach. *Science and Engineering Ethics, 24*(2), 505–528. https://doi.org/10.1007/s11948-017-9901-7

Costanza-Chock, S. (2020). *Design justice: Community-led practices to build the worlds we need*. MIT Press. https://doi.org/10.7551/mitpress/12255.001.0001

Fjeld, J., Achten, N., Hilligoss, H., Nagy, A., & Srikumar, M. (2020). *Principled AI: Mapping consensus in ethical and rights-based approaches to principles for AI* (Berkman Klein Center Research Publication No. 2020-1). https://doi.org/10.2139/ssrn.3518482

Floridi, L., Cowls, J., Beltrametti, M., Chatila, R., Chazerand, P., Dignum, V., … Schafer, B. (2018). AI4People: An ethical framework for a good AI society: Opportunities, risks, principles, and recommendations. *Minds and Machines, 28*(4), 689–707. https://doi.org/10.1007/s11023-018-9482-5

Gebru, T., Morgenstern, J., Vecchione, B., Wortman Vaughan, J., Wallach, H., Daumé III, H., & Crawford, K. (2021). Datasheets for datasets. *Communications of the ACM, 64*(12), 86–92. https://doi.org/10.1145/3458723

Hagendorff, T. (2020). The ethics of AI ethics: An evaluation of guidelines. *Minds and Machines, 30*(1), 99–120. https://doi.org/10.1007/s11023-020-09517-8

Jobin, A., Ienca, M., & Vayena, E. (2019). The global landscape of AI ethics guidelines. *Nature Machine Intelligence, 1*(9), 389–399. https://doi.org/10.1038/s42256-019-0088-2

Kroll, J. A. (2018). The fallacy of inscrutability. *Philosophical Transactions of the Royal Society A, 376*(2133), 20180084. https://doi.org/10.1098/rsta.2018.0084

Lipton, Z. C. (2018). The mythos of model interpretability. *Communications of the ACM, 61*(10), 36–43. https://doi.org/10.1145/3233231

Long, D., & Magerko, B. (2020). What is AI literacy? Competencies and design considerations. In *Proceedings of the 2020 CHI Conference on Human Factors in Computing Systems* (pp. 1–16). ACM. https://doi.org/10.1145/3313831.3376727

Mehrabi, N., Morstatter, F., Saxena, N., Lerman, K., & Galstyan, A. (2021). A survey on bias and fairness in machine learning. *ACM Computing Surveys, 54*(6), 1–35. https://doi.org/10.1145/3457607

Microsoft. (2023). *Ethical AI governance framework.* https://www.microsoft.com/ai/responsible-ai

Mitchell, M., Wu, S., Zaldivar, A., Barnes, P., Vasserman, L., Hutchinson, B., & Gebru, T. (2019). Model cards for model reporting. In *Proceedings of the Conference on Fairness, Accountability, and Transparency* (pp. 220–229). https://doi.org/10.1145/3287560.3287596

Mittelstadt, B. (2019). Principles alone cannot guarantee ethical AI. *Nature Machine Intelligence, 1*(11), 501–507. https://doi.org/10.1038/s42256-019-0114-4

Morley, J., Floridi, L., Kinsey, L., & Elhalal, A. (2020). From what to how: An initial review of publicly available AI ethics tools, methods, and research to translate principles into practices. *Science and Engineering Ethics, 26*(4), 2141–2168. https://doi.org/10.1007/s11948-019-00165-5

Mozilla Foundation. (2023). *Mozilla AI transparency toolkit.* https://foundation.mozilla.org/en/initiatives/responsible-ai/

OECD. (2019). *OECD principles on AI.* https://www.oecd.org/going-digital/ai/principles/

Partnership on AI. (2023). *Multi-stakeholder collaborations and reports.* https://partnershiponai.org/

Raji, I. D., Smart, A., White, R. N., Mitchell, M., Gebru, T., Hutchinson, B., … Barnes, P. (2020). Closing the AI accountability gap: Defining an end-to-end framework for internal algorithmic auditing. In *Proceedings of the 2020 Conference on Fairness, Accountability, and Transparency* (pp. 33–44). ACM. https://doi.org/10.1145/3351095.3372873

Reisman, D., Schultz, J., Crawford, K., & Whittaker, M. (2018). *Algorithmic impact assessments: A practical framework for public agency accountability.* AI Now Institute. https://ainowinstitute.org/aiareport2018.pdf

Reuters. (2024, March 1). Legal transparency in AI finance: Facing the accountability dilemma in digital decision-making. https://www.reuters.com/legal/transactional/legal-transparency-ai-finance-facing-accountability-dilemma-digital-decision-2024-03-01/

Rudin, C. (2019). Stop explaining black box models for high stakes decisions and use interpretable models instead. *Nature Machine Intelligence, 1*(5), 206–215. https://doi.org/10.1038/s42256-019-0048-x

Stanford HAI. (2023). *Human-centered AI research initiatives.* https://hai.stanford.edu/

UNESCO. (2021). *Recommendation on the ethics of AI.* https://unesdoc.unesco.org/ark:/48223/pf0000380455

Veale, M., & Zuiderveen Borgesius, F. (2021). Demystifying the draft EU AI Act. *Computer Law Review International, 22*(4), 97–112. https://doi.org/10.9785/cri-2021-220402

West, S. M. (2018). Data capitalism: Redefining the logics of surveillance and privacy. *Business & Society, 58*(1), 20–41. https://doi.org/10.1177/0007650317718185

Whittaker, M., Crawford, K., Dobbe, R., Fried, G., Kaziunas, E., Mathur, V., … Schwartz, O. (2018). *AI Now Report 2018*. AI Now Institute, New York University. https://ainowinstitute.org/AI_Now_2018_Report.pdf

Winfield, A. F., & Jirotka, M. (2018). Ethical governance is essential to building trust in robotics and AI systems. *Philosophical Transactions of the Royal Society A, 376*(2133), 20180085. https://doi.org/10.1098/rsta.2018.0085

Yeung, K., Howes, A., & Pogrebna, G. (2019). AI governance by human rights-centred design, deliberation and oversight. In M. D. Dubber, F. Pasquale, & S. Das (Eds.), *The Oxford handbook of ethics of AI* (pp. 77–106). Oxford University Press. https://doi.org/10.1093/oxfordhb/9780190067397.013.4

7 Ethical Considerations of Autonomous AI Decision-Making

7.1 OVERVIEW OF AUTONOMOUS AI AND ETHICAL CONSIDERATIONS

Autonomous AI systems can perform tasks and make decisions without human intervention, in contrast to traditional software, which follows a strict set of instructions or rules. Autonomous AIs are more capable of learning from their experiences through data assimilation; that is, they can gather information, adjust to new information, and operate at a speed and scale of action that human beings cannot easily monitor. As such, there are numerous areas of activity where autonomous AI systems can currently be found, including but not limited to assisting with medical diagnosis, credit evaluations, content moderation, self-automated vehicles (i.e., self-driving cars), and predictive policing and law enforcement. Autonomous AI systems offer advantages such as increased efficiency and consistent performance; they can process large volumes of data, automate many repetitive tasks performed by humans, and improve decision-making in complex environments. However, the characteristics that make autonomous AI a valuable tool introduce complex ethical concerns. First, when an AI decides to use an opaque method, the reasoning behind the AI's decision will be unclear; therefore, questions arise as to whether the AI's decision is fair and what the AI's level of accountability is if the AI's decision causes harm (Floridi et al., 2018).

A significant ethical issue associated with the development and implementation of autonomous AIs is the shift in responsibility for making important decisions from humans to machines. Because autonomous AI systems can execute decisions without human involvement or monitoring when they are being executed, established accountability systems that rely upon human judgment, intent, and monitoring cannot exist. If an autonomous AI system makes a negative or biased decision, it may not be possible to establish a single point of accountability for that decision because responsibility may be shared among developers, data suppliers, system users/operators, and organizational owners (Cath et al., 2018). Another significant challenge of autonomous AI is the opaque nature of many modern AI algorithms. Although high-performing AI systems, particularly those that employ deep learning algorithms, can produce results with a high degree of accuracy, there is often no clear explanation of how the AI produced those results, making it difficult for

DOI: 10.1201/9781003679974-7

users, regulators, and affected stakeholders to understand or challenge AI decisions. This lack of transparency poses a serious concern for applications in critical domains such as healthcare, law enforcement, and finance, where AI-enabled decision-making can have profound consequences for individuals' lives and rights (Lipton, 2018). This chapter reviews and analyzes the multitude of ethical dilemmas caused by autonomous AI systems and provides an assessment of the ethical concerns of responsibility, transparency, justice, human oversight, privacy, and safety issues. While the discussion of these ethical dilemmas is a central focus of this chapter, the authors prefer to emphasize the applicable pragmatic implications and governance approaches of the ethical implementation of autonomous AI by industry instead of being overly conceptually vague. The overarching goal of this chapter is to identify and discuss possible methods for identifying, managing, and mitigating the distinct ethical challenges of autonomous AI systems and their practical applications (Winfield & Jirotka, 2018).

7.2 FUNDAMENTAL ETHICAL DILEMMAS IN AUTONOMOUS DECISION-MAKING

The ethical issues raised by autonomous AI systems are not associated with their function as machines; rather, ethical issues arise from the extent of the effect autonomous AI systems have on people's lives because of their decisions (which are usually implemented on a massive scale and with very little opportunity for human input). This section reviews the most common ethical dilemmas associated with autonomous decision-making.

7.2.1 Obligation and Liability

The assignment of authority to an autonomous system has created uncertainty regarding the assignment of responsibility. In a traditional context, responsibility is usually assigned to the individual or organization that directly made the decision. In the case of an autonomous AI system, the decisions created by the system can be attributed to a variety of factors, such as design, training data, model behavior, and deployment environment. One potential cause of a negative outcome may stem from failure due to bias from training data, a design limitation in the model, or a lack of adequate human oversight during deployment, leading to an accountability gap (i.e., there is no single entity to which responsibility can be readily assigned for the outcome) (Cath et al., 2018). Without a clear way to hold people accountable, an organization can avoid taking responsibility for the outcome by blaming the system. We must impose explicit responsibility before deploying autonomous AI systems to ensure ethical use and implementation. Developers design and train the system, organizations use it, and operators monitor and intervene when necessary. Creating comprehensive documentation and checklists will be critical in establishing who is responsible for any system failure (Winfield & Jirotka, 2018).

7.2.2 Clarity and Comprehensibility

To evaluate the decision-making of today's AI systems, we need to understand how they work and why they make the decisions that they do. The transparency of an autonomous system, often because of the complexity of its underlying technology and the difficulty in interpreting the results of these systems' decision-making processes, limits our ability to fully evaluate the decision-making processes of these technologies. For example, in cases where decisions directly affect people's lives, such as a physician's diagnosis, approval for a loan, or sentencing for a crime, the need for explainability becomes paramount. Those affected by decisions cannot contest or change them if they don't understand why they were made. The loss of trust, along with fears of inequity and invalidity stemming from this lack of understanding, can be particularly damaging to those affected by technology. Consequently, it will be increasingly difficult for affected individuals and communities to participate in the development of the technology that affects them (Lipton, 2018). Although complete transparency regarding technological systems may not always be feasible, there is an ethical imperative to provide sufficient practical explanations for users and stakeholders. We should clearly define a system's goals and objectives, the technology's limitations, and the evaluation criteria to facilitate user and stakeholder understanding. An explanation of the reasons for a decision should be designed to enable users and stakeholders to review, appeal, and hold the technology accountable, rather than simply being an exercise in generating technical specifications (Arrieta et al., 2020).

7.2.3 Prejudice, Equity, and Inequity

Autonomous AI systems use historical data to learn how to operate. If the historical data used by the autonomous AI system contains social, economic, or institutional bias, the autonomous AI systems can mimic or even amplify the same patterns. Given the scalability of AI systems, biased choices made by autonomous AI systems can quickly and uniformly affect many people. Autonomous decision-making processes in various fields, such as hiring decisions, credit assessments, predictive policing, and healthcare risk assessments, have documented numerous instances of bias. These biases have often been unintentional owing to the use of imbalanced datasets, the use of proxy variables, and the design of the technology without consideration of the social context (O'Neil, 2016). To reduce bias in the autonomous decision-making process, more than just a technical solution is needed; to ethically implement autonomous AI systems, data must be carefully selected, fairness must be continuously monitored, and the contribution of automated decisions to existing disparities must be acknowledged. Without these considerations, technology is likely to lead to increased discrimination and the appearance of neutrality.

7.2.4 Human Agency, Consent, and Control

Autonomous AI systems have been used to reduce the level of human input in the decision-making process. Concerns are growing that this will reduce the degree of human choice in decision-making. Many people remain unaware that AI systems make decisions for them when they use automated decision-making technology. A person should be fully aware of how an AI system uses automated decision-making to create decisions regarding him/her. Unfortunately, in several existing systems, many people either lack this understanding or are unable to fully grasp the implications that automated decision-making may have on their ability to make decisions. This lack of understanding often leads to a person's difficulty in contesting or opting out of any automated decisions made, especially in instances where those decisions may have significant effects on the individual (Danaher, 2019). The use of a human preserver implies that humans can act autonomously. A human preserver means that systems are available to facilitate human engagement, evaluation, and override in all circumstances in which human input is required. Human-in-the-loop and human-on-the-loop models are critical in cases involving an individual's rights, safety, and long-term effects.

7.2.5 Privacy and Data Management

To provide the best user experience, autonomous AI relies heavily on the collection and use of a user's personal data, including data related to behaviors, biometrics, and context. Constant data collection can make it difficult to differentiate between the benefits of customization and the dangers of surveillance. The inability to govern such data creates an environment in which they are susceptible to exploitation through unauthorized use and function creep (the continued use of data for purposes other than their original intent). The risks associated with this type of data collection will increase in an environment where an autonomous system operates independently and learns continually throughout its lifecycle (Zuboff, 2019). Establishing sound data governance systems to oversee the collection and use of user data is necessary for the ethical deployment of autonomous AI systems in the workplace. Data governance should include limiting the amount of data collected (data minimization), explicitly defining why the data are being collected (purpose limiting), securing the stored data, and establishing user rights regarding the collection and use of their data. Furthermore, privacy protection should be included in the design of an autonomous AI system rather than simply being considered a secondary concern.

7.3 PRACTICAL IMPLEMENTATION OF TRANSPARENCY AND ACCOUNTABILITY

Transparency and accountability are usually regarded as ethical considerations, but the effectiveness of such principles relies on the way they are organized to achieve a specific organizational objective (i.e., transparency and accountability). With respect to autonomous AI systems, transparency cannot simply be achieved by explaining the algorithms used; it requires explicit documentation, verifiable processes of decision-making, and delineated lines of accountability through all phases of the autonomous system's lifecycle. A successful approach to transparency begins with a specific purpose that is clearly defined. Therefore, organizations must specify the purpose, intended environment, and limitations of an autonomous system. If organizations leave the definition of the intended use of an autonomous system open-ended, there will be an increased risk that users will misappropriate those systems or use them in environments for which they were never intended (Floridi et al., 2018).

7.3.1 Documentation of Models and Systems

One way to promote better operational transparency in a model is to create a structure that documents all the components. This includes the model's goals, data sources, success measures, usage limits, and failure examples. When creating documentation for a model, it is not necessary to include proprietary information; however, it must be sufficient to provide a means for others to review the documentation internally and hold those responsible for external accountability. Documenting design decisions and reasoning is necessary to assign responsibility for the events within a model. Documenting the design decisions and assumptions provides a means to trace how a system behaves based on those design decisions and the thought process that led to them. This should allow for a more efficient investigation after an incident and reduce the tendency to attribute problems solely to the system rather than to the developers' or users' decision-making (Winfield & Jirotka, 2018).

7.3.2 Data Transparency and Traceability

The reliability of autonomous artificial intelligence (AI) relies heavily on the quality of the data used to train and operate the system. When we understand how the data were collected and who they represented as data transparency, we can make a more informed judgment about whether there is bias, fairness, and appropriateness for a specific context. Without this understanding, it is difficult to assess a system's bias, fairness, or appropriateness. Traceability is an important concept because systems change over time owing to changes in data distributions and operational parameters, and an overall decrease in performance is quite likely. A reduction in performance increases the likelihood of unintentional harm. Companies can monitor their systems and data for any type of error before they have a significant impact by using data audits and maintaining a record of all versions of the data and systems (Gebru et al., 2021).

7.3.3 Transparency in Decision-Making and the Right to Explanation

High-stakes situations require a transparent view of both the standard operating procedure for the system and the specific decisions it makes. This transparency enables those affected by the decision to understand the reasoning behind it, regardless of the complexity of the model used to reach this conclusion. Decision-level transparency allows for a meaningful analysis and appeal of the decision. When a person cannot contest a decision or seek clarification about it, the responsibility for that decision consists of being a symbolic act only, rather than operational. While it is not always possible to provide comprehensive explanations, delivering reasoned explanations at an appropriate level will enhance procedural fairness as well as trust in the process (Arrieta et al., 2020).

7.3.4 Responsibility Throughout the AI Lifecycle

To effectively manage the risks associated with autonomous AI systems, an organization that deploys an autonomous AI system should ensure that it has established an accountability framework throughout the lifecycle (from design to deployment) and has tracked accountability throughout its entire operation. Developers should establish accountability for the model architecture, training decisions, and testing methodology, whereas the organization deploying it should establish accountability for the specific contextual implementation, oversight, and intervention of the system (although this can vary widely depending on the type of system). Establishing explicit accountability responsibilities within AI systems requires a clear delineation of the actions required to address AI degradation. If organizations do not have a clearly defined delineation of their accountability for any role during the degradation of AI systems, they will likely have trouble acting on incidents of harm (for example) resulting from AI systems and will likely experience a delay in implementing corrective actions. Furthermore, as outlined in the article "Accountability Frameworks for AI: A Policy Perspective" (Cath et al., 2018), establishing clear accountability frameworks prior to deploying an AI system is highly recommended because organizations will subsequently find it difficult to implement the necessary corrective actions effectively if they do not already have a clearly articulated framework for enforcing accountability when required (for instance).

7.3.5 Regulatory and Organizational Conformity

As regulators push for more openness and responsibility through rules and laws, there is a stronger focus on keeping track of the choices made by AI systems, identifying the risks linked to them, and giving more support and power to those creating and using high-risk AI systems under new rules. This shift from voluntary ethical guidance to mandatory governance has significantly changed how organizations operate in both the private and public sectors. Organizations that have integrated their internal processes with existing regulatory regulations have found themselves to be better positioned to manage risk and demonstrate accountability. Transparency and accountability should not be viewed as impediments to compliance; rather, they should be viewed as ways in which transparency and accountability can be integrated into the culture of an organization, thus improving the quality, dependability, and trustworthiness of AI systems, ultimately creating better public trust (Veale & Zuiderveen Borgesius, 2021).

7.4 GOVERNANCE AND RISK MANAGEMENT FOR AUTONOMOUS ARTIFICIAL INTELLIGENCE

Well-established governance frameworks provide definitions and formality for transparency and accountability. The governance framework provides regulations, responsibilities, and procedures that govern the design, development, monitoring, and correction of autonomous AI systems over their operational lifetime. Without a governance framework, ethical principles may appear as lofty goals and prove challenging to implement. AI governance also relies on effective risk management. Autonomous AI systems exhibit unexpected behaviors when deployed in complex and changing environments. Ethical governance assumes that failures will occur and focuses on reducing the likelihood of failure, reducing the impact of failure, and responding effectively when they do occur (Floridi et al., 2018).

7.4.1 Governance Based on Lifecycle

Rather than viewing autonomous AI simply as a product, effective governance sees the autonomous AI lifecycle as a complete system comprising all phases through which data are collected, developed, and deployed. Within each of these phases, ethical risks exist that result from collecting data and building models (data gathering), training those models (training), putting the model into operation (deployment), and changing how the system operates (post-deployment modification). Organizations should conduct a structured assessment of the risks prior to deploying their autonomous AI solutions, which includes examining the potential for harm that may occur, who the affected stakeholders will be, what the conditions are that will prevent or enable the organization to mitigate such risks, and what level of autonomy and human oversight is required for that type of activity. Following the deployment of an autonomous AI solution, organizations should implement ongoing monitoring of the system to identify situations where the performance of the autonomous AI solution has degraded, the level of bias has increased, or the autonomous AI solution has demonstrated characteristics that were not anticipated at the time of training (Winfield & Jirotka, 2018). The autonomous AI lifecycle requires continuous evaluation. One cannot assume that autonomous AI solutions are safe and just based solely on the results of their original testing. The development of autonomous AI solutions will continue to evolve as new technologies emerge and new datasets and operating conditions are developed.

7.4.2 Mechanisms for Human Oversight and Intervention

Autonomous AI systems require human supervision to safeguard against risks. While autonomy can help increase the productivity of an organization, the removal of human oversight increases the risk of inaccuracies, mistakes, and faulty ethical decisions by increasing the number of opportunities for errors in the judgment of the system and removing the ability to detect them. The extent of oversight varies according to the application. In high-risk industries, human-in-the-loop (HITL) and human-on-the-loop (HOTL) methods allow humans to evaluate the decisions of an automated system, intervene when they observe a problem, and reverse the outcome of an automated process if necessary. These approaches enable humans to maintain ultimate accountability for decisions, which is critical to ensure that automated systems do not replace human decision-making. Unquestionably, the guidelines and basis for intervention should primarily use objective criteria, not just subjective opinions, to determine when to act. To clearly define when intervention occurs, there should be uniformity in the protocols for intervening, as well as criteria for when intervention needs to happen, notifications to inform decision-makers when intervention is warranted, and escalation procedures specifying who must intervene in what order. By standardizing the response process and having clear definitions of each step in the process for all parties involved, the uncertainty associated with each situation is reduced, and uniformity in how to respond is achieved.

7.4.3 Auditing and Independent Evaluation

The auditing of AI systems can be performed objectively by following independent processes that objectively evaluate autonomous AI systems, as many organizations do not fully assess their AI systems internally. An independent audit can help identify any hidden biases, performance limitations, and governance issues that are present within the AI system and have not been uncovered by the organization itself. The audit may also evaluate other aspects of the AI system, including data integrity, model performance, decision outcomes, and compliance with relevant ethical and legal standards. Regular auditing of AI systems will create accountability by documenting the actual content of an organization's governance commitments (Cath et al., 2018).

In applications of AI that have significant consequences for human beings, the results of the audits will influence decisions concerning the ongoing deployment, modification, or termination of the AI system. As such, audits should be considered formal instruments of governance rather than token activities to build trust in AI systems and create institutional accountability.

7.4.4 Incident Reporting and Response

When effectively administered systems fail, ethical risk management must have clear event reporting and response protocols. An event can consist of poor judgment calls, discriminatory outcomes, breaches of security, or issues related to safety. Organizations must create avenues for stakeholders (i.e., users, operators, and affected individuals) to voice their concerns without fear of retaliation. Once an issue is identified, the organization's responses (i.e., how the organization investigates and documents the incident and implements corrective actions) are addressed using established response protocols. In addition to preventing incidents, they are important to learn from because they continue to promote improvement and the establishment of corporate responsibility (Floridi et al., 2018).

7.4.5 Harmonizing Governance with Regulation and Organizational Culture

Statutory requirements and organizational principles guide the development of the governance framework. There is an increasing emphasis on documentation, risk categorization, and oversight regarding the use of autonomous artificial intelligence

(AI) technology imposed by new legislation, especially where the technology presents a high level of risk to society. Entities that embrace these requirements within their Internal Governance Frameworks will be in a better position to comply with and receive ethical reviews of their AI technology (Veale & Zuiderveen Borgesius, 2021). Ethical AI governance should not be limited to compliance checklists. To effectively govern an ethical AI strategy, it must be part of the business culture through leadership commitment, training, and the creation of well-defined accountability frameworks. This allows the ethical AI strategy to be part of the decision-making processes on a day-to-day basis rather than as something that is separate from business functions.

7.5 CASE STUDIES ON AUTONOMOUS DECISION-MAKING FAILURES AND ACQUIRED INSIGHTS

In understanding the ethical risks posed by autonomous AIs, the study of case studies is critical, as it helps illustrate the potential issues faced by an autonomous AI system. Generally, we use the study of real-life incidents of failure to explain concepts such as transparency and accountability. The case studies below illustrate how ethical issues emerge in real-life situations and affect the appropriate use of decision-making systems that rely on the autonomy of AI.

7.5.1 Autonomous Decision-Making in Healthcare

Increasingly, artificial intelligence systems are being introduced into healthcare to enhance diagnosis, risk assessment, and treatment prioritization. These AI systems provide consistency, timeliness, efficiency, and reliability; however, their failure to accurately predict risks can adversely affect patient outcomes. The use of historical healthcare data to build clinical risk prediction instruments has also been criticized. In some cases, algorithms did not accurately reflect the level of health risk for some patient populations because of the use of historical healthcare expenditure data as a surrogate for medical necessity. Owing to historical inequities in access to care, these AI systems have learned patterns based on systemic bias instead of clinical risk. The ethical failure in this situation is not due to a failure of AI technology itself, but rather a decision made by developers to use a proxy variable that appeared to be appropriate but included an implicit societal bias. The lack of transparency with respect to data selection and testing among demographic groups resulted in an ongoing risk of bias in this study.

Lessons Learned:

- Proxy variables for data must be thoroughly evaluated for ethical implications, in addition to prediction accuracy.
- Healthcare AI systems must be evaluated and monitored for biases in different population groups.
- Transparency in the data sources used and the assumptions made is necessary to provide clinical accountability.

7.5.2 Autonomous Systems in Criminal Justice and Law Enforcement

The introduction of autonomous decision-making tools to the criminal justice system for purposes such as the evaluation of risk and predictive policing of crime has assisted in decisions regarding bail, sentencing, and the distribution of patrol officers. These assessment instruments disproportionately classified individuals from underrepresented communities as "high-risk" because the data used to create these instruments were derived from arrest and law enforcement records, which reflected long-standing structural inequalities rather than actual crime rates. The ethical issue is related to scale and authority. The decision to classify individuals as lower or higher risk using automated decision-making tools is executed uniformly and has institutional legitimacy. Automated tools may limit an individual's ability to understand and challenge the outcome of any determination.

Findings include:

- Automation amplifies the societal biases captured by historical data.
- The need for transparency at the level of decision-making in a system with an effect on an individual's legal rights; and
- Autonomous decision-making tools may not replace human decision-making regarding an individual's liberty and due process rights.

7.5.3 Autonomous Vehicles and Safety-Critical Determinations

Automotive autonomy is an example of an ethical question raised by safety-critical systems that require further investigation. Safety-critical systems require rapid decision-making capabilities in complex and uncertain environments. Consequently, insufficient information provided through sensors and decision-making by machines, as well as a lack of adequate oversight by humans, can lead to severe consequences. Investigations into autonomous vehicle accidents have revealed that individual companies bear partial responsibility for these failures. As a result, consumers received inadequate information and developed unreasonable expectations of the product. The distribution of accountability among the various components of the overall system is challenging. If the cause of failure is unclear, it may be hard to learn from it, and public trust may fall.

Lessons Learned:

- When establishing human oversight responsibilities, it is important that the assignments be practical and clearly defined.
- The development and use of safety-critical autonomy necessitate a cautious approach to the development and supervision of this class of technologies and systems.
- Accountability must be assigned to the entire system lifecycle, not just at the time of failure.

7.5.4 Integrative Ethical Insights from Case Studies

The case studies presented here exemplify common ethical trends across many disciplines. First, many cases of failure are not purely technical errors but rather due to poor design and governance decisions. Second, the lack of transparency limits the ability of affected individuals and organizations to contest or correct the automated results. Third, the absence of accountability results in weakened responses to harm and delays in remediation. Collectively, these case studies support the assertion that we have already identified ethical risks associated with autonomous AIs, many of which are preventable. A strong governance structure, significant openness, and a well-defined accountability system can greatly reduce the likelihood of adverse events and their resultant impact.

7.6 PRACTICAL GUIDELINES FOR THE ETHICAL IMPLEMENTATION OF AUTONOMOUS AI

Ethical standards play an important role only when they guide the development and use of independently operating artificial intelligence systems. To help companies reduce the ethical risks of creating autonomous agents while preserving their commercial benefits, this report outlines the specific steps that companies should take. These guidelines do not belong to any single category of technology or industry and can therefore be adapted to various situations.

7.6.1 Clearly Define Purpose and Boundaries

Before an autonomous AI system is put into action, AI must be clearly defined by outlining its intended purposes, the types of autonomous decisions it can make, and identifying which areas require human involvement and which do not. Multiple issues arise when we use AI outside its intended design context. A solid boundary will also minimize the risk of misuse and ensure that we do not become overly dependent on using automated decisions in inappropriate circumstances (Floridi et al., 2018).

7.6.2 Designate Accountability Prior to Implementation

Prior to a system transitioning into an operational state, the responsibility must be distributed. This includes identifying the individuals responsible for each design aspect, such as data selection, deployment timing, and ongoing oversight once the system becomes operational.

Responsibility should be clearly defined so that companies can quickly act on any identified errors and maintain significant accountability. Vague responsibilities often allow ethical concerns related to an outstanding error to be shifted away from the company instead of being eliminated, which adversely affects confidence and the ability to take corrective action (Cath et al., 2018).

7.6.3 Incorporate Transparency into System Design

To be effective, transparency should be treated as a foundational design concept rather than a bonus. This means that as much information as possible has been retained regarding the assumptions made during model creation, where the training data came from, what limitations there are regarding performance, and what risks have been identified with that model.

For transparency to work in practice, access to model outputs must be provided in a way that can be evaluated from multiple perspectives. The explanation of outputs will not necessarily involve providing detailed descriptions of the technology used to create them but will allow users or those affected by them to supervise, appeal, and make informed decisions (Arrieta et al., 2020)

7.6.4 Assessment for Bias, Safety, and Contextual Relevance

To ensure that autonomous technologies operate at optimal performance, assessments should include evaluations of accuracy, bias, robustness, and safety in real-world settings. Testing will include various types of datasets, such as scenario testing, which simulates the environment in which the automation systems will operate, allowing for the identification of any potential detrimental effects before they are launched into the market. The evaluation of an automated system is an ongoing practice that must be conducted regularly. An automated system that changes over time based on input data requires continued assessment for fairness and safety as the contextual environment continues to change (O'Neil, 2016).

7.6.5 Guarantee Significant Human Supervision

Human oversight is necessary for autonomous AI systems to function properly, particularly when safety is at risk. Oversight mechanisms should allow for human observation and intervention with respect to automated decision-making when appropriate, as well as enable the human operator to reverse automated decisions made by the system in certain circumstances. An effective oversight mechanism should implement a clear procedure for escalating decisions made by the system based on a specific context rather than the personal discretion of the decision-maker. This ensures a uniform response from all decision-makers and a rapid response to any erratic or malfunctioning behavior by the system (Russell, 2019).

7.6.6 Implement Monitoring and Incident Response Protocols

After the launch of an automated or autonomous product or system, an organization has a continuing obligation to monitor the product's or system's operation for degradation in performance, unusual behavior, and emerging risks (Winfield & Jirotka, 2018). Developing a systematic way to report and respond to incidents can allow an organization to learn from its failures and prevent them from recurring. By treating an incident as an opportunity to improve rather than assigning blame for it, an organization is more likely to develop a reliable and ethically sound automated or autonomous system.

7.6.7 Synchronize Practices with Legal and Regulatory Standards

Regulatory regimes increasingly require documentation, risk evaluation, and oversight of autonomous AI systems. Consequently, to comply with applicable regulations and maintain public accountability, organizations must integrate internal governance into the evolving regulatory framework. Rather than viewing regulatory requirements as restrictions on the organization, meeting ethical standards in accordance with legal requirements will provide increased quality of their systems and greater public trust (Veale & Zuiderveen Borgesius, 2021).

7.6.8 Consider Ethics as a Continuous Organizational Obligation

The ethical applications of technology surpass the need for technical safety measures alone. The practical use of autonomous or AI technologies is greatly affected by educational support for users, the commitment of leaders to being role models in the use of such technologies, and the type of corporate culture established by those who lead an organization (Floridi et al., 2018). Ethics should be considered a continuing and evolving responsibility for organizations as they continue to create and implement new technologies, rather than simply a list of tasks to complete before using or implementing them (Floridi et al. 2018). By viewing ethics this way, organizations can adapt to changing risks and societal norms as they arise (Floridi et al., 2018).

7.7 CONCLUSION AND PRINCIPAL INSIGHTS

AI autonomous technologies represent the advancement of academic research to real-world applications. They represent an entirely new way of creating, tracking, and deploying technology, including how people have historically interacted with it and the potential risks it poses to society. The autonomous decision-making capabilities associated with these systems could allow organizations to implement large-scale solutions with minimal human supervision. However, this also alters the organizational dynamics between humans and machines regarding trust, control, and responsibility. Many of the ethical considerations associated with autonomous decision-making technologies outlined in this chapter are driven more by how we design, manage, and use them than by their inherent autonomy. This chapter highlights that we can predict many ethical risks associated with autonomous decision-making technologies. For example, the combination of unclear accountability, limited transparency, biased outcomes, reduced user autonomy, and privacy concerns can lead to ethical dilemmas, especially when developing systems for real-world deployment without establishing appropriate boundaries and governance. These ethical risks are not inevitable; they usually stem from design process shortcuts, insufficient documentation, or dependence on automation devoid of human oversight. Many ethical dilemmas associated with autonomous decision-making technologies can be addressed through transparency and accountability; however, transparency and accountability must be addressed through practical, real-world applications rather than abstract concepts. Documentation, traceability, decision-making rationales, and well-defined accountability frameworks assist companies in understanding how their systems perform in the real world and in responding appropriately when they encounter problems. Without these processes, companies' ethical obligations to these systems are largely symbolic and impossible to enforce. The case studies in this chapter show that autonomous decision-making technologies are not solely responsible for most failures. They are the result of decisions concerning how to use data, train users, and where to deploy systems. These examples illustrate the importance of lifecycle governance, continuous monitoring, and human oversight (especially in critical sectors such as healthcare, criminal justice, and transportation). Ultimately, this chapter illustrates that ethical oversight is not a one-time requirement but an ongoing process. The continuous development and evaluation of frameworks to establish system objectives, assign accountability, assess bias and safety, and develop response plans for incidents require continuous investment from organizations to support ongoing development and periodically evaluate how these systems develop and the impact they will have on society.

- Proper design and oversight can mitigate the ethical risks associated with autonomous decision-making technologies.
- Transparency cannot simply clarify technology; instead, it is needed to provide opportunities for accountability, evaluation, and contestation.
- Accountability must be established throughout the entire lifecycle of an AI system to ensure accountability.
- Human oversight is critical for making decisions regarding rights, safety, and long-term consequences.
- Organizational culture, governance, and technical design have equal impact on the ethical implementation of these systems.

As technology continues to develop, so must the decision-making processes associated with it. Ultimately, the way to ensure responsible autonomy is to eliminate the possibility of individual human involvement while continuing to develop the capacity of individuals to design, develop, and manage these technologies effectively. This requires an ongoing commitment from organizations to facilitate this process, and it is equally important to continue supporting it to promote public trust in these systems and align autonomous AI with human and social objectives.

REFERENCES

Arrieta, A. B., Díaz-Rodríguez, N., Del Ser, J., Bennetot, A., Tabik, S., Barbado, A., García, S., Gil-López, S., Molina, D., Benjamins, R., Chatila, R., & Herrera, F. (2020). Explainable Artificial Intelligence (XAI): Concepts, classifications, opportunities, and problems in the pursuit of responsible AI. *Information Fusion*, *58*, 82–115. https://doi.org/10.1016/j.inffus.2019.12.012

Cath, C., Wachter, S., Mittelstadt, B., Taddeo, M., & Floridi, L. 2018. The stance of the US, EU, and UK towards artificial intelligence and the ideal society. *Science and Engineering Ethics*, *24*(2), 505–528. https://doi.org/10.1007/s11948-017-9901-7

Danaher, J. (2019). *Automation and Utopia: Human prosperity in a labor-free society.* Harvard University Press.

Floridi, L., Cowls, J., Beltrametti, M., Chatila, R., Chazerand, P., Dignum, V., Luetge, C., Madelin, R., Pagallo, U., Rossi, F., Schafer, B., Valcke, P., & Vayena, E. (2018). AI4People—An ethical framework for a beneficial AI society: Opportunities, risks, principles, and recommendations. *Minds and Machines*, *28*(4), 689–707. https://doi.org/10.1007/s11023-018-9482-5

Gebru, T., Morgenstern, J., Vecchione, B., Vaughan, J. W., Wallach, H., Daumé III, H., & Crawford, K. (2021). Datasheets for the datasets. *Communications of the ACM*, *64*(12), 86–92. https://doi.org/10.1145/3458723

Lipton, Z. C. (2018). The mythology of model interpretability. *Communications of the ACM*, *61*(10), 36–43. https://doi.org/10.1145/323323

O'Neil, C. (2016). *Mathematical weaponry: The manner in which big data exacerbates inequality and jeopardizes democracy.* Crown Publishing Group.

Russell, S. (2019). *Human compatibility: The challenge of controlling artificial intelligence.* Viking.

Veale, M., & Zuiderveen Borgesius, F. (2021). Clarifying the proposed EU Artificial Intelligence Act. *Computer Law Review International*, *22*(4), 97–112. https://doi.org/10.9785/cri-2021-220402

Winfield, A. F. T., & Jirotka, M. (2018). Ethical governance is crucial for establishing trust in robotics and artificial intelligence systems. *Philosophical Transactions of the Royal Society A*, *376*(2133), 20180085. https://doi.org/10.1098/rsta.2018.0085

Zuboff, S. (2019). *The era of surveillance capitalism: The struggle for a human future at the new frontier of authority.* Public Affairs.

8 Navigating Regulation and Governance in Generative AI

8.1 OVERVIEW

As GenAI continues to become increasingly complex, there are now greater needs for establishing effective governance and regulation (Brundage et al., 2018). Instead of the previous generations of artificial intelligence (AI) where systems could easily be understood, GenAI operates in very complex sociotechnical systems, is trained on vast amounts of data, and generates results that cannot be explained with a transparent process to the user. To add to these risks, GenAI also involves methods of computing that do not use determinism to provide results and therefore cannot provide a level of accountability for any identified impacts. As a result, GenAI's many issues create problems for traditional regulatory mechanisms, which rely almost exclusively upon supporting determinism and providing accountability.

As a direct result of this lack of predictability due to GenAI's opaque nature, existing legal frameworks have not provided a solution to the need for a comprehensive governance model that integrates the legal, ethical, and technical standards associated with GenAI (Calo, 2020; Floridi & Cowls, 2019). Presently, the global regulations for GenAI vary significantly, with the European Union leading because of its recently implemented AI Act based upon a risk-based regulatory framework, while the United States has opted for a more voluntary sector-specific regulatory approach to GenAI regulation. Additionally, several countries such as China are attempting to implement a state-mandated regulatory model for AI governance, which takes into consideration issues of national security and socio-political agendas (Taddeo & Floridi, 2018). The difference between these global regulatory approaches is extremely divergent and creates many challenges in creating globally consistent rules due to differing political ideologies, commercial structures, and cultural values. As GenAI models begin to traverse borders, this disparity in regulation will create opportunities for jurisdictional arbitrage and exploitation. Furthermore, simply having national regulatory strategies will not address the fundamentally global implications of GenAI, such as misinformation campaigns, synthetic identity theft, and cross-border data transfers. These challenges illustrate the need for globally aligned governance mechanisms based on democratic accountability and multilateral cooperation. Although organizations such as UNESCO, OECD, and G7 have begun creating high-level principles to guide AI policy development, most of these

DOI: 10.1201/9781003679974-8

efforts are advisory and non-binding (UNESCO, 2021; OECD, 2019). To develop effective regulatory frameworks for GenAI, we must transition from principles to enforceable and interoperable policy. This chapter explores these topics through three interrelated objectives. It provides an in-depth review of the current regulatory frameworks addressing AI industry regulation. It addresses the role of ethical principles (such as transparency, equity, and human oversight) in shaping governance. Finally, it provides an analysis of several important case studies that illustrate new methods of regulating AI and collaboration on a global scale. This chapter aims to bridge normative aspirations with institutional realities by providing a blueprint for a responsible governance framework for GenAI that promotes the protection of human rights.

8.2 THE PRESENT STATE OF AI REGULATION

AI regulation, especially that of GenAI, represents a complex, developing, and often ambiguous regulatory body. Each government is trying to attain the right balance between encouraging new ideas and making sure there are enough protections in place, which leads to many countries having different laws about how much they will regulate and enforce these rules, as well as the reasons behind those laws. These differences reflect not only the types of technologies being developed but also the political beliefs, economic interests, and values that drive their growth and development. Therefore, it is critical to understand these differences to properly evaluate the strengths and weaknesses of existing governance models and the possibilities for convergence at the global level.

8.2.1 The European Union: Leading in Risk-Based Regulation

The EU has placed itself at the forefront of establishing a comprehensive regulatory framework with its proposed AI Act, which groups artificial intelligence (AI) according to its level of risk, from minimal to unacceptable. GenAI systems are considered medium- or high-risk, including foundational models such as GPT and generative image-generating systems (Image Generators), which will be required by law to meet various standards, including transparency and documentation, and have post-market surveillance for the regulation of these products (European Commission, 2021). The proposed AI Act indicates a shift toward a rights-based approach, introducing social and ethical values such as human control over machines, anti-discriminatory practices, and safety in the legal context. Some believe that the regulatory process behind the AI Act may be too rigid and no longer allow for any flexibility in what are rapidly evolving technologies or the unexpected impacts of GenAI (Veale & Borgesius, 2021).

8.2.2 The United States: Sector-Specific and Decentralized Regulation

The United States utilizes a decentralized approach with sector-specific regulations predominantly based on existing laws and voluntary guidance from various industry groups. Among these groups is the NIST, which has created an AI Risk Management Framework that provides non-binding guidance regarding Transparency, Reliability, and Privacy. Additionally, several Executive Orders from the White House have been issued directing Federal Agencies to develop governance frameworks for AI and establish a prioritization of safety, civil rights, and innovation in AI.

However, the United States does not yet have any overarching AI statutes; therefore, the implementation of the regulations (as described) is different across all 50 states and various industries in the United States. Owing to the current state of this regulatory environment, critics have argued that there is not enough protection against the negative consequences of the implementation of GenAIs, particularly concerning misinformation, biometric surveillance, and job discrimination (Binns, 2018).

8.2.3 China: Governance Centered on the State and Focused on Security

The Chinese government has enacted a state-oriented approach to the regulation of AI (and thus, the broader landscape of AI development) by integrating the governance model for GenAI into their larger strategic and geopolitical agendas. The Cyberspace Administration of China (CAC) passed new laws regulating generative AI on March 12, 2023, which require developers to evaluate the security of their offerings, provide information about the origin of the data they use, and operate in accordance with principles related to socialist ideology. The approach to artificial intelligence (AI) and Generative AI by the People's Republic of China focuses primarily on ensuring China remains secure, maintaining harmony in presenting it while at the same time controlling digital information being presented to individuals, which is very different from a rights-based model as it would be in one of the western Liberal Democracies. Although such laws have been successful in enforcing compliance with the ideology of the Chinese government, they also have created barriers to the ability of individuals to express themselves freely and have provided little opportunity for the general public to participate in a discussion about the creation and usage of AI technologies and have established an example of how to prevent dissent. This illustrates the conflict underlying the state's control of AI and the concept of pluralism or ethical plurality in the context of AI governance (Taddeo & Floridi, 2018).

8.2.4 Innovative Frameworks: Canada, Singapore, and the United Kingdom

Canada, Singapore and the UK are also beginning to implement hybrid and adaptable regulatory frameworks for AI and data, with Canada passing its AI and Data Act (AIDA), which establishes a risk-based compliance framework for AI developers and also provides the Privacy Commissioner with the enforcement authority to ensure compliance with AIDA (Government of Canada, 2022); Singapore's

Model AI Governance Framework utilizing a co-regulatory approach through the creation of voluntary toolkits and industry-specific guidelines to build trust and increase adaptability (IMDA, 2020); and a sectoral regulator (e.g. healthcare/finance) being responsible for enforcing AI compliance with existing laws in the UK. Each of these specific regulatory frameworks demonstrates an increasing recognition that common regulatory frameworks are an inappropriate method of regulating increasingly complex technological products, such as GenAI; therefore, the use of an anticipatory regulation strategy will enable the development of flexible regulatory frameworks that adapt with the evolving nature of technology and society.

8.2.5 Principal Obstacles in the Regulatory Framework

GenAI's growing volume of activities has created problems. The type of framework that is needed to audit and explain GenAI models has yet to be developed, and as a result, these types of frameworks are unable to accomplish this because GenAI models are often treated as black-box systems. There has been a high level of technological advancement, and legislative and regulatory developments have not kept up with technology, making it difficult for organizations to meet any regulatory requirements that currently exist. In addition, developers can take advantage of the difference in regulations around the world by setting up shops in other countries where there are lower or no regulations and therefore not meeting the standards of international regulation (Figure 8.1).

The necessity of countries and regions to work together to create and maintain good governance systems as well as to follow through with democratic principles and reduce the impact of large-scale global threats due to technological changes can be highlighted by addressing these significant hindrances to introducing new governance models.

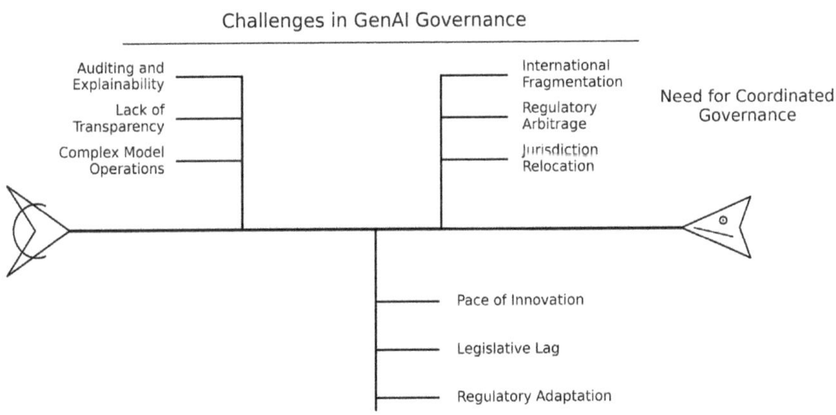

FIGURE 8.1 Obstacles to effective governance of GenAI. Source: Authors.

8.3 THE SIGNIFICANCE OF ETHICAL GOVERNANCE

The legal framework provides an overall structure for the monitoring of AIs; but ethical governance must accompany that structure. Because GenAI is becoming increasingly prevalent and affecting how individuals and society are making decisions and shaping opinions, the need for ethical principles in their design, application, and assessment is even more necessary. Ethical governance is defined as a collection of standards, conversations, and values that will ensure that AI systems are built to operate in alignment with human values, social justice, and the collective good (Floridi & Cowls, 2019).

8.3.1 Transparency: A Fundamental Element of Democratic Oversight

The most significant aspect of transparency regarding the GenAI system is providing an open process to the user for training the models. There are many variables to take into consideration when looking at transparency, including how the model was trained, what data was used to train it, and what risks were associated with both training the model and producing the respective output from the model. Having an appropriate level of transparency will help all stakeholders make informed decisions about whether to accept, challenge, or reject an algorithmic decision made by an algorithm without a human directly involved in the decision-making process. If transparency becomes inadequate for end users (policymakers, developers, etc.), those end users will eventually not have access to this transparency and create an explosion of confusion which is referred to as the "black box problem" (Burrell, 2016). The ethical mitigations required to govern GenAI will require using interpretability (explainability) as a tool of ethical governance; therefore, the model's output will need to be rationalized in a stakeholder (end user) understanding. This is especially important in areas that may impact human life, such as healthcare (i.e., medicine) and criminal justice (i.e., crime), finance, etc. Nevertheless, achieving this level of transparency within the language model still presents tremendous challenges that must first be addressed through improved auditing methods for language models, improved interpretive methodology, and improved documentation processes (i.e., model cards and data sheets) (Mitchell et al., 2019).

8.3.2 Accountability: Correlating Authority with Obligation

The growing sophistication and independence of GenAI systems make it crucial to establish clear accountability measures for these new technologies, as there will be more examples of adverse consequences resulting from their use in the future. Unlike other software, which is deterministic in nature (i.e., it produces the same result given the same inputs), GenAI systems create novel content and produce non-deterministic results. Therefore, determining who is accountable for the results produced by these systems is likely to be more complex than previously thought. To help solve this problem, attempts to create ethical guidelines for GenAI development include algorithmic impact assessments, restitution for individuals adversely affected by these technologies, and assigning organizational accountability to those who develop and deploy them (Rahwan et al., 2019). In addition, assigning individual responsibilities is preferable to diluting individual accountability. Thus, GenAI system developers, platform operators, and end users have ethical duties proportional to their ability to cause harm to others. Therefore, institutions developing these technologies should establish internal ethical review boards and a charter for ethical AI development as a mechanism for instituting accountability throughout the AI technology's lifecycle.

8.3.3 Equity and Non-Discrimination

It appears that Generative AI technologies will replicate and magnify social inequities reflected in their training datasets. For example, if the training corpus consists of historical documents, Generative AI may have learned to encode racial, gender, and cultural stereotypes (Bolukbasi et al., 2016). Ethical governance of AI technologies should establish that fairness is both an ethical framework and a necessary criterion for designing and evaluating AI technologies.

To achieve this, generative AI systems should be continuously monitored for the possibility of producing disparate impacts owing to biased training data and the application of restrictions that create fairness during the generative AI training phase. The evaluation of generative AI models must also involve testing from multiple perspectives, including those of members of various populations or groups that have historically been the target of discrimination and bias.

Fairness must also be defined on a contextual basis, as it is defined mathematically and cannot be evenly distributed among different cultures (Binns, 2018).

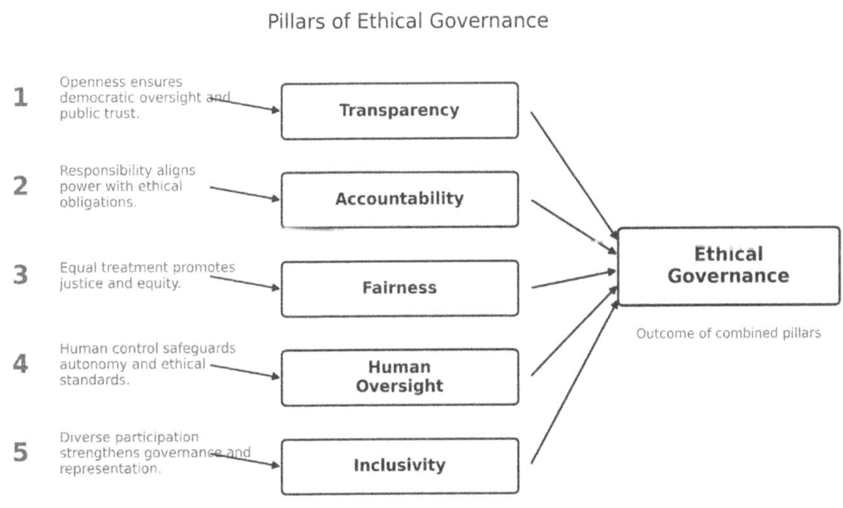

FIGURE 8.2 Pillars of Ethical Governance (Source: Authors)

8.3.4 Human Supervision and Autonomy

Ethical governance ensures that people continue to have agency over their decisions, especially with the use of GenAI technology in education, media, and government. This technology can enhance human agency rather than eliminate it. Humans must identify and evaluate GenAI-generated materials before disseminating them to the public. This will help mitigate the risk of manipulation, cascading effects on the public, and erosion of public faith (Zuboff, 2019). Ultimately, the European Commission's High-Level Expert Group on Artificial Intelligence and the ABA's ethical guidelines are aimed at establishing adequate means of placing humans in the decision-making loop of AI-based (artificial intelligence system) decisions while ensuring that humans have sufficient oversight over the decision-making processes of these systems and can hold them accountable (European Commission, 2019). Therefore, these guidelines provide for the necessity of having appropriate mechanisms to prevent AI from becoming an unaccountable black-box system while retaining human authority to make independent decisions.

8.3.5 Inclusivity and Stakeholder Engagement

The essential components of ethical governance are participatory design and inclusive deliberation. To that end, information for decisions regarding GenAI deployment should be gathered from a broad coalition of stakeholders (including marginalized communities, civil society and subject matter experts) who wish to participate in the GenAI decision-making process. To make the process of assessing the impact and legitimacy of society's actions clear, public engagement techniques such as citizen juries, algorithmic impact assessments, and ethical review boards will clarify context-specific issues and enhance the legitimacy of actions taken by society (Morley et al., 2020). Without inclusive governance, there is a significant possibility of narrow elites utilizing AI to promote their values and interests throughout the world. In this regard, ethical oversight should not only ask, "What works well?" but also, "Who does it work well for? At what cost?"

8.4 GLOBAL COLLABORATION AND THE NECESSITY FOR INTERNATIONAL AI REGULATION

As GenAI technology does not have physical borders, it necessitates a worldwide cooperative approach to be successful in its use. While traditional industrial innovations have primarily affected localized communities where they originated, GenAI technologies will influence various communities worldwide, regardless of their development location, because these systems are trained using global data and shared through cloud computing systems. For instance, Africa could use a North American Large Language Model (LLM) to help with education, Europe could use an LLM to moderate content, and Asia could use an LLM to help with customer service. The worldwide reach of GenAI creates enormous potential but also poses profound governance challenges, including legislative fragmentation, diverging values, and the ability of some countries to benefit ethically from the advances made by others (Cihon, 2019).

8.4.1 The Issue of Fragmentation and Regulatory Arbitrage

AI regulations at the national and regional levels are driven by various social and political systems, as well as by differing conceptions of what constitutes effective governance. For instance, the European Union's AI Act focuses on protecting human rights and adopts a risk-based approach to regulation. In comparison, the United States will use a more sectoral approach for AI self-regulation, while in China, GenAI will be required to adhere to ideologically based preservation of content (Mozur et al., 2023). As a result of these different regulatory approaches, a fragmented regulatory system exists that permits multinational developers to take advantage of regulatory arbitrage by developing their products in jurisdictions that do not impose strict regulations. Fragmentation caused by varying regulatory approaches to AI compromises developers' ability to comply with ethical practices throughout their development across numerous, sometimes conflicting, legal frameworks. An additional issue with the absence of alignment across borders is the inability to hold developers accountable for their use of AI, the lack of sharing best practices in the development of AI, and the protection of fundamental human rights, including data privacy and algorithmic transparency (Winfield and Jirotka, 2018).

8.4.2 Multilateral Institutions and Their Functions

To address the problems associated with AI governance, international organizations have begun to build broad principles and frameworks for collaboration on AI governance. In 2019, the Organisation for Economic Co-operation and Development (OECD) played a leading role in developing broad principles for the development of artificial intelligence (AI). It produced detailed guidelines that provide guidance on how to create an effective, equitable, and transparent AI system (OECD, 2019). More than 40 countries have signed the principles, now using them as a framework for their national strategies. UNESCO's 2021 recommendation for the ethical use of artificial intelligence, which is built on a common global ethical framework that includes human rights, sustainability, and inclusiveness, is an important move toward creating a wide set of universal ethical principles for AI. This calls for global cooperation to prevent technologies that incorporate AI from exacerbating poverty or diminishing the cultural heritage of different nations. The Hiroshima G7 Process (established in 2023) aims to address the specific challenges posed by large-scale algorithmically generated texts and foundation models through the creation of agreements to govern and monitor their safety, governance, and transparency. As highlighted by these developments, there is increasing international recognition that unilateral regulation of technological activity that occurs globally is no longer viable or acceptable.

8.4.3 The Necessity for Binding, Interoperable Frameworks

Many international instruments allow providers of such technologies to take advantage of them for personal and business purposes. However, these instruments are still primarily non-binding legal agreements or recommendations that operate based on the goodwill of countries that wish to develop their own national security policies in line with them. As a result, they are currently limited in the degree to which they will impact a provider's conduct and a state's ability to develop national security policies regarding an artificial intelligence system that does not have any uniformity across jurisdictions (Cath, 2018). To hold states accountable and avoid ethical collapse, we must move beyond principle-based regulations and develop a harmonized, enforceable framework that incorporates cross-border statutory sandboxes, mutual recognition agreements for AI systems, and possibly binding international treaties on AI ethics and governance comparable to existing international treaties on cybersecurity, nuclear non-proliferation, and climate change.

Interoperability must also extend beyond compliance with these legal obligations and include developing a unified framework governing documents, risk classifications, and audits. A prime example of efforts to provide international standards for AI is ISO/IEC JTC 1/SC 42; however, efforts to develop these standards have been considerably disparate and heavily biased toward the Global North.

8.4.4 Comprehensive and Fair Global Governance

Global governance structures are necessary for all values, needs, and risks to be represented equally across the globe. Currently, there are no standards bodies for GenAI creating standards in developing countries; thus, there is a large imbalance between what is prioritized by different entities based on their individual needs, values, and risks. Without international representation of those most affected by AI, it will continue to cause harm (Mohamed et al., 2020). To reduce the potential risk of digital colonialism, multilateral institutions must create participatory opportunities and empower low- and middle-income countries, Indigenous populations, and civil society. This can occur through funding capacity building, investment in better accessibility to technology, and developing infrastructure necessary to ensure adequate representation during international discussions around AI.

8.5 REGULATORY CASE STUDIES

To learn about effective ways to regulate generative AI (GenAI) we will examine case studies of different governance models from around the world. These models represent various levels of development, different ways they enforce their rules, and their ethical frameworks. This paper compares three examples: the European Union's Artificial Intelligence Act, Canada's Artificial Intelligence and Data Act, and the Singapore Model AI Governance Framework. Each of these provides a different way to address the difficult balance between innovation and risk management and how to provide ethical oversight. These three case studies offer practical illustrations of how to apply institutional, legal, and cultural differences to the governance of GenAI technology.

8.5.1 Case Study 1: The European Union's AI Act—A Proactive Rights-Based Framework

The European Union (EU) proposed Artificial Intelligence (AI) Act is the largest effort to build a legal structure through legislation to regulate AI cross sectorally. The AI Act was a new piece of legislation created in 2021 that applied a classification system based on risk to AIs and provided regulations based on the level of risk. Additionally, the AI Act includes regulations for various aspects of GenAI systems (a.k.a., foundational AI models and general-purpose AIs), including but not limited to safety measures, transparency, and human oversight (European Commission, 2021).

The AI Act requires GenAI providers to inform people about AI-generated content, provide summaries of the training data they have used, and have some type of technical protection mechanism in place to prevent illegal results. The AI Act indicates the European Union's (EU) strong commitment to transparency, accountability, and protection of human rights in accordance with the Charter of Fundamental Rights. Many critics of the AI Act argue that it will be unable to provide enough flexibility to accommodate rapidly changing technology and that it will create an unreasonable burden on small inventors and companies. In contrast, the AI Act serves as a demonstrable example of democratic governance by showing how large and comprehensive laws can work with innovation, particularly when these laws are created inclusively and responsively (Veale & Borgesius, 2021).

8.5.2 Case Study 2: Canada's Artificial Intelligence and Data Act (AIDA)—A Risk-Based Compliance Framework

In Canada, the Artificial Intelligence and Data Act (AIDA) was created under Bill C-27 in 2022 to allow for a shift in the way artificial intelligence (AI) creates and influences human and automated systems (GenAI) through a compliance-driven and risk-based approach. The AIDA provides fewer specific definitions of what constitutes "high-impact" AI instances compared to a multi-tier hierarchy used in the European Union (EU), which provides clearer directives related to the obligations of businesses that design or utilize "high-impact" AI. In addition, the AIDA establishes requirements for AI Developers to create monitoring mechanisms to identify the actual or potential threat that AI systems pose; establish that an AI created by an AI Developer is explainable; and evaluate the effect of AI on marginalized populations. In addition, the AIDA establishes an independent AI and Data Commissioner responsible for ensuring compliance with the AIDA and for the enforcement of penalties for non-compliance; thus, it represents one of the most robust examples thus far in successfully combining ethics and regulation through an iterative policy development process.

8.5.3 Case Study 3: Singapore's Model AI Governance Framework—Co-Regulation and Soft Law

Singapore has created a non-binding, structured framework for: Co-Regulation and Industry Engagement. This is called the Model AI Governance Framework and was created by both: The Infocomm Media Development Authority (IMDA) and the Personal Data Protection Commission (PDPC). This framework contains all the universal benchmarks that define how AI should be deployed and operated in an accountable and responsible manner, including: Transparency; Explainability; Robustness; and Accountability. Rather than creating regulatory frameworks based on ethical considerations, Singapore is attempting to empower firms to create responsible AI by providing them with tools to succeed, which include Toolkits; Sandboxes; and Best practices/Guides for Creating Responsible AI. The particular focus of these guidelines is on the necessity for human oversight. Additionally, they require that all results from any type of AI (including generative) must have the ability to be checked and understood. These guidelines further require that explainability be incorporated into the AI product design architecture and consider the concept of Contextual Justice in developing AI products. Many have criticized the model for being non-binding, and therefore an insufficient approach to AI governance. However, the model has been praised for fostering trust through discussion rather than by using coercive means. Moreover, this method allows for quicker iterations by allowing regulatory bodies and developers to redefine governance structures based on the ebb and flow of technology advances. Singapore's soft-law strategy has made it synonymous with being one of the world's foremost leaders of Innovation in AI ethics and policy (Chander, 2021).

8.5.4 Instructional Lessons and Comparative Insights

The three models are similar in their assessments of risk; however, they diverge in how they conduct the assessment. All three models contain a wide range of risk assessments, but each country (EU, Canada, and Singapore) has also developed a unique way to assess risk. The degree to which each country has implemented its regulations through legislation differs significantly. The EU has enacted legally binding regulations, Canada conducts investigatory monitoring and will only monitor compliance if there is concern for regulatory compliance or lack of compliance, and Singapore has no legal obligation for compliance on the part of its respective stakeholders. The concept of ethical pluralism contrasts with regulatory minimalism, as it espouses multiple norms for evaluating an entity and allows for the opportunity to achieve maximum regulatory compliance. Based on the EU experience, the EU provides an environment whereby regulators can develop robust regulations through the incorporation of ethical norms into the regulatory framework of the respective jurisdictions, whereas Singapore is characterized by providing regulatory flexibility to address specific business circumstances through a more pragmatic approach. Ultimately, the three case studies indicate that there is no universal model for GenAI governance. Therefore, the opportunity for regulators to effectively address and develop a hybrid framework incorporating both strong enforcement measures (with appropriate regulatory oversight) and flexible participatory processes through regulatory trials demonstrates their ability to adopt an environment conducive to the development of a regulatory framework that can effectively guide the development of GenAI.

8.6 CHALLENGES AND CRITIQUES OF EXISTING GOVERNANCE MODELS

The growing awareness among countries and organizations regarding the importance of regulating GenAI has led to the emergence of several governance frameworks; however, there are several institutional, technical, and philosophical barriers that adversely affect the effectiveness of these early-stage frameworks. In addition to being practical barriers, these barriers highlight a fundamental contradiction between innovation and regulation, transparency and authority, and global collaboration and autonomy. This section evaluates existing regulatory frameworks based on five interrelated viewpoints: legal inertia, technical opacity, regulatory capture, ethical relativism, and global imbalances.

8.6.1 Legal Inertia and the Velocity of Innovation

A major problem with artificial intelligence (AI) is that it cannot keep up with the rapid pace at which technology is evolving. This means that AI regulation typically ends up being a long, drawn-out, regimented activity that is based on the long-standing legal approach of "the linear model of technological advancement." In contrast, generative AI (GenAI) has been developed and improved at an unprecedented pace. Basic models of GenAI (currently) increase by orders of magnitude within a few months after their initial introduction to the market (Bommasani et al., 2021). Consequently, regulatory agencies take an increasingly long time to develop regulations that have little or no relevance as soon as they are introduced to the market. In addition, many current regulatory laws are not specific enough to provide guidance on how to address the hazards associated with generative AI, such as synthetic media manipulation, the distribution of deepfakes, and content hallucinations (Crootof & Ard, 2021).

8.6.2 Technical Opacity and the Constraints of Explainability

Most GenAI systems operate as opaque entities, making decisions through the interplay of numerous intricate parameters and training sets that are exceedingly challenging to elucidate or comprehend, even for their developers. Thus, it is impossible to maintain the standards of transparency, auditability, and due process (Burrell, 2016).

While the field of explainable AI (XAI) has developed as a research area, the methods currently available are often limited and only provide approximate or post hoc explanations that do not satisfy the legal or ethical requirements of many critical areas. The lack of transparency associated with these systems inhibits accountability, making it impossible to determine the intent, cause, or liability for the harm caused.

8.6.3 Risk of Regulatory Capture and Corporate Self-Regulation

Businesses are becoming more reliant on cooperating with government agencies for AI regulation as they develop their products. Companies that are cooperating with governments are leveraging these relationships to ensure the creation of AI regulatory frameworks in multiple government jurisdictions that reflect their interests as opposed to being established to enhance societal welfare through regulation (Zuboff, 2019). When no actual enforcement mechanisms exist to enforce voluntary commitments or ethical charters, there may not be genuine accountability for the effects of those commitments or charters being ineffective forms of normative action, particularly when self-regulation is promoted as a solution (Pasquale, 2015).

8.6.4 Ethical Relativism and Absence of Normative Coherence

The increasing number of AI ethical guidelines across the globe varies significantly with respect to their core concepts. There are numerous interpretations of the ideas of fairness, trust, and human-centeredness across a variety of cultures, legal systems, and political systems, leading to inconsistencies on a normative basis. Because there is no shared moral lexicon to support these various interpretations, it is challenging to create a common understanding of AI, which ultimately impacts the legitimacy of the AI governance structure. For instance, in Western democracies, a commitment to freedom of speech can conflict with the current state of restrictions on the content allowed on GenAI systems in countries governed by authoritarian regimes. As a result of the continuing inability to establish common ethical standards, interoperability continues to be an aspiration rather than a reality (Cath, 2018; Fjeld et al., 2020).

8.6.5 Global Disparities and the Threat of AI Colonialism

The way we now govern technology is set up in a way that keeps alive the inequalities between technologically advanced and technologically disadvantaged countries worldwide regarding technical capability, development of standards, and formulation of policies. Stakeholders in the developed world, primarily the United States, the European Union, and China, heavily influence most current regulations related to GenAI. In contrast, low- and middle-income countries (LMICs) have very little influence on the policy-making process. Digital colonization occurs when AI systems built on culturally influenced layers of big data are used in different parts of the world without adequate localization, representation, or accountability. Furthermore, many LMICs lack the necessary frameworks to use or implement AI safeguards appropriately. Therefore, populations living in LMICs may be exposed to an unfair or disproportionate amount of risk without any benefit from AI use (Mohamed et al., 2020).

8.6.6 Advancing Reflexive, Inclusive Governance

The challenges posed by GenAI indicate that the future of governance needs to be responsive to change; as such, there is a greater need for a governance model that is adaptive to advancements in technology. Currently, regulatory approaches take one form and are often viewed as finalized products. However, the development of regulatory strategies should involve continuous development through the incorporation of stakeholder feedback and testing the effectiveness of these strategies over time. The role of international organizations is equally important, as they represent multiple views on regulation and allow stakeholders from all areas of society to participate in developing and supporting regulations. A reflexive governance approach views the regulation of technologies as a continual learning, adaptive, and innovative system that responds to the impacts of social changes caused by GenAI.

8.7 PROSPECTIVE TRAJECTORIES: ADVANCING ADAPTIVE AND INCLUSIVE AI GOVERNANCE

The effective regulation of GenAI will require a shift in regulatory frameworks from traditional "prescriptive" and "static" methods of regulating GenAI toward regulatory systems that are dynamic (i.e., adaptable), inclusive (i.e., adaptive), and agile (i.e., responsive) to the ongoing evolution of GenAI technologies. To achieve this, the way we evaluate the governance of GenAI will have to be changed from a "static" model that focuses on prescriptive compliance with rules and regulations to a "dynamic" approach that considers multiple ethical points of view and applies technology to solve problems as they arise (for example, GenAI), engages stakeholders, and fosters institutional resilience (i.e., institutional capacity to adapt to changing conditions such as GenAI), among other things. Therefore, to assure future generations of effective governance of GenAI, we need to develop an anticipatory approach to the governance of GenAI that is a set of anticipatory policies, procedures, and structures so that our future governance of GenAI will have an adaptable structure and an empowered democratic process for implementation (as part of a broader governance framework).

8.7.1 Adaptive Regulation and Anticipatory Governance

Anticipatory governance has become an effective method for creating rules and regulations for new technologies (especially those that change quickly and unpredictably) rather than traditional forms of governance. It employs several techniques, such as developing foresight methodologies, scenario planning, and prototyping public policy, to minimize the risk of harm while also encouraging innovation to proceed in an ethical manner (Guston, 2014). Unlike a retrospective compliance model, where the focus is on regulatory compliance after harm has occurred, anticipatory governance focuses on the pre-regulatory setting of social norms and institutions prior to the occurrence of harm. In the case of GenAI, anticipatory governance will likely include the use of regulatory sandboxes in which innovators can test their models under controlled conditions, with the support of ongoing auditing systems to monitor their performance while deployed. Additionally, owing to the rapid pace of technological advancement, these systems should be designed to be iterative in nature; as such, the instruments used to govern GenAI will need to evolve alongside the development of new technologies through continuous feedback and learning.

8.7.2 Collaborative and Multi-Party Governance

Democratizing AI governance requires inclusive dialogue and participatory policy-making processes. Generally, the governance systems currently in place are established top-down, either by governmental bodies or by leading engineers. The socioeconomic impacts of GenAI mean that new governance models must incorporate diverse lived experiences, including those of people who have historically been marginalized and excluded (Leins et al., 2020). Citizen assembly processes, algorithmic impact assessments, and the development of public consultation platforms to facilitate transparency in AI governance and build legitimacy are incorporated into the governance structure of generative AI. The Canadian government has developed an Algorithmic Impact Assessment Tool that mandates the release of all automated decision-making systems utilized in the federal government to the public, along with an assessment of the risks associated with their use, to ensure transparency. This framework can also be applied to GenAI applications (Government of Canada, 2020). In addition, generative AI governance can be aided by multi-stakeholder entities, including representatives from the government, civil society, academia, industry, and international organizations. This approach allows for the reconciliation of conflicting interests, fills gaps in technical expertise, and creates added legitimacy in AI governance. This approach is particularly important in multinational settings, as they face a wide range of challenges, including differences in ethical standards and disparities in resources, when developing AI standards.

8.7.3 Establishing Global AI Governance Frameworks

To create a worldwide governing system for GenAI, such as the International Atomic Energy Agency, formal laws (rather than just recommendations) governing GenAI are required. While there are currently several initiatives (OECD AI Principles, UNESCO AI ethics proposals, and the G7 Hiroshima Process) that provide normative direction, they do not provide any authority to enforce compliance. Global communities should consider developing formal governance institutions (such as the International Atomic Energy Agency or Intergovernmental Panel on Climate Change) and create a governance system that will develop nationally appropriate regulations relating to GenAI (Cihon et al., 2021). To this end, we recommend establishing an International AI Observatory, possibly linked to the United Nations. This observatory would provide oversight on the development of generative AI, conduct annual risk assessments for generative AI development, and develop coordinated responses to global threats such as disinformation campaigns and synthetic identity fraud. Consideration must be given to developing a governance system that allows for democratic participation and inclusion of the Global South, in addition to preventing any one country or region from monopolizing the technology. Creating an internationally recognized interoperability framework, which includes a standardized process for auditing models, safety criteria for testing AI systems, documentation standards for data used to train AI models, and accountability standards for AI algorithms, is essential to ensure cohesive and equitable enforcement across all countries worldwide. The need to establish a cohesive regulatory framework for generative AI is particularly critical for established foundation models, which are most often deployed across multiple platforms, languages, and nations.

8.7.4 Ethics by Design and Technological Alignment

Ethics by design refers to the requirement for ethical considerations to be integrated throughout the entire GenAI life cycle, from data acquisition, model creation, and deployment to post-market follow-up. This creates an environment where ethical social science, engineering, and policy-making professionals can work collaboratively to develop sociotechnical (rather than purely technical) solutions for GenAI systems. To implement ethics by design, organizations should consider employing some or all of these techniques: identification of bias and inequity within the training process; providing clear documentation, such as the use of datasheets and model cards; creating red teams and using hostile testing to uncover unwanted behaviors; and designing explainability layers and establishing human-in-the-loop verification points. These methods ensure that ethical alignment becomes a core tenet of the GenAI architecture rather than an ancillary aspect or afterthought.

8.7.5 Empowerment and Worldwide Inclusion

Fair governance of GenAI requires a focus on building capacity in developing nations. Due to a lack of access to education, technological infrastructure, and lawmaking capabilities, many countries currently find themselves passive consumers of imported AI technologies not knowing whether those technologies reflect their own values and needs (Brevini, 2021). By establishing global funding mechanisms (i.e., AI equity funds) and creating regional AI laboratories, we will be able to support the development of locally based innovation, infrastructure, research and development by developing and cultivating future generations of leaders, innovators, and regulators who will have the ability to engage in global conversations regarding how to regulate technology. To ensure inclusion in the governance of GenAI, we must expand the understanding of epistemic justice by allowing for the inclusion of different forms of knowledge systems, cultures, and ethical principles in the governance of GenAI.

8.8 CONCLUSION

The regulation of GenAI is transforming as GenAI becomes more complex and its effects on society increase in significance. The increased complexity of GenAI presents challenges to current regulatory regimes; thus, new frameworks must be developed that will facilitate the continued development of GenAI while still being compliant with ethical and legal standards. Furthermore, the regulation of GenAI must evolve along with the technology and future effects of GenAI; therefore, there needs to be an assessment of relevant regulatory developments in multiple jurisdictions, as well as identifying the core ethical standards and evaluating the institutional regulatory frameworks, so that recommendations for the creation of a more responsive and inclusive global system can be made to meet the needs of all affected parties. While modern regulatory frameworks are quite aspirational in their intent, they have struggled to develop due to stagnation in many jurisdictions, obstacles for developing new policy, inconsistent values, and the economic divides between nations. Singapore, Canada, and the European Union collectively illustrate that while there are no single regulatory structures for the effective monitoring of GenAI, hybrid approaches will need to be developed to balance both the compulsory legislative actions required and the inclusive participatory models that create a bridge between normative aspirations and their ultimate enforcement. Global cooperation will also be critical in the future. As AI technology is implemented globally, disparate national regulatory initiatives will not effectively address the multifaceted challenges and risks of GenAI, nor will they provide a consistent framework for international consensus on issues related to fairness, transparency, and accountability. The OECD, UNESCO, and G7 have all started to create multilateral frameworks to create a unified approach to the regulatory issues created by GenAI; however, for these organizations to be effective, they will need to continue evolving into binding regulatory structures with interoperability. The future of governance should use anticipatory regulations, ethics by design, and inclusive policy making in developing better governance, which will apply the latest technological solutions as well as reflect the cultural and institutional changes needed for democratic governance of technology in the future. The governance of GenAI must respond to current needs and ultimately believe that GenAI can provide a path forward for society while continuing to respect the values of human dignity, agency, and justice. In conclusion, creating a unified governance framework for addressing the potential risk posed by new technological development requires collective global action, and only through collective efforts can we create a successful governance model to regulate the risks associated with emerging technologies and ensure fair and responsible technologies. Through such efforts, GenAI can become a transformative force for society rather than simply accelerating or further entrenching current inequities.

REFERENCES

Binns, R. (2018). Fairness in machine learning: Lessons from political philosophy. *Proceedings of the 2018 Conference on Fairness, Accountability, and Transparency*, 149–159. https://doi.org/10.1145/3287560.3287583

Bolukbasi, T., Chang, K. W., Zou, J. Y., Saligrama, V., & Kalai, A. T. (2016). The relationship between a man and a computer programmer is similar to that between a woman and homemaker: Debiasing word embeddings. *Advances in Neural Information Processing Systems, 29*, 4349–4357. https://doi.org/10.48550/arXiv.1607.06520

Bommasani, R., Hudson, D. A., Adeli, E., et al. (2021). *On the opportunities and risks of foundation models*. Stanford Center for Research on Foundation Models. https://arxiv.org/abs/2108.07258

Brevini, B. (2021). *Is AI good for the planet?* Polity Press.

Brundage, M., Avin, S., Clark, J., et al. (2018). *The malicious use of artificial intelligence: Forecasting, prevention, and mitigation*. arXiv. https://doi.org/10.48550/arXiv.1802.07228

Burrell, J. (2016). How the machine 'thinks': Understanding opacity in machine learning algorithms. *Big Data & Society, 3*(1), 1–12. https://doi.org/10.1177/2053951715622512

Calo, R. (2020). Artificial intelligence policy: A primer and roadmap. *University of California Law Review, 107*(2), 399–435. https://doi.org/10.2139/ssrn.3015350

Cath, C. (2018). Governing artificial intelligence: Ethical, legal, and technical opportunities and challenges. *Philosophical Transactions of the Royal Society A: Mathematical, Physical and Engineering Sciences, 376*(2133), 20180080. https://doi.org/10.1098/rsta.2018.0080

Chander, A. (2021). Singapore's approach to AI governance: Soft law and co-regulation. *Harvard Journal of Law & Technology, 34*(1), 147–173.

Cihon, P. (2019). Standards for AI governance: International standards to enable global coordination in AI research & development. *Futures, 115*, 102475. https://doi.org/10.1016/j.futures.2019.102475

Cihon, P., Maas, M. M., & Kemp, L. (2021). Should AI governance be centralised? Design lessons from history. *Proceedings of the AAAI/ACM Conference on AI, Ethics, and Society*, 260–266. https://doi.org/10.1145/3461702.3462630

Crootof, R., & Ard, B. (2021). Structuring techlaw. *Yale Law Journal, 130*(5), 1225–1302.

European Commission. (2019). *Ethics guidelines for trustworthy AI*. https://digital-strategy.ec.europa.eu/en/library/ethics-guidelines-trustworthy-ai

European Commission. (2021). *Proposal for a Regulation of the European Parliament and of the Council laying down harmonised rules on artificial intelligence (Artificial Intelligence Act)*. https://eur-lex.europa.eu/legal-content/EN/TXT/?uri=CELEX:52021PC0206

Fjeld, J., Achten, N., Hilligoss, H., Nagy, A. C., & Srikumar, M. (2020). Principled artificial intelligence: Mapping consensus in ethical and rights-based approaches to principles for AI. *Berkman Klein Center Research Publication, 2020-1*. https://doi.org/10.2139/ssrn.3518482

Floridi, L., & Cowls, J. (2019). A unified framework of five principles for AI in society. *Harvard Data Science Review, 1*(1). https://doi.org/10.1162/99608f92.8cd550d1

Government of Canada. (2020). *Algorithmic Impact Assessment tool*. https://www.canada.ca/en/government/system/digital-government/digital-government-innovations/responsible-use-ai/algorithmic-impact-assessment.html

Government of Canada. (2022). *Digital Charter Implementation Act, 2022*. https://www.ic.gc.ca/eic/site/062.nsf/eng/h_00108.html

Guston, D. H. (2014). Understanding 'anticipatory governance'. *Social Studies of Science, 44*(2), 218–242. https://doi.org/10.1177/0306312713508669

IMDA. (2020). *Singapore's model AI governance framework* (2nd ed.). https://www.imda.gov.sg/resources/press-releases-factsheets-and-speeches/press-releases/2020/model-ai-governance-framework

Leins, K., Balding, C., & Halpert, E. (2020). Artificial intelligence and the future of global development. *Third World Quarterly, 41*(4), 577–593. https://doi.org/10.1080/01436597.2019.1702637

Mitchell, M., Wu, S., Zaldivar, A., et al. (2019). Model cards for model reporting. *Proceedings of the Conference on Fairness, Accountability, and Transparency*, 220–229. https://doi.org/10.1145/3287560.3287596

Mohamed, S., Isaac, W., & Png, M. (2020). Decolonial AI: Decolonial theory as sociotechnical foresight in artificial intelligence. *Philosophy & Technology, 33*(4), 659–684. https://doi.org/10.1007/s13347-020-00405-8

Morley, J., Floridi, L., Kinsey, L., & Elhalal, A. (2020). From what to how: An initial review of publicly available AI ethics tools, methods, and research to translate principles into practices. *Science and Engineering Ethics, 26*, 2141–2168. https://doi.org/10.1007/s11948-019-00165-5

Mozur, P., Zhong, R., & Krolik, A. (2023, April 3). A new law in China seeks to regulate generative A.I. tools. *The New York Times.* https://www.nytimes.com/2023/04/11/technology/china-ai-rules.html

OECD. (2019). *OECD principles on artificial intelligence.* https://oecd.ai/en/ai-principles

Pasquale, F. (2015). *The Black Box Society: The secret algorithms that control money and information.* Harvard University Press.

Rahwan, I., Cebrian, M., Obradovich, N., et al. (2019). Machine behaviour. *Nature, 568*(7753), 477–486. https://doi.org/10.1038/s41586-019-1138-y

Taddeo, M., & Floridi, L. (2018). How AI can be a force for good. *Science, 361*(6404), 751–752. https://doi.org/10.1126/science.aat5991

UNESCO. (2021). *Recommendation on the ethics of artificial intelligence.* https://unesdoc.unesco.org/ark:/48223/pf0000380455

Veale, M., & Borgesius, F. J. Z. (2021). Demystifying the draft EU Artificial Intelligence Act. *Computer Law Review International, 22*(4), 97–112. https://doi.org/10.9785/cri-2021-220402

Winfield, A. F., & Jirotka, M. (2018). Ethical governance is essential to building trust in robotics and AI systems. *Philosophical Transactions of the Royal Society A: Mathematical, Physical and Engineering Sciences, 376*(2133), 20180085. https://doi.org/10.1098/rsta.2018.0085

Zuboff, S. (2019). *The age of surveillance capitalism.* PublicAffairs.

9 Developers' Responsibilities in Promoting Ethical AI

9.1 DEVELOPERS AS ETHICAL DECISION-MAKERS IN ARTIFICIAL INTELLIGENCE SYSTEMS

A growing number of developers have started to create AIs that assist with or influence various decisions related to employment, healthcare, public safety, access to services, and civic engagement. This phenomenon places the developer in a position of practical authority over AI that exceeds its technical employment. Developers' choices affect the implementation, data interpretation, result production, and prioritization of AI systems. Thus, AI research is not purely an engineering exercise; it is a process of ethical and social decision-making (Mittelstadt, 2019).

The point of distinction between AI development processes and traditional software development processes is that AI has access to all previous data. Furthermore, AIs will have unpredictable behaviors in environments that may vary greatly from previous data, making the outcomes much more difficult to change once they are implemented. Subsequently, even if the AI system's concept does not address ethics, a developer makes ethical decisions at every stage of the system's design, including the data used for development, the use of proxy variables, the goals pursued through the data, and the context in which AI will be implemented.

The requirement for developers to identify as ethical decision-makers shifts the responsibility from the abstract idea of "ethical AI" to the concrete and professional obligations of the developer. Where "ethical AI" envisions a morally perfect individual, ethical responsibility here means that the developer has a responsibility to predict foreseeable harm, adequately share the limitations of the product, and reject the development of systematic practices that disadvantage vulnerable individuals or groups.

9.1.1 Mitigating Harm Beyond Technical Malfunction

This is often understood as the duty to prevent the failure of safety-critical systems, and in AI systems, harm can occur even when the models work. A technically correct algorithm that applies to a biased model trained on a biased dataset can produce a biased output, discriminatory classification, or poor inference. Examples include the bias of automated hiring and screening technologies, whereby models learn the

DOI: 10.1201/9781003679974-9

gender/racial differences already present in human hiring decisions (Buolamwini & Gebru, 2018; Dastin, 2018). Harm is not merely a secondary issue; it is an inherent part of the design, resulting from choices that prioritize efficiency over equity. Developers take on the responsibility for everything from technical correctness to contextual harm, contemplating how their output will be interpreted, distorted, or magnified for different groups, and how to interrogate their definition of success and proxy variables (Bender et al., 2021).

9.1.2 Transparency as a Prerequisite for Accountability

While transparency is sometimes regarded as a value or ethical principle, for developers, it becomes a necessary condition of accountability. When the system behaves in an inexplicable or undocumented manner, it becomes challenging to determine who is responsible for specific issues, making it difficult to repair and foster trust.

Developers can increase transparency in both technical and non-technical ways. Explainability seeks to clarify why a model does or does not yield a particular output, and much of the work on transparency comes in the form of documentation: conveying intent (what the system is meant to do), provenance (where the data came from), and how the system is supposed to perform (what are its limits, what are its worst failures, and where it is erroneous). What are the dangers (Mitchell et al., 2019; Gebru et al., 2021)? Model cards and datasheets for datasets do not make every decision clear but rather make assumptions and limits clear.

It is also important to be clear about this uncertainty and the fact that it will continue to exist in the future. Far too often, users receive probabilistic forecasts and mistakenly treat them as outcomes, trusting that the system is correct and delaying their engagement. This poses a risk, especially in applications such as healthcare, finance, and criminal justice, where AI outputs may hold excessive decision-making authority (Lipton, 2018).

9.1.3 Ethical Agency and Professional Disagreement

Developers are often thought to be in the hands of companies. However, developers possess unique and privileged knowledge of the ethical implications of their skills. Therefore, they must stop, question, and reject ideas that pose known risks, even if they are institutionally and financially beneficial. The rebellion of Google employees against the abuse of AI for Project Maven is a beneficial example of developer dissent shifting the company priorities. This makes it evident that ethical responsibility in AI research is simultaneously personal and collective, relying on shared, understood norms of the profession and one that relies upon collective action (Wagner, 2018).

Dare I say, unless courage is? Individual courage is no match for unemployment and disgrace. Organizations must build enabling environments for ethical dissent, such as whistleblower hotlines, ethics review boards, and ethical leadership that sees ethical concerns as part of proper engineering rather than walls of sludge holding back innovation. We hold people accountable but do not assign them specific tasks or responsibilities.

9.2 INTEGRATING ETHICS THROUGHOUT THE AI DEVELOPMENT LIFECYCLE

Ethical AI development cannot be achieved through selective design choices or post hoc compliance testing. Ethics must be integrated throughout the development lifecycle, influencing not only what problems to solve but also what data to curate, how to train and deploy models, and how to monitor system performance over time. Developers must understand that ethical responsibility is cumulative in nature: it constrains the space of options in initial decisions, and minor technical decisions can have outsized societal impacts as systems scale. We present ethical integration not as a restriction on innovation but as a system maturation discipline that increases resilience, legitimacy, and longevity.

9.2.1 Ethical Anticipation in Problem Identification and System Architecture

Before any model is trained, ethical choices are often incorporated; the framing of a problem determines the results we prioritize, the people we consider, and the boundaries around the trade-offs. Without embedding ethical considerations into the framing layer, technical fixes cannot cure deeper faults (Selbst et al., 2019). Developers can apply ethical insights ex ante to frame problems. Is automation advisable for this study? Who are the relevant recipients of this system? Stakeholder mapping, value-sensitive design, and scenario analysis can turn implied into explicit measures (Friedman & Hendry, 2019). By framing predictive policing as a crime optimization problem, we ignore a host of other social problems that plague the problem space, such as past histories of excessive policing and the current root of trust. Developers using ethical foresight in the design stage can identify these early and push back against problems in deep layers that contribute to structural inequalities.

9.2.2 Data Curation as an Ethical Obligation

Data are not neutral inputs; rather, they reflect past practices, institutional agendas, and power structures. Where one chooses to source often influences how one collects labels or simply omits particular people or information for uses and purposes or for useful reuse. Changes in the data used throughout data curation for one project can have downstream consequences, affecting model system performance, and hence, risks and incentives. Thus, they should be considered a foundational ethical responsibility of AI developers, rather than, for example, a preliminary step (Paullada et al., 2021). Data responsibility entails obtaining permission and privacy consent, documenting data provenance, and scrutinizing the representativeness of the data for the individuals and contexts in which the systems are deployed. Annotation techniques are particularly worthy of study because human judgments are often encoded in how we label data with the utmost implications for their behavior, perception, and use of human behavior. Data ethics "failures" are thus evident in emotion detection and behavioral inference, but also more broadly when datasets are collected naively without concern for the context of use, producing misleadingly exoticized or culturally biased model outputs. This has led researchers to abandon the idea of data governance as a technoscientific duty and to consider it a design problem (Gebru et al., 2021).

9.2.3 Equity and Responsibility in Model Development

There are various causes of bias in an AI system, as these are all entangled: data distributions, modeling choices, optimization objectives, and evaluation metrics intertwine with one another. As a result, developers are primarily the ones who are tipped off to sources of disparity within training pipelines and how they can go about mitigating them.

Explanations of fair models cannot simply telescope down to overall accuracy numbers. Developers must measure relevant subgroups and trade off the beneficial objectives of their design, such as efficiency, fairness, and interpretability. Fairness-aware training approaches and post hoc auditing tools can help; however, developers should use their personal discretion on what disparities they can live with.

Model documentation is a manifestation of model accountability. We explain why we chose this model, why we did not use the alternatives, and how ethical issues affected the final design decisions for traceability. Running a model and having it answer questions is less complicated, and institutions are responsible for any adverse side effects of an AI system.

9.2.4 Human-Centric Assessment and Implementation

Even better-than-average ethical models can cause harm if they are not carefully embedded in the real world. A human-centered evaluation approach understands how humans make sense of, interact with, and respond to AI outputs. Developers can't just stay in "this model is technically beneficial" mode; they need to shift to "this model should explain itself here," "this model should be usable here," and "this model should be calibrated for trust here."

Human-centered evaluation approaches, such as usability studies, co-creation workshops, and limited releases, assist in identifying areas where a system falls short and where people over-rely on or misuse it (Amershi et al., 2019). In sensitive domains such as health, AI should augment human judgment rather than replace it. Developers must ensure that results are interpreted, uncertainty is communicated to the user, and suggestions are consistent with decision-makers' actions. If we overlook these aspects, we risk underuse, misuse, and naive trust, which can lead to ethical harm.

9.2.5 Ongoing Surveillance and Post-Implementation Accountability

Ethics does not end with deployment. Over time, changes in data distributions, human behavior, and social context can degrade performance or introduce new risks.

Therefore, developers should consider deployment as the start of their ongoing ethical obligations.

Post-deployment obligations include monitoring drift in system performance, auditing for creeping bias, and providing ways for users and those affected to provide feedback. Regular audits are crucial for any system operating in dynamic or high-risk settings, as life can quickly deteriorate from old assumptions (Wynants et al., 2020). By promoting this kind of thinking, ethics becomes a subject we learn and must continually review, rather than just a box to tick on our end-of-project checklist; ethics will evolve, like any other aspect, alongside technology and society.

9.3 ORGANIZATIONAL CONDITIONS FACILITATING ETHICAL AI DEVELOPMENT

The abilities or intentions of individual developers do not entirely determine the ethical fate of AI. The organization in which developers work influences, enables, or constrains their ethical decisions by determining the incentives they pursue, the priorities and tensions they face, the colleagues who mediate their work, and the powers and systems of governance that can undermine any ethical considerations that may arise in the process. A developer given ethical duty without the right kind of organizational environment—the right incentives, accountability, and a shared framework for doing things right—may find themselves confronted by difficult questions without sufficient space or power to answer them. Here, we discuss how to knit together organizations to create conditions in which developers can act primarily on ethical judgment as part of their technical work, rather than as a risky and unusual case.

9.3.1 Ethical Instruction as Professional Proficiency

Many AI engineers learn to be technical experts without being adequately prepared to recognize and address ethical risks; as a result, legal or policy teams come to see ethical risks as a separate constraint sitting outside the context of the system they are building. Organizations can fill this gap by treating ethics as a component of professional skill. Successful tactics include embedding ethics in technical training, delivering scenario-based talks on real-world development issues, and pairing engineers with experts in the social sciences, law, or health. These techniques help developers view ethical risks as design problems rather than as theoretical ethical challenges (Greene et al., 2022). Embedded ethics initiatives demonstrate the ability to integrate ethical reflections into technical work processes without hindering technical development. Developers are more likely to engage with and apply ethics training in routine engineering decision-making.

9.3.2 Team Diversity as a Risk Identification Mechanism

Homogeneous development teams may overlook issues that primarily affect populations they do not represent. A diverse mix of gender, color, geography, discipline, and experience across AI teams increases the range of perspectives they contribute to the design and review. Diverse teams are better at spotting biased assumptions, querying narrow problem definitions, and predicting corner cases than homogeneous teams. Research has shown that systems built without awareness of linguistic, cultural, or demographic diversity often have unreliably high performance on different populations and often reinforce existing inequality (West et al., 2019; Koenecke et al., 2020).

Diversity is insufficient if the culture in the organization excludes minorities. Developers should feel free to speak up about problems, and children should have their voices heard. Psychological safety and diverse decision-making processes are key components of diverse teams.

9.3.3 Governance Frameworks That Facilitate Ethical Decision-Making

Formal organizational processes should encourage an ethical culture within organizations. In the absence of governance institutions, ethical thinking may collapse into informality, inconsistency, or call for some human initiative.

Having internal ethics committees, cross-functional decision bodies, and systematic points where ethical risks are weighed prior to deployment all help assess ethical hazards before production. When done well, these processes should not serve as bottlenecks for approvals but as forums for discussion, where developers can voice their concerns and document trade-offs (Metcalf et al., 2021).

Finally, ethical governance works better if it lives within development pipelines rather than existing as an external audit. Baking ethical reviews into agile cycles, model validation stages, or deployment approvals makes it more likely that they can fit in with traditional engineering processes.

9.3.4 Leadership, Dissent, and Ethical Responsibility

Organizational leadership also plays a significant role in ethical culture formation. Leadership that sees speed, growth, or commercial advantage as more pressing issues than a possible downstream effect on ethical issues is more likely to marginalize the issue. When leadership views ethical risk as a valid engineering issue, accountability appears to be more collective than placing all the blame on subordinates. Developers should have permission and empowerment to discuss ethical issues beyond the fear of retribution or adverse career impact, which could include protected reporting routes, known escalation pathways, and transparency in accountability leaks. Cases where developers publicly challenge companies for ethics/technology clashes are well-known examples where collective action affected the organization's operational decisions. We hope that everyday actions, not just extraordinary instances, will change exploitative organizations. A culture that facilitates cultural dissent does not stifle creativity but rather increases accountability and reduces the chances of spontaneous and damaging innovation disasters from do-it-all technology.

9.3.5 Ethics as an Organizational Practice Rather Than a Slogan

Organizations' perception of ethical delivery as a standard business function rather than a virtue signal ultimately determines the future of ethical AI. Codes of ethics, principles, and public pledges, without incentive structures, resource allocation, and accountability, come to little use. Organizations that are successful in developing ethical AI align KPIs with responsible outcomes, provide time and resources for ethical scrutiny, and reward the delivery of ethical leadership as a meaningful part of professional roles. In this situation, individuals are not required to choose between their ethical duties and the success of the organization; instead, they are rewarded for the outcomes of a mutually reinforcing relationship.

AI developers are no longer just engineers of technical systems. They shape choices in terms of decision rights, power allocation, and risk assignment. As AI systems become more autonomous and consequential, the importance of development decisions becomes increasingly grave. Here, we argue that ethical AI does not fall from the sky as an angelic idea, nor is it encoded in regulations or even noble goals; rather, it sits in the mundane decisions developers make daily and the messy conditions in organizations in which those decisions are embedded. We began by establishing the developer as an ethical decision-maker rather than an amoral implementer. Decisions regarding data, modeling objectives, performance measures, and contexts for use are not neutral. They embed basic assumptions about fairness, legitimacy, and permissible harm. Recognizing this basic truth is a welcome and essential starting point for accountability in AI development and deployment.

We then observed that moral accountability cannot be restricted to one period of the AI pipeline. Rather, ethics must be supported throughout the lifecycle of an AI system, from problem conception through data exploration and curation to model training, usage, and post-use monitoring. Decisions made at the design stage constrain options later in the process, and work lost to supervision and evaluation robs even the most well-intentioned systems of their potential. Treating ethics as an ongoing activity rather than a given action increases technical integrity and social legitimacy. Finally, we established that individual responsibility is insufficient. Developers work in organizations that shape incentives, minimize disagreements, and set boundaries on what is taken seriously. Building ethical AI relies on organizational conditions that foster ethical education and practice, promote diversity within teams, establish appropriate governance structures, and ensure that leaders value responsibility as much as innovation. Without such conditions, ethical responsibility shifts to those powerless to address the responsibility at hand. Collectively, these arguments establish that AI developers serve as ethical stewards of increasingly powerful systems rather than naive technologists. (Ethical stewardship does not imply moral purity or infallibility; rather, it requires alertness to harm, willingness to be challenged, dedication to documenting and rationalizing choices, and commitment to capturing learning opportunities from systems that fail.) As AI systems are applied in more organ systems of human life, their ethical future will be less determined by wishful thinking and more determined by developers' and companies' willingness to do the hard work of being serious about ethics.

REFERENCES

Amershi, S., Weld, D. S., Vorvoreanu, M., et al. (2019). Guidelines for human–AI interaction. *Proceedings of the 2019 CHI Conference on Human Factors in Computing Systems*, 1–13. https://doi.org/10.1145/3290605.3300233

Bender, E. M., Gebru, T., McMillan-Major, A., & Shmitchell, S. (2021). On the dangers of stochastic parrots: Can language models be too big? *Proceedings of the ACM Conference on Fairness, Accountability, and Transparency*, 610–623. https://doi.org/10.1145/3442188.3445922

Buolamwini, J., & Gebru, T. (2018). Gender shades: Intersectional accuracy disparities in commercial gender classification. *Proceedings of Machine Learning Research, 81*, 1–15.

Dastin, J. (2018). *Amazon scraps secret AI recruiting tool that showed bias against female applicants*. Reuters.

Friedman, B., & Hendry, D. (2019). *Value sensitive design: Shaping technology with moral imagination*. MIT Press.

Gebru, T., Morgenstern, J., Vecchione, B., et al. (2021). Datasheets for datasets. *Communications of the ACM, 64*(12), 86–92. https://doi.org/10.1145/3458723

Greene, D., Hoffmann, A. L., & Stark, L. (2022). Ethical AI as critique. *Proceedings of the ACM on Human-Computer Interaction, 6*(CSCW1), 1–29. https://doi.org/10.1145/3512938

Koenecke, A., Nam, A., Lake, E., et al. (2020). Racial disparities in speech recognition systems. *Proceedings of the National Academy of Sciences, 117*(14), 7684–7689. https://doi.org/10.1073/pnas.1915768117

Lipton, Z. C. (2018). The mythos of model interpretability. *Communications of the ACM, 61*(10), 36–43. https://doi.org/10.1145/3233231

Metcalf, J., Moss, E., Watkins, E. A., & Raji, I. D. (2021). Algorithmic impact assessments and accountability: The co-construction of impacts. *Proceedings of the ACM Conference on Fairness, Accountability, and Transparency*, 735–746. https://doi.org/10.1145/3442188.3445935

Mittelstadt, B. D. (2019). Principles alone cannot guarantee ethical AI. *Nature Machine Intelligence, 1*(11), 501–507. https://doi.org/10.1038/s42256-019-0114-4

Mitchell, M., Wu, S., Zaldivar, A., et al. (2019). Model cards for model reporting. *Proceedings of the ACM Conference on Fairness, Accountability, and Transparency*, 220–229. https://doi.org/10.1145/3287560.3287596

Paullada, A., Raji, I. D., Bender, E. M., Denton, E., & Hanna, A. (2021). Data and its (dis)contents: A survey of dataset development and use in machine learning research. *Patterns, 2*(11), 100336. https://doi.org/10.1016/j.patter.2021.100336

Selbst, A. D., Boyd, D., Friedler, S. A., Venkatasubramanian, S., & Vertesi, J. (2019). Fairness and abstraction in sociotechnical systems. *Proceedings of the ACM Conference on Fairness, Accountability, and Transparency*, 59–68. https://doi.org/10.1145/3287560.3287598

Wagner, B. (2018). *Ethics as an escape from regulation*. Amsterdam University Press.

West, S. M., Whittaker, M., & Crawford, K. (2019). *Discriminating systems: Gender, race, and power in AI*. AI Now Institute.

Wynants, L., Van Calster, B., Collins, G. S., et al. (2020). Prediction models for diagnosis and prognosis of COVID-19: Systematic review and critical appraisal. *BMJ, 369*, m1328. https://doi.org/10.1136/bmj.m1328

10 Future Directions
Toward Sustainable and Ethical AI Development

10.1 OVERVIEW

GenAI has moved on from the research laboratory to the secret corner of every social, institutional, and economic life we are familiar with. AI that can make for us some meaningful integration of text, believable images, audio, and code is now out there in places we are all using with millions of daily users. It assists us with our work, but it is already changing how we know, interpret, and do things. As generative models are widely deployed and generalized, the question of how they are governed grows urgent.

One of the challenges is progress itself; generative model updates come too thick and fast to be governed by regulators fast enough. Previous technologies were deployed piece by piece, but GenAI is a single click worldwide, fast to deploy, and often mysterious in the training data, design constraints, and intended use. This uncompromising speed of progress widens the gap between the competence of technologies and the institutions we have designed to safeguard risk, responsibility, and moral accountability (Brundage et al., 2020).

GenAI systems also obscure the line between tools and agents; they make some text that seems to be authoritative, creative, or prescriptive, but they are simply techniques. Their output is produced by matching statistical patterns rather than understanding or wanting. New challenges for trust show up when the output of generative systems is indistinguishable from what people produce. Mistakes and fabrications are "plausible, quickly produced and apologetic," and problems spread quickly, badly helped by tools designed to help and amplify dissemination. Understanding these generative systems involves going beyond the technical understanding. GenAI appears in messy sociotechnical situations where model behavior weaves through user expectations, institutional structures and cultures, and social norms. The choices made during the concrete design and rollout of the model have tangible consequences on how each generation can be relied upon or challenged by users, as well as how the model can be adjusted to change the results of the generated text. From this perspective, the necessary governance of GenAI involves less algorithmic control and more management of the conditions under which systems affect us (Rahwan et al., 2019).

In this chapter, we describe an approach to experimentally managing GenAI using foresight, ethical scalability, and inclusiveness. Looking not only toward more reactive regulation but also management that accounts for at least some of the critical

DOI: 10.1201/9781003679974-10

uncertainties, power imbalances, and long-term importance of AI, we recall GenAI in wider society and institutions to engage in reflections on the governance of emergent technologies to assist in building public trust and improving social welfare.

10.2 ENHANCING REGULATORY AND POLICY FRAMEWORKS

Robust regulatory and policy frameworks are necessary to ensure the responsible, equitable, and democratic development of GenAI. The patchwork of governance that currently exists is lagging behind the rapid development of technology, with many countries' national AI strategies prioritizing innovation, economic growth, or strategic competitiveness, sometimes at the expense of longer-term considerations for how AI will affect society. The increasing global reach of GenAI elements and actions, each with unique applications or uses, poses major challenges for international cooperation; an entity developing a GenAI system in one area may be distributing and utilizing that same system throughout the world within a short timeframe (Cihon et al., 2021). The broad nature of GenAI systems and the domestic nature of national regulations has resulted in significant gaps in regulation; regulations that were implemented to address a specific case often do not fully address how these same systems would function on a generalized basis. Specifically, governmental entities developing regulations for directed use of GenAI systems have created regulations that can be easily circumvented because they were developed based on a specific application at a specific location in a specific manner. The complexities created by the rapid emergence of unanticipated applications from GenAI systems will limit the effectiveness of the regulatory frameworks being developed for the GenAI systems because those regulations will become outdated very quickly after they have been developed and implemented. There has not been sufficient scholarly research into creating regulatory frameworks that are proactive, flexible, and integrated into institutional frameworks as well as national laws to address the chaotic or mutable nature of GenAI. These regulatory frameworks must be created to accommodate the undefined or unanticipated consequences of social behavior and perception of GenAI technology, as opposed to simply regulating against negative behaviors after they have occurred.

10.2.1 Proactive Regulation and Adaptive Governance

Traditional methods of regulation tend to only address the harm caused by technology after it has occurred. However, the deployment of GenAI systems can be particularly detrimental because society may not fully comprehend the potential harm they could inflict. Anticipatory regulation, or regulation that prioritizes foresight, early and continuous engagement, and updated learning throughout the technology lifecycle, promises to be an effective antidote to this challenge (Guston 2014).

Anticipatory governance aims to align the development of regulatory approaches with the paths of new technology rather than activating regulation after the fact of the technology alone. This involves considering multiple, sometimes risky, futures, including anticipating the potential harm and opportunities of new GenAI capabilities. Scenario analysis and design fiction methods can help policymakers recognize potential future uses of GenAI that could cause harm or abuse before they become entrenched.

The next step involves the "prototyping of policy." Law and ethics are tested in controlled environments to understand their efficacy and to brainstorm potential outcomes "before humans push the button." For instance, regulatory "sandboxes" for AI help developers and regulators alike understand how a "sandboxed" governance model for using GenAI in a particular real-world application area works before systems are used more widely. These systems also allow for mutual learning, where each group learns layer-by-layer from the other to further develop their systems with strategic ethical and legal implications in mind.

The third component of anticipatory regulation is the systematic iteration and reshaping of regulations in accordance with technological advancements. What is happening today: Static rules preventing the use of GenAI fall behind the rapid pace of innovation in GenAI's capabilities and applications "once in the wild." Dynamic governance requires a process for close understanding, review, reform, and "sunsetting" of regulations to prevent stale rules from getting stale.

The European Union's proposed AI Act is an example of an effort to vigorously institutionalize anticipatory regulation. Designed to ensure protective proactive power rather than reactive defenses, the Act organizes all AI systems according to a taxonomy of risk and requires high-risk systems to undergo assessment for conformity before they can go to market. Some note that this project contains real challenges due to GenAI's tendency to be "general purpose" and the burdens of catching harms of use that often follow deployment after the fact (Veale & Zuiderveen Borgesius, 2021).

Institutions must have the ability to adapt to dynamic governance. One of the principles should be that regulatory bodies are both transdisciplinary and nimble, allowing them to adapt to necessary policy changes, such as capturing new usage terms and preventing human/technology loss without being constrained by a lengthy political cycle. This may be achieved through the creation of rapid multi-stakeholder task teams, progressive technical standards for GenAI deployment, or adaptive licensing rules that evolve with promised societal feedback loops, evidence of harm, and emerging technologies.

10.2.2 International Alignment and Transnational Regulation

GenAI technologies have been created, deployed, and used worldwide. A single-language model developed in one jurisdiction can generate legal documents in another, assist disinformation efforts in a third, and be embedded in public services regulated under an entirely different framework. The international dimension renders national governance approaches inadequate and, in some cases, detrimental to the environment. Without international coordination, regulatory fragmentation is likely to occur. Importantly, diverse national norms can lead to inconsistent levels of protection, incentivize regulatory arbitrage, and push ethical responsibility to the most fragile regions of the globe. In this scenario, when governance failure occurs within one jurisdiction, the consequences of that failure can radiate well beyond its borders (Cath, 2018).

Globally coordinated, contextually relevant, and interoperable governance systems are required to address these challenges. Many global efforts are underway in this space, including the G7 Hiroshima AI Process, UNESCO's Recommendation on the Ethics of Artificial Intelligence, and the OECD's AI Principles. While these are important steps in the normative direction, most are based on voluntary compliance and lack the mandatory mechanisms to foster it.

There is growing awareness that soft law tools must be scaled up into more robust systems of international governance. One such avenue may be the proposed setting up of international conventions or treaties on AI, which could set out some basic ethical and legal principles for the development and use of GenAI, such as international agreements on climate change or cybercrime (Brundage et al., 2020).

Another possible direction may be the creation of global AI observatories and independent audit consortia that oversee the development of GenAI models, send real-time notifications when potential safety failures arise, and perform independent evaluations of high-impact systems, which allow for collective scrutiny rather than reliance on developer and company self-reporting.

Mutual Recognition Agreements (MRAs) as governance efforts may facilitate the acknowledgment of regulatory decisions across countries (e.g., safety certificates or audit results) and thereby minimize rework while ensuring that some degree of regulatory independence prevails in local countries. Such agreements involve holistic regulation.

Global alignment should not only react to current AI systems and how they are built and integrated into society but also address the existing uneven power dynamics, where many countries in the Global South lack the necessary institutional capacity, infrastructure, and political representation to shape global AI governance standards to their interests. If we do not take action to address this issue, the most technologically powerful entities may benefit from the design of global systems instead of the masses. Long-term investment in enhancing skills, sharing information through South-South cooperation, building a system of open-access infrastructure, and providing opportunities for the voices of marginalized people to be raised are all necessary to achieve inclusive and fair governance (Mohamed et al., 2020). For GenAI to produce benefits to all parties involved, lack of adequate global cooperation means that increased inequality and heightened geopolitical tension will occur because of GenAI. Improving national and international regulatory and policy frameworks is not only a problem of technology, but also a requirement for proper governance based on ethics and fairness.

10.3 EXPANDING ETHICAL CONSIDERATIONS IN AI ENGINEERING AND IMPLEMENTATION

As GenAI increasingly becomes integrated into real-world products and services, traditional forms of ethical supervision struggle to keep pace. Manual risk reviews, ad hoc ethics assessments, and one-and-done compliance checklists are functional but not set up for the scale and speed required for GenAI research. These systems are deployed continuously, updated on a rolling basis, and embedded in complex infrastructures across many companies and countries. Going forward, ethics supervision needs to be scalable and repeatable and should not be conducted through human-only assessments but by integrating ethical thinking into the engineering workflows.

The problem is not a lack of introspection or ethical awareness in the AI community but rather an agonizing gap between our systems of supervision and the technologies as they exist. GenAI can introduce slowly accruing, contextually contingent, and subtly nuanced risks (not to mention the familiar perils of hallucination and automation bias): bias amplification, misleading outputs, and emergent social harms. Thus, mitigating these risks is best achieved via techniques that integrate ethical thinking and technical work processes rather than keeping them apart. This means that upcoming technologies will integrate ethics directly into AI systems, be capable of automation, and ensure oversight and corporate accountability.

10.3.1 Automation of Ethical Audits and Risk Prediction

Companies are more frequently turning toward automated tools to conduct ethical auditing on a large scale to address ethical risks. Automated ethical auditing tools comprise software-based programs that allow organizations to monitor model behavior and changes made to models during their deployment, while also monitoring for potential negative impacts on society caused by the deployment of these models. These tools are designed to be used in conjunction with human judgment rather than replacing human judgment, providing extra insight for humans into the nature, likelihood, and scale of emerging ethical risks and highlighting ethical risks that are otherwise difficult to identify in a scalable manner during their deployments. The tracking of these types of ethical effects is accomplished with a set of tools specifically designed to track ethical impacts. The tools measure changes in model behavior over time, including monitoring the shifts that occur in output distributions, monitoring the performance gaps occurring in output outcome distributions, and monitoring the model's performance on various demographic groups because of the deployment of the model. In addition, an organization can provide real-time or near-real-time updates using dashboards to allow employers to monitor and address the unintended consequences a model may create before these potential impacts become widespread (Raji et al.,2020). Another area of growth in automated auditing tools is related to automated bias testing of models. Automated bias testers automatically examine a model's output for a variety of characteristics (e.g., gender or ethnicity) when it produces a result that is affected by sensitive characteristics, to provide evidence of discrepancies that do not appear in overall average performance statistics. Fairness is not the same as equity; both Fairlearn and AI Fairness 360 have been developed to illustrate the use of many definitions of fairness, with a focus on implementing fairness measurements so that they are consistent over time. While bias testing tools such as these have many benefits, they also require careful interpretation of their results since fairness measurement can involve trade-offs between multiple dimensions, and situational evaluations of fairness do not universally apply across all people.

Several new methodologies have emerged in the last several years that aim to further improve "predictive" governance by allowing organizations to anticipate ethical risks before deploying their models. By leveraging knowledge gained from previous model deployments, as well as using contextual clues to identify potential ethical risks, automated tools can predict future model behaviors. Within the literature on machine learning, AI systems are not just passive calculators, but rather active participants in complex social environments. Therefore, it is essential that as researchers explore the ethics of AI systems, they understand that AI will not be limited to defined or anticipated environments. Learning how to improve predictability and accuracy in understanding ethical risks will be important to developing models that will behave appropriately in complex sociotechnical environments (Rahwan et al.,2019).

One approach to addressing the ethical risks of deploying AI systems is the creation of "ethics-as-code" solutions. In this research study, we developed a new way to incorporate human ethics into any RL (reinforcement learning) agent by developing ethics-as-code methodologies through the application of formal, semi-formal, and computer science methods. Using an open-source toolkit designed to provide a framework for teaching ethical principles and values to any RL agent, we aim to design training programs that teach RL agents to predict appropriate behavior based on their original goals, but with the added constraint that the behavior will be based on ethical standards. We anticipate that through the development of ethics-as-code solutions, we will create an opportunity for any algorithm to develop a framework for establishing ethical values, including some form of virtue-based assessments of ethical behavior and some form of disgust toward unethical behavior (Arnold et al., 2017). Although automated ethical audits represent a positive step toward addressing the ethical risks of deploying AI systems, developing an automated ethical auditing process has many challenges associated with its development. One significant obstacle to developing automated ethical audits is related to access to the data necessary for conducting audits; many of these challenges also raise significant questions related to privacy and governance. Based on quantitative measurements, they may fail to address ethical questions that are, at their core, qualitative, core-sensitive, and context-dependent. Automated systems will be decision-support tools rather than dictating ethical decisions; they will broaden our attention rather than abolishing ethical choices.

10.3.2 Integrating Ethics into Development Pipelines

Though automated audit methods are necessary, they cannot stand alone as solutions. Implementing sustainable governance of GenAI necessitates incorporating ethical considerations into the AI engineering process, as opposed to simply retroactively adding or addressing them; ethics should be considered and integrated into the development cycle as a matter of course. The operationalization of ethics is typically viewed as a framework through which organizations can make the necessary changes in their policies, infrastructure, processes, and culture (Morley et al., 2021) for ethics to become an integral aspect of their day-to-day work. In order to do this successfully, it can be useful to incorporate ethical considerations during early phases of designing new items. For instance, the use of ethics checklists during design sprints can encourage design team members to think about harmful effects from the outset, who will be impacted by their solutions, and what potential negative outcomes may occur downstream from these projects, thus ensuring that ethics are considered early in the design process. Treating ethical concerns as part of determining overall success alongside technical features and performance (as opposed to treating ethics as just an additional consideration if time allows) will greatly enhance the industry's progress in this direction. Another example of an innovative method for integrating ethics into ML and AI engineering workflows is providing ethics-informed version controls. Like software engineering, many ML initiatives cannot proceed without a complete version history of all prior versions; thus, having written documentation about ethics trade-offs, assumptions, and risk evaluation for every model and dataset version is beneficial. This appropriate documentation increases institutional memory; therefore, others will have reference points that increase understanding about the type of decisions made and why. A third technique is to employ typical technical integrations of ethical behavior into existing technical systems/processes. Adding explainability modules, safety, and fairness models directly into CI/CD will ensure automatic and deterministic ethical evaluations; if ethical evaluations are built into normal quality assurance, they are more likely to survive the production grind. Various tools in the industry reflect these concepts. Model cards and other formats for documenting fairness can allow companies to report constraints on models and their intended use cases, as well as risks, in a consistent format across the page cycle. By making the ethical thought process explicit and documentable, they build transparency for companies internally and for their audiences.

Collaborative approaches that incorporate all perspectives into the creative process (whether collaboration between engineers and ethicists or between domain experts and other representatives of affected communities exposed to the model's outputs) also highlight specific local dangers that are difficult to identify through technical exploration alone. This is especially true for GenAI systems, the meaning of whose outputs can be radically adjusted based on the (cultural, linguistic, and social) norms of a given situation.

Ethics does not need to result in moral boilerplates. It involves creating controlled situations where people feel validated to recognize, discuss, and document ethical problems. Organizations that reward ethical clarity and responsibility in technology skills will create an environment for responsible innovation.

By explicitly and visibly bolting ethics onto infrastructure through measurable interventions, organizations might bake ethics-driven GenAI development without stifling innovation. This will often create more trust among end users, regulators, and partners.

10.4 MITIGATING THE RISKS ASSOCIATED WITH SYNTHETIC CONTENT AND MISINFORMATION

A major challenge of GenAI is the rapidity of the ability to create synthetic media such as photos, videos, text, and voice recordings that closely resemble (mimic) human-created media. Improvements to generative models now allow large-scale content creation of extremely convincing CGI with little technical knowledge (in case of further use). While these capabilities help with creativity, accessibility, and personal expression, they also pose major threats to democratic institutions, public trust, and the integrity of our collective systems of knowledge (Rastogi et al., 2022; Weidinger et al., 2021).

Synthetic content can cause harm by undermining our ability to determine which things are genuine and which things are false. The proliferation of GenAI will subject our information ecosystem to greater risk from aggregated misinformation, identity stripping, and bot-driven influence operations. To effectively deal with these issues, a governance strategy is needed that will create a governance framework to enhance systemic resiliency and accountability to build a credible, long-lasting relationship based upon trust. The following sections will provide ideas on how future research and governance processes can respond to the risks associated with digital manipulation, truth decay, and synthetic disinformation by focusing on the social and institutional components of trust regarding AI-generated content.

10.4.1 Deepfakes, Misinformation, and Public Confidence

Generative AI is enabling hyper-realistic creation of synthetic media. Deep fake manipulated versions of audio or video of real people are being produced with ease using commercially available tools and limited computing power. As a result, the production of false audio and video is on the rise and includes instances of purposely fraudulent (financial) use; generation of non-consensual images of real persons for sexual or criminal purposes; and widespread generation of political disinformation and false reputational depictions of real people (Weidinger et al., 2021).

The problem created by generative AI misinformation is beyond the usual undertaking of debunking an individual instance, as the magnitude and pace of false information combined with the illusion of legitimacy and credibility contribute to cascading threats to public trust. Sustained exposure to incorrect but credible information results in disassociation and exhaustion, a phenomenon described as "truth fatigue," leading ultimately to feelings of disillusionment due to constant questioning regarding the existence of truth. Individuals who experience repeated uncertainty about the truth will experience fatigue leading to a breakdown of the common social fabric of trust and connection. Additionally, generative AI poses both asymmetrical threats by using synthetic information to create targeted influence and manipulation of individuals and non-state actors; e.g., interfering with elections, increasing polarization among political groups, and spreading disinformation in the areas of health and science communication. Generative AI also enables decentralized efforts to conduct coordinated and systematic misinformation campaigns with little or no investment in physical assets.

The widespread availability of deepfake technologies provides plausible deniability to public figures who deny involvement with false representations and statements about real events. Instances of publicly available video footage (created with AI) negate the credibility of both actual and false occurrences. Therefore, generative AI is facilitating increased opportunities for deception and limiting accountability (Chesney &

Citron, 2019). To mitigate these threats, a robust system of governance will be required. Governments may leverage technical methods to detect manipulation via anomalies in language, visual artifacts, or signs of synthetic information as part of their media forensic strategy to validate and verify information. In addition to supporting and promoting public awareness of technology and digital literacy, the capability to effectively utilize critical thinking skills to assess the information being presented, identify manipulated information, and identify trusted sources of information will improve the capacity for all users to discern valid from invalid information. Legal actions can provide deterrents against generative AI; however, any changes to laws regarding impersonation, consent, or defamation that provide an impediment to the manipulation of synthetic media require corresponding modification to ensure enhanced deterrents and accountability. The development of synthetic media has the potential to yield an ongoing arms race between developing generative AI and adversarial actors who use automated methods to detect generative AI as future generative models continue to improve.

Governance systems that effectively enhance the integrity of information will be required overall. Transparent governance over social platforms from the industry, independent auditors, autonomous regulatory bodies, and increased governance and standards for information integrity from trusted institutions are necessary to restore and maintain clarity. The goal is not to eliminate synthetic media, as it serves numerous purposes, but rather to strengthen the resilience of information systems against state media manipulation.

10.4.2 Authenticity Framework and Digital Provenance

As GenAI blurs the line between true and false, the future of trustworthy digital communication may depend on authenticity infrastructure, the technical and institutional infrastructure through which users can determine if and how digital content has been altered and by whom. Rather than relying on post hoc detection, this emerging class of infrastructure introduces a trust chain for the media to provide users with the tools they need to interpret its meaning.

Digital provenance is a key concept in this framework. Provenance systems allow users to confirm who or what was responsible for the creation and any subsequent alterations to a piece of digital material by digitally signing the creation, editing, and distribution of content. One way to do this is to embed content credentials directly into a piece of media, with information such as who created it, when and how it was edited, and what changes were made (Adobe, 2022). If widely adopted, such credentials allow viewers to determine the origin of a piece of content and then assess the alterations from there.

Alternatives explore other means of blockchain-based verification, where the digital fingerprints of materials are stored on immutable ledgers to build tamper-proof audit trails. Meanwhile, industry efforts, such as the Coalition for Content Provenance and Authenticity (C2PA), aim to standardize media authentication on various platforms, devices, and production tools.

A news image with C2PA-compliant credentials allows you to verify its origin, determine whether it has been changed, and identify its creator or modifier. Using this type of approach to this problem may result in a greater sense of trust in what can be achieved when trying to identify the origin of a piece of content. Showing where a piece of material originates from or its history rather than concealing it gives the end user increased confidence that it is credible and reliable. Although this kind of trust could be generated, there are many obstacles to establishing provenance systems. For example, if provenance systems are being extensively used, they will require some degree of interoperability among potentially hundreds of millions of digital devices, social media platforms, and content authoring tools that are located all over the world. Additionally, privacy issues abound on the Internet. Anonymity is typically very important for people such as activists, journalists, or whistleblowers; therefore, exposing their identity within a provenance system is considered an invasion of privacy. Malicious users could misuse provenance systems by falsifying documents, deleting metadata, and creating fictitious documents. Considering these problems, constructing an infrastructure for dependable verification of genuineness is extremely important for developing a healthy information environment. To achieve this, all parties will need to tussle: governments, standards bodies, tech companies, and civil society. Provenance systems may yet live in the background, in a position equivalent to SSL certificates in today's web security outfits, making the complicated status quo trustworthy.

10.5 GUARANTEEING EQUITY, ACCESS, AND INCLUSION IN GENAI FUTURES

GenAI has the potential to expand access to knowledge, empower creativity, and accelerate discoveries across a wide range of fields. Existing social, economic, and geopolitical systems, which are fundamentally unjust to the Global South, are responsible for the development and deployment of all these technologies. Unless we actively work to change the course we are on, GenAI will be captured by the most powerful technology stewards, further marginalizing already disadvantaged communities. To maximize the chances that GenAI can help equip networks for egalitarian futures, we need to maintain an ongoing focus on power, access, and inclusion at every level of the technology's lifecycle.

Widespread access to technology alone will not ensure equity in the use of GenAI. It is important to consider who controls the data, whom we pay attention to in our systems of knowledge, and whose communities are prioritized for building. Autonomously generating text and applications has the potential to reshape industries, bring terraforming tools to new communities, and catalyze radical new applications of tools such as large language models. In this section, we explore how inclusive governance and design techniques can help set GenAI on a course of social benefit rather than extractive or discriminatory outcomes.

10.5.1 Mitigating Data Colonialism

Data is the lifeblood of GenAI. The power of enormous models is developed using vast amounts of text, photos, audio, and videos from the world's activities. Much of this data is harvested without substantial consent, situational awareness, or a fair sharing system. Often, the groups whose digital footprints furnish AI systems have less control over their use or monetization than they aspire to have.

Cultural data colonialism is the practical manifestation of extractivism, a contemporary iteration of colonial exploitation patterns. Data colonialism invokes the thoroughgoing expropriation of digital traces, local rights and meanings, and mutuality, just as colonial extractivism does in the exploitation of land or resources (Couldry & Mejias, 2019). In GenAI, this may take the form of models powered by the work of people in cultural domains but return few benefits to the communities that create that labor.

Colony data expropriations occur in many entangled manifestations. Well-trafficked languages and urban domains, especially Western domains, may furnish more training data than other domains, reflecting limited normative assumptions in models. Indigenous peoples and other marginalized populations may perceive the utilization of cultural, linguistic, and even creative assets as inadequate recognition, compensation, and protection of their rights. Models developed and trained on outside digital data may participate in monetization schemes that further disembody profits from remuneration or social goods for their initial contribution people or communities.

Such outcomes necessitate the reconsideration of data governance practices for GAI. Participatory data governance suggests a method of expressing the priority of those likely to benefit or be harmed by data in how these data are gathered and utilized, kept, and let go: a data paradigm that is understood as local and socially contextual, rather than as a generic resource.

Support for region- and community-enabled AI is also essential. Community-first initiatives that focus on local languages, traditions, and relevance may help mitigate some of the negative impacts arising from the uniform makeup of large models, while in parallel, data sovereignty frameworks can be leveraged to support this shift and confirm Indigenous and Global South communities' legal and moral sovereignty over their digital products (Mohamed et al., 2020).

There are exemplars of this work. Project examples like the African Language Technology Partnerships illustrate how open models can create equitable access to language resources while also helping build local infrastructure capacity in a way that is not based on extraction. To ensure GenAI is established as a true global public good, we need productive critique and rethinking the extractive affordances of the training pathways leading to its successes. We need to transition from simply collecting data for efficiency to developing ethical frameworks around data use based on reciprocity, accountability, and local creativity.

10.5.2 Designing Culturally Attuned AI Systems

The communities that are typically presented in the data used to train GenAI systems all demonstrate similar cultural values, norms, and methods of communication. Furthermore, all these communities are typically found in Western-style societies that are heavily represented in English, have a rich history of technological development, and are primarily reliant upon electronic forms of communication. This similarity in the cultural context helps to explain how and why GenAI systems will often operate effectively within those cultural settings. However, it also places the experiences of communities whose knowledge systems and representation practices are not supported by the dominant design and development paradigms of GenAI at risk of being corrupted, oversimplified, and rendered invisible.

Culturally intelligent GenAI acknowledges that meaning is contextually dependent upon a range of cultural variables. Different cultures will assign different meanings to different words, images, gestures, and stories, and that a word or [gesture] which is non-threatening in one context may have the potential to be very harmful or false in another. Many knowledge systems, such as oral history, visual expression, ritual knowledge, and land-based systems, are difficult (if not impossible) to reduce to standardized models and typically do not consider the written word to be the most important form of knowledge.

Failure to respect these cultural intersections can result in cultural corruption, discrimination against certain groups, erasing historical records, and denying certain groups access to their own existence, as well as inflicting severe emotional and/or mental trauma on individuals within some of the most privileged forums such as education, journalism, and cultural conservation.

To ensure that GenAI is culturally relevant, it must be culturally adapted. Culturally adapting GenAI will involve a significant shift away from simply adding more training data to the available datasets. It will also require that those involved in the design and development of GenAI consciously make design decisions that prioritize those languages, dialects, and communication styles that have been underrepresented. The development of multilingual and multicultural corpora will require that the same co-design process that is carried out with communities also takes place to ensure that these systems accurately portray the lived experiences of individuals, rather than utilizing theoretical models for evaluation. Contextual sensitive generation techniques would also help to make GenAI more aware of local customs and the backgrounds of users.

Algorithmic humility is also a core component of GenAI; generative systems must be developed to communicate that they do not have the answer to a given question and must withhold any output from a user when the software output does not have a sufficient background in local culture. Saying you do not know something would be far more ethical than providing a user with an erroneous output that you were confident in its accuracy. The work that has been done incorporating Indigenous knowledge systems, using relational ethics, and incorporating these techniques into AI demonstrates the opportunity for using this approach to expand and shift the conversation about the development of AI: "This work re-centres Indigenous means of knowing, through the relationships, ethics, and respect for Indigenous peoples, and providing opportunity for the development of emergent language and a commitment to respect, reciprocity, and accountability" (Lewis et al., 2020). Cultural responsiveness should not be viewed as something to be added to the design and development of GenAI. Rather, it should be seen as a philosophical approach that is core to the design and development of GenAI; Given the diversity of populations that GenAI is designed to serve, generative models cannot be designed or developed safely or effectively without consideration of the experiences of all individuals, including those who belong to non-dominant cultures with differing beliefs, languages, and customs; therefore, empathy, pluralism, and respect for human experience must guide the design and development process.

10.6 PROMOTING MULTIDISCIPLINARY AND HUMAN-CENTRIC AI RESEARCH

Technical expertise in isolation cannot solve the ethical, social and practical challenges presented by GenAI. GenAI systems are situated at the intersection of technology, culture, law and political power; therefore, they will alter the ecology of how we communicate, learn and make decisions. As such, the future of GenAI research should be a pluralistic, rigorous and diverse body of work, drawing from social sciences and humanities, design and art, as well as various domain expertise. This indicates a growing awareness that GenAI systems are not neutral technologies or products; they are sociotechnical systems with roots in and operating within both political and economic systems. The aspects not captured by performance benchmarks will probably express themselves here, just as most questions around legitimacy, justice, and trust are difficult, if not impossible, to address via a purely technical lens. Human-centered research workflows in this space are critical to understanding how GenAI represents evolution, not revolution, in its complex relationship with the practices and values of the world.

10.6.1 Interdisciplinary Collaboration

The effective governance and design of GenAI systems will depend on interdisciplinary collaboration, in which philosophers and ethicists help identify value conflicts and highlight normative aims, social scientists and anthropologists study the effects of GenAI on institutions, identity, and social connection, designers and artists explore engaging and expressive practices, and lawyers and policymakers identify legal issues and implications for rights. This collaboration can be seen in interdisciplinary research centers and initiatives working to characterize human-centered AI and discover ways in which varying forms of expertise can contribute to contextually sensitive and responsible innovation. However, true substantive collaboration involves more than just consulting with or co-authoring with others; it requires collaborative governance of research problems, methods, and assessment criteria. Non-technical considerations are often introduced too late in the development process to make a difference in the core design choices of the project. A genuine teamwork approach values both qualitative insights and quantitative data, making social awareness a focus rather than a bonus. The aim is to structurally create co-creation environments, where builders, engineers, artists, activists, and citizens all come together at project inception and throughout. As GenAI spreads in areas such as healthcare, education, law, and the arts, collaboration across different fields will be essential to protect systems that support people instead of harming them.

10.6.2 Incorporating End-User Perspectives

While research institutes, companies, and regulators lead the frontiers of GenAI, end users will experience the results of these efforts. Users will someday interact with AI systems in diverse and rich contexts, whether through authoring tools, translation services, media verification tools, or decision-making systems. However, design and implementation probably do not adequately represent user perspectives (Sloane et al., 2020).

Innovatively including end-user perspectives involves going beyond the presumptions about optimal usage. Participatory design approaches allow users to set their metrics of success, understand where pitfalls await, and design interfaces that satisfy their needs and values. The AI-generated information must also be accessible and easily understandable for users ranging from toddlers to retirees, accommodating various reading levels and cultural values worldwide.

To create a sense of security for users interacting with AI systems, there needs to be effective channels for giving users feedback regarding the problems they encounter or their desire to opt out of certain AI-based functions. By performing an ethnographic review of the GenAI experience, we can help identify and examine how GenAI is used in everyday life and identify unmet expectations from these experiences. When designing systems that pose a risk to oneself or others, especially in time-sensitive circumstances or ones that create emotional attachments, if we do not consider user experience, we risk developing advanced technologies that contradict the social values of the individuals who use them, which will create confusion regarding the nature of technology, who it impacts, how it impacts, and how it got to the point that it did.

10.7 ADVANCING A SUSTAINABLE AND EQUITABLE AI ECOSYSTEM

It is clear from the above considerations that the question is not whether we can create more powerful systems of General Intelligent Agents (GenAI), but rather if those systems can be designed and steered in a responsible, inclusive, and sustainable manner. Governance (the systems and processes we use to manage our societies), engineering practice (the actual work done to create a system), information integrity (such as the accuracy of the data we use), equity (the fairness of our society), and research into humanity's needs face many interrelated challenges and opportunities. To support a well-functioning GenAI ecosystem, we must design our systems responsibly while utilizing ethical audits that scale with time, employing normative values at key points in our development pipeline, having systematic approaches to authentically mitigate misinformation by creating authenticity-bound infrastructures and working toward mitigating global inequities, resisting the ongoing move toward data colonialism, and incorporating local contextual design by partnering with regional interests and utilizing end-users for input and collaboration in defining our systems. This imperative for multiple disciplines across all areas of design (engineers, ethicists, designers, social scientists, legal scholars, and affected communities) to collaborate with one another as co-creators of mutual power rather than just as symbolic partners is where interdisciplinary collaboration comes into play. All these initiatives are tied together by common threads; engineers, ethicists, designers, social scientists, legal scholars, and those impacted by GenAI have an obligation to collaborate with one another, standing side by side in the mud as they discuss the power to structure data sets, build frameworks, and establish decision-making standards.

To succeed in developing the social benefits of GenAI, we must do much more than implement technical solutions or temporary regulatory stops. We need to build the institutions we have reorganized, commit to obtaining necessary behaviors/resources from the public, and enter new cross-country collaborations based on an ethical obligation to provide fair access to the benefits of new technologies. If we invest our resources now in proactive inclusive practices and equity-based methods, we can create the potential for GenAI to be a tool to develop the common opportunities that allow us all to live, learn, and thrive within an overall culture of integrity.

REFERENCES

Adobe. (2022). *Content authenticity initiative: Building trust and transparency in digital content.* https://contentauthenticity.org

Arnold, T., Kasenberg, D., & Scheutz, M. (2017). Value alignment or misalignment: What will keep systems accountable *Proceedings of the 2017 AAAI Workshop on AI Ethics and Society.*

Brundage M., Avin S., Clark J., et al. (2020). *Towards trustworthy AI development: Mechanisms for supporting verifiable claims.* arXiv. https://arxiv.org/abs/2004.07213

Cath, C. (2018). Governing artificial intelligence: Ethical, legal, and technical opportunities and challenges. *Philosophical Transactions of the Royal Society A, 376*(2133), 20180080. https://doi.org/10.1098/rsta.2018.0080

Chesney, R., & Citron, D. K. (2019). Deepfakes: A looming challenge for privacy, democracy, and national security. *California Law Review, 107*(6), 1753–1819.

Cihon, P., Maas, M., & Kemp, L. (2021). Artificial intelligence and global governance: A review of governance initiatives and future directions. *Global Policy, 12*(4), 462–476. https://doi.org/10.1111/1758-5899.12942

Couldry, N., & Mejias, U. A. (2019). *The costs of connection: How data is colonizing human life and appropriating it for capitalism.* Stanford University Press.

Guston, D. H. (2014). Understanding anticipatory governance. *Social Studies of Science, 44*(2), 218–242. https://doi.org/10.1177/0306312713508669

Lewis, J. E., Arista, N., Pechawis, A., & Kite, S. (2020). Making kin with the machines: Indigenous protocols for artificial intelligence. In *Indigenous Protocol and Artificial Intelligence Position Paper.* https://indigenous.ai

Mohamed, S., Isaac, W., & Png, M. T. (2020). Decolonial AI: Decolonial theory as socio-technical foresight in artificial intelligence. *Philosophy & Technology, 33*(4), 659–684. https://doi.org/10.1007/s13347-020-00405-8

Morley, J., Floridi, L., Kinsey, L., & Elhalal, A. (2021). From what to how: An initial review of publicly available AI ethics tools, methods and research to translate principles into practices. *Science and Engineering Ethics, 27*(4), 1–26. https://doi.org/10.1007/s11948-021-00307-3

Rahwan, I., Cebrian, M., Obradovich, N., et al. (2019). Machine behaviour. *Nature, 568*(7753), 477–486. https://doi.org/10.1038/s41586-019-1138-y

Raji, I. D., Smart, A., White, R. N., et al. (2020). Closing the AI accountability gap: Defining an end-to-end framework for internal algorithmic auditing. In *Proceedings of the 2020 Conference on Fairness, Accountability, and Transparency* (pp. 33–44). https://doi.org/10.1145/3351095.3372873

Rastogi, C., Mishra, S., & Gaur, L. (2022). Deepfake generation and detection: A review of threats, challenges, and future directions. *IEEE Access, 10*, 121559–121576. https://doi.org/10.1109/ACCESS.2022.3220984

Sloane, M., Moss, E., Awomolo, O., & Forlano, L. (2020). Participation is not a design fix for machine learning. In *Proceedings of the 2020 Conference on Fairness, Accountability, and Transparency* (pp. 344–354). https://doi.org/10.1145/3351095.3372874

Veale, M., & Zuiderveen Borgesius, F. (2021). Demystifying the draft EU Artificial Intelligence Act. *Computer Law Review International, 22*(4), 97–112. https://doi.org/10.9785/cri-2021-220402

Weidinger, L., Mellor, J., Rauh, M., et al. (2021). *Ethical and social risks of harm from language models*. arXiv. https://arxiv.org/abs/2112.04359

Index

Accountability, 82, 85, 91, 106, 122; *see also* transparency
  algorithmic auditing and impact evaluations, 91
  autonomous decision-making, 106
  decision-making responsibility, 108
  documentation and record-keeping, 92
  legal and regulatory compliance, 92
  public disclosure systems, 92
  responsibility and liability, 92, 104
Adaptive governance, 131, 146; *see also* anticipatory governance
AI autonomy, 103, 124; *see also* Autonomous AI
AI colonialism, 130, 154
AI creativity, 7, 12
AIDA, *see* Artificial Intelligence and Data Act
AI development lifecycle, 41, 108, 139, 150
AI engineering, 148
AI ethics, 9, 43, 103, 139; *see also* Ethical AI
  committees and review boards, 11, 91
  development tenets, 9
  ethical quandaries, 12
  future directions, 43, 145
  professional disagreement, 138
AI governance, 60, 91, 122, 132, 142; *see also* governance frameworks; regulation
  calibration, 60
  committees, 91, 142
  global frameworks, 132
  organizational conditions, 141
  regulatory guidelines, 99
AI literacy, 96
AI models, 48, 52, 61; *see also* calibration
  ethical calibration, 48, 61
  fairness and neutrality, 56, 61
  model training calibration, 52
  post-processing calibration, 52
AI regulation, 119, 124, 146; *see also* regulation
  Canada, 120, 127
  China, 120
  European Union, 119, 127
  fragmentation, 125
  Singapore, 120, 128
  United Kingdom, 120
  United States, 119
AI systems, 82, 83, 87, 106; *see also* accountability; transparency
  complexity and opacity, 87
  data provenance, 87
  documentation, 107
  public disclosure, 92
  transparency, 83, 89
Algorithmic auditing, 91, 110
Algorithmic opacity, 87
Anticipatory governance, 131
Artificial Intelligence and Data Act, 127
Artificial intelligence systems, *see* AI systems
Auditing, 90, 91, 110, 149; *see also* algorithmic auditing; ethical audits
  autonomous audits, 90
  ethical audits, 149
  impact evaluations, 91
  independent evaluation, 110
Autonomous AI, 103, 108; *see also* autonomous decision-making
  governance and risk management, 108
  human oversight, 109, 114, 124
  incident reporting and response, 110, 114
  lifecycle governance, 109
  regulatory alignment, 110
Autonomous decision-making, 103, 104, 111; *see also* AI autonomy
  criminal justice and law enforcement, 112
  ethical dilemmas, 104
  healthcare, 111
  human agency and control, 105
  safety-critical determinations, 112
  vehicles, 112
Autonomous systems, *see* Autonomous AI

Bayesian Neural Networks, 52
Benchmarks, 88
Bias, 7, 22, 38, 50, 105; *see also* bias mitigation; fairness
  AI-generated content, 38
  AI-powered hiring tools, 59
  data provenance, 87
  facial recognition technology, 24
  gender bias, 25, 38
  healthcare solutions, 40, 59
  imbalanced datasets, 57
  recruitment algorithms, 24
  training data, 22, 25
Bias mitigation, 25, 33, 38, 41, 43; *see also* bias; fairness
  AI development lifecycle, 41
  bias-free AI future, 45
  feedback mechanisms, 42

policy and regulation, 44
representative data, 33, 34
synthetic data, 37
Black box, 83
Brier score, 55

Calibration, 48, 49, 52, 56, 58, 60; *see also* Brier score; Expected Calibration Error; Isotonic regression; Platt scaling
bias mitigation, 50
ethics, 48
fair lending decisions, 58
fairness via calibration, 49
healthcare, 59
imbalanced datasets, 57
metrics and instruments, 55
multidimensional fairness, 58
post-processing methods, 52
precision-fairness compromise, 56
training, 52
Canada, 120, 127
Case studies, 12, 24, 58, 73, 93, 111, 126
autonomous decision-making failures, 111
biased artificial intelligence, 24
calibration, 58
ethical quandaries, 12
privacy-centric approaches, 73
regulation, 126
transparent and accountable AI, 93
Chatbots, 6
China, 120
Civil society, 96
Clarity and comprehensibility, 105
Collaborative AI, 90
Collaborative governance, 132
Commerce, 6
Computer vision, 33
Consent, 66, 105
Criminal justice, 112
CT scans, 5
Culturally attuned AI systems, 155

Data collection, 28, 66; *see also* training data
ethical practices, 28
privacy risks, 66
third-party data, 69
Data colonialism, 154
Data curation, 139
Data management, 106
Data provenance, 87, 107
Data quality, 21
Data transparency, 107
Data utilization, 68
Data visualization, 25
Data volume and heterogeneity, 21
Deepfakes, 12, 152; *see also* synthetic content
creativity and deception, 12
misinformation, 152
public confidence, 152
Deep learning, 1
Differential privacy, 71
Digital provenance, 153
Discriminatory algorithms, 24
DL, *see* Deep learning
Documentation, 89, 92, 107
models and systems, 107
record-keeping protocols, 92
standardized AI instruments, 89
Drug discovery, 6

Education and awareness, 15
End-user perspectives, 158
Equity, 8, 33, 49, 105, 123, 140, 154; *see also* fairness
AI-driven healthcare solutions, 40
calibration, 49
data colonialism, 154
non-discrimination, 123
training data, 33
Ethical agency, 138
Ethical AI, 9, 28, 139, 145; *see also* AI ethics; Responsible AI
development lifecycle, 41, 139
organizational practice, 143
professional proficiency, 141
sustainable development, 145
Ethical audits, 149
Ethical governance, 122; *see also* AI governance
accountability, 122
equity and non-discrimination, 123
human supervision and autonomy, 124
inclusivity and stakeholder engagement, 124
transparency, 122
Ethical relativism, 130
Ethics by design, 133
Ethics committees, 11, 91
Ethics review boards, 11, 91
EU AI Act, *see* European Union Artificial Intelligence Act
European Union Artificial Intelligence Act, 93, 119, 127
Expected Calibration Error, 55
explainability, 89, 107, 121; *see also* Explainable AI; interpretability
Explainable AI, 52, 83, 89, 105, 121; *see also* Interpretability; LIME; SHAP

Facial recognition technology, 24
Fair lending decisions, 58
Fairness, 8, 49, 56, 105, 123, 140; *see also* bias; bias mitigation; equity
calibration, 49, 56

data representativeness, 33
decision-making systems, 105
model development, 140
multidimensional fairness, 58
Federated learning, 70
Feedback mechanisms, 42, 93
Fragmentation, 125

GANs, *see* Generative Adversarial Networks
Generative Adversarial Networks, 1, 26
Generative AI, 1, 3, 7, 65, 118; *see also* training data
applications, 3
art and entertainment, 3
commerce, 6
ethical framework, 9
ethical frontiers, 7
governance and regulation, 10, 118
healthcare innovation, 5, 14
privacy challenges, 65
responsible future, 15
Generative models, 14
Global AI governance, 132
Global collaboration, 124
Governance frameworks, 129, 131, 142; *see also* AI governance; ethical governance; regulation
adaptive and inclusive governance, 131
organizational decision-making, 142
reflexive governance, 131
risk-based compliance, 127
Governance models, 129

Human agency, 105
Human-centric AI, 16, 140, 157
Human oversight, 27, 109, 114, 124
Human supervision, 114, 124

Imbalanced datasets, 57
Impact evaluations, 91
Incident reporting and response, 110, 114
Inclusive AI, 28, 124, 154; *see also* equity
culturally attuned systems, 155
future directions, 30
stakeholder engagement, 124
Independent evaluation, 90, 110
Innovation, 68, 129
Interdisciplinary collaboration, 41, 157
International AI regulation, 124
International alignment, 147
Interpretability, 89, 105; *see also* Explainable AI
Isotonic regression, 52

Large language models, 118
Leadership, 98, 142
Legal inertia, 129

Liability, 92, 104
Local Interpretable Model-agnostic Explanations, 83, 89, 107
Local Interpretable Model-agnostic Explanations, *see* LIME

Machine learning, 1
Medical images, 5
Misinformation, 152
Mitigating bias, *see* bias mitigation
ML, *see* Machine learning
Model documentation, 89, 107
Multidisciplinary collaboration, 95, 157
Multilateral institutions, 125

Neural networks, 1
Neutral AI models, 61
NN, *see* Neural networks
Non-discrimination, 123
Non-maleficence, 137

OpenAI GPT, 93
Open-source AI, 90
Organizational culture, 110, 143
Organizational governance, 98, 142

Participatory AI development, 95
Platt scaling, 52
Policy and regulation, 10, 44, 76, 90, 119, 146
Prejudice, *see* bias
Privacy, 8, 65, 106; *see also* differential privacy; federated learning; privacy by design
data collection risks, 66
data utilization, 68
differential privacy, 71
financial services, 75
GenAI, 65
healthcare, 73
privacy-preserving techniques, 75
social media platforms, 74
third-party data vulnerabilities, 69
user privacy, 70
Privacy by design, 70
Privacy-preserving techniques, 75
Public disclosure systems, 92
Public involvement, 98

Racial prejudice, 24, 39
Recruitment algorithms, 24
Regulation, 10, 44, 76, 90, 119, 146; *see also* AI governance; policy and regulation
adaptive regulation, 131
global collaboration, 124
legal inertia, 129
regulatory arbitrage, 125
regulatory capture, 130

risk-based regulation, 119, 127
sector-specific regulation, 119
Regulatory arbitrage, 125
Regulatory capture, 130
Regulatory compliance, 92, 108
Regulatory frameworks, 90, 99, 119, 146
international alignment, 147
proactive regulation, 146
transparency requirements, 90
Representative data, 26, 34
Research, 97, 157
academic institutions, 96
end-user perspectives, 158
independent think tanks, 97
multidisciplinary research, 157
Responsible AI, 15, 139, 145; *see also* Ethical AI; Sustainable AI development
Risk-based regulation, 119, 127
Risk management, 108

Secure multiparty computation, 72
Shapley Additive Explanations, 83, 89, 107
SHAP, *see* Shapley Additive Explanations
Singapore Model AI Governance Framework, 128
Social media platforms, 74
Stakeholder engagement, 93, 124
Structured data, 19
Sustainable AI development, 145, 158
Synthetic content, 151; *see also* deepfakes
Synthetic data, 37

Team diversity, 141
Technical opacity, 129
Third-party data, 69
Traceability, 107
Training data, 19, 21, 22, 25, 28; *see also* bias; data quality
bias, 22, 25
categories, 19
definition, 19
ethical collection practices, 28
future directions, 28
quality, 21
representative data, 26, 34
structured data, 19
unstructured data, 19
volume and heterogeneity, 21
Transparency, 10, 29, 82, 83, 89, 106, 122, 138; *see also* accountability; Explainable AI
AI documentation, 89
autonomous decision-making, 107
democratic oversight, 122
explainability and interpretability, 89
public disclosure systems, 92
regulatory requirements, 90
transparency-by-design, 89
Transparency-by-design, 89
Trust, 77

United Kingdom AI regulation, 120
United States AI regulation, 119
Unstructured data, 19
User privacy, 70

VAE, *see* Variational Autoencoders
Variational Autoencoders, 1
Virtual assistants, 6, 25

Whistleblower safeguards, 93

For Product Safety Concerns and Information please contact our EU
representative GPSR@taylorandfrancis.com
Taylor & Francis Verlag GmbH, Kaufingerstraße 24, 80331 München, Germany

www.ingramcontent.com/pod-product-compliance
Ingram Content Group UK Ltd.
Pitfield, Milton Keynes, MK11 3LW, UK
UKHW020205200926
475702UK00004B/624
9781041153184